BROKEN FOR THE MASTER'S USE: THE 828 WOMAN

NOTHING IS WASTED

TERESA T.S. DANGWA

Copyright © 2019 Teresa Dangwa

Cover design by Makaita Vivian Taruvinga-Rance
Graphics © 2019 Viv's Creative Studio

All rights reserved. This book or any portion thereof may not be reproduced, transmitted, or used in any form or any manner electronic or mechanical, including photocopying, or any information storage and retrieval system whatsoever without the express written permission of the publisher except for the use of brief quotations in a book review. For inquiries, please contact thediasporapastor@gmail.com.

MMC Publishing
Atlanta, Georgia USA
gyrlfriendcollective.com

MMC Publishing Company titles may be purchased in bulk for ministry, educational, business, fund-raising, or sales promotional use.

Scripture quotations are taken from or paraphrased from the New King James Version®. Copyright © 1982 by Thomas Nelson. Used by permission.

THE HOLY BIBLE, NEW INTERNATIONAL VERSION®, NIV® Copyright © 1973, 1978, 1984, 2011 by Biblica, Inc.® Used by permission.

The publisher is not responsible for websites (or their content) that are not owned by the publisher.

ISBN: 978-1-734184907

Printed in the United States of America

DEDICATION

THIS BOOK IS DEDICATED to my grandson, Errol the prince, whose presence in my life introduced me to an unexplainable level of human love. It is not that I love my son, Nyasha, any less; it is just a different level of love that God has reserved solely for grandparents. To my son, Nyasha, whose birth forever changed the trajectory of my life. Outside of the day I received Christ Jesus of Nazareth as my Lord and personal Savior, being his mother is one of three of the most emotionally charged events of my life so far. To my Mother Dearest, Christina Watambwa-Dangwa, my #1 fan, my defender, my confidante, my first love. Without my mother, I wouldn't have the courage to be. Gambiza, you have taught me resilience, commitment, unconditional love and hard work just to name a few. You're my hero, my phenomenal woman. To my Father, Togara Rutendomari Dangwa, to whom I owe my stubbornness, my resolve and my love for my birth country. Every patriotic bone in me, is from you, Mudhara Countryman. My sisters, Perpetua and Janet Zigumi (late) and my dear brothers, Russell (late) Tinashe and Tonderai best siblings anyone could ever have. We don't always see eye-to-eye, but the womb we shared makes us indestructible. To my late little sister, Janet, for being Nyasha's legal guardian while I work out the Diaspora life. You loved my son like he came out of your womb and for that I will be forever grateful. To my late big brother Russell Tamboaga Mumanikwi Dangwa, whom I am grateful gave his life to the Lord in the end. When I was leaving Zimbabwe part of his encouragement speech to me as we walked in the streets of Harare for what would be the last walk together on this side of Heaven - just the two of us - was to be etched in my memory forever. He said, "You're one lucky fool to be so blessed twice to go out of Zimbabwe to spread your wings – do not blow it". At the airport as if foreseeing the future, I could hear him sing as I walked to the airplane that evening of Sept 11, 1997 – "Tionanazve tionane, tionane Achida, Ave nemi tionanazve. Till we meet, till we meet. God be with you till we meet again". To this day over two decades later after that 11th September day and 13 years after his untimely departure from this earth, I still cannot sing that song without tearing up – heck I am tearing up as I write this book. To my creative and extremely talented Muzukuru Makaita Vivian Taruvinga, your love, respect and support renders me speechless.

To my best friend, Misheck Saineti, my move to America cannot be told without you. You're the destiny helper who just would not let go until I got on that plane on September 11, 1997. I will forever be in your debt.

To my girlfriends who became Sistas along the way–Tarisai Kungwengwe, Lydia Madzima, Joyce Mangwiro, Margaret Manyamba,

Sis Caro Manyika, Patricia Muti, Nokuthula Sibanda, Lucia Barbra Sibanda, Christine Chikurunhe-LeRoux, Iris Holy-Skinner (late and oh how I miss her), Lisa Austin, 'Mum' Carol Bayle, Kristen Groff, Theresa Marangas, Sue Kline, Pastor Asante Shipp-Hilts and Pink Makeleni, - your love, encouragement and support is unparalleled. Iris was the first to know and encourage me to write this book which she was going to publish under her brand, Mustard Seed. She would have been so proud. Last, but in no way the least, to all the women mentors I've met along the way and every woman who has been through the wringer, who is in the wringer right now, or who is about to go through the wringer, I SALUTE YOU! YOU MATTER! YOUR STORY MATTERS! YOU HAVE MORE THAN PLENTY TO OFFER THE BODY OF CHRIST and THE WORLD! YOU ARE *The 828 Woman*!

And we know that all things work together for good to those who love God and are called according to His purpose." Romans 8:28

And the Lord said, "Simon, Simon, Satan has desired to have you that he may sift you like wheat. But I have prayed for you, Simon, that your faith may not fail. And when you have repented and turned back to me, strengthen your brethren." Luke 22:31-32

"And I will restore to you the years that the locust hath eaten, the cankerworm and the caterpillar and the palmerworm, my great army which I have sent among you." Joel 2:25

CONTENTS

CHAPTER ONE | Hijacked Innocence & Love   1
- Bondolfi Mission
- The Transition: Rhodesia to Zimbabwe
- An Encounter with a Snake

CHAPTER TWO | Disowned, Rejected and Abandoned   58
- A Big Misunderstanding
- The Marondera Experience

CHAPTER THREE | The Escape   114
- Angels on Assignment
- God Orders My Steps
- Stubborn as Stubborn Does
- So What Happened to Patrick?
- The Stubbornness Runs Deep But This Time It Met Its Match

CHAPTER FOUR | The Church – Sadly, not Always a Safe Haven   154
- So Many Bumps Under This Rug
- Arise Oh Zion Arise!

CHAPTER FIVE | Blessings in Disguise   215
- When God Does What God Does
- There are no Coincidences
- Are You the Woman I am Looking For?
- More Angels on Assignment

CHAPTER SIX | The Blessing of Motherhood   266
- Nyasha, my First True Love
- Errol, my Prince

CHAPTER SEVEN | Betrayal & Forgiveness - a Necessary Partnership   309
- Falling in Love
- The Marriage that Never Was
- Why not End it All?
- Taking Responsibility
- Healing, the Children's Bread

CHAPTER EIGHT | A Ministry in the Making 404

➢ I Am Enough!
➢ The Forgotten Dream – 2007
➢ Ezekiel 12 and an Unlikely Mentorship
➢ The Assignment

CHAPTER NINE | The Power of a Vision Board 453

➢ Israel Diary

FOREWORD

FATHER, THANK YOU for the grace to share my story and experiences to help someone out there who needs to know and feel your grace. My desire, Lord, is that with this book, your name be glorified as you have made it abundantly clear that most of the experiences you put on me had more to do with others than they were or are about me. I am the vessel you chose to use to deliver your message and as painful as it was going through the wringer, now in retrospect, I am eternally grateful that your grace and mercy located me. I recognize that everything I went through was because you had faith in me and my loyalty to you as my Lord and Savior. I know now that. Like with Job in Job 1:8, you said to the Devil, *"Have you considered my servant [Teresa]?"* For that, I am also grateful. As always, Lord, I decrease so you may increase in me. I ask all this in the name that is above every name, Jesus Christ the Messiah. Amen!!!

There is a purpose in every pain. My job (and yours) is to seek God's face so He can reveal that purpose to me (and you). Nothing just happens…everything is orchestrated; yes, even the pain is orchestrated! Nothing happens without the Lord permitting it. You don't believe me? Well, come along with me throughout the Word of

God for examples of some of such cases. Sarah, Joseph, Moses, Naomi, Ruth, widow woman of Zarephath, Esther, Job, David, Solomon, Jonah, Samaritan woman at the well and the list goes on. One such incredible story is that of Jabez. Even his name means pain.

<u>Sidebar: Healing begins at the point of surrender. End of Sidebar.</u>

After months of not talking to God except to express my anger, I needed to surrender. Depending on the day, my anger was directed in one of three main directions. First, I was angry at God. I didn't know why He saw this coming and still let me walk right through the eye of the storm. *God, you are Omnipresent, Omnipotent, surely you could have prevented this from happening to me!* Second, I was angry at my husband – *how did he say he loved me and still chose to deliberately hurt me like this?* Third, I was angry at myself. Boy was I angry at myself. Truth be told, I was angrier with myself than I was with God or my husband. *How could I be so stupid! How could I allow myself to be in this position? Nekungwara kwese uku? In other words, with all the smarts I have, how could I have been so* stupid? With all the education, life experiences and the exposure – how could I not see this one coming?

Then, I would go into trying to figure out the root cause or what could have possibly triggered this reaction. *Could this be payback for all the affairs I had with other people's husbands? Maybe it was the sex outside of marriage? Or was it the resentment I carried for a long time for my father and those who had hurt me? But then again, I repented many moons ago and turned my life around, so God, are you backpedaling on your word? In Isaiah 1:18 where you say, "...Though your sins are as red as scarlet, they shall be like snow, though they are crimson, they shall be like wool, I remember them no more"? But then again, my spirit knows that in Numbers 23:19 you say, "You're not a son of a man that you should lie; nor a human being that you should change your mind. Do you not say it and then not act? Do you promise and not fulfill?". Romans 8:1 is an old' time memory verse, "There is therefore now no condemnation to them which are in Christ Jesus, who walk not after the flesh but after the Spirit". So what gives, God? I'm so confused. Why God? Why is this happening to me? I am a good person...I know at times I can be too much but aren't you the one who created me and gave me this personality? What have I done to deserve this? Why are you silent? Answer me now! Is it because I am Black? A woman? A single parent? What now? (with a dragged exaggerated Nigerian accent). God did I ask you for this man? Did I not tell you, "no pastor" for a husband? Seriously? I thought you said you will give me the desires of my heart?* I tried to guilt-trip God as if He can be manipulated.

When it seemed like God remained silent, my questions were directed to my husband – not that he cared to answer them. "What was the purpose of proposing if the intention was never to "leave" your siblings?" "You're a pastor for crying out loud?" How do you interpret Genesis 2:24? (*Therefore shall a man leave his father and mother and shall cleave unto his wife; and they shall be one flesh.*)" "And these are your siblings you are having a hard time leaving and God did not even make them part of the marital equation?" I would ask these questions face to face, in texts, in emails, over the phone and into the abyss to no avail.

<u>Sidebar: This is my testimony. I have no intention to expose or put anyone on blast, but to share my testimony, praying and hoping that someone</u>

will be helped along their way to becoming who God intended for them to be. So, my dear reader, if you and I have had the fortune to cross paths and you know in part my story and you are looking for names or sordid details, you will be sorely disappointed because that is not the intent of this book. If you're reading this and you happen to identify yourself in my story (directly or indirectly), let's help each other heal. For those of you looking to grow; to be delivered from the world of secrecy - especially in the church - or you desire to be an intercessor for the Body of Christ, then you are in the right place. I am also sharing my story because I truly believe that the longer you fester and keep unhealthy secrets, the greater the hold and power those secrets and the devil have over you, your family, your life and your community. There is an urgent need for us as individuals and as a collective

> Body of Christ to retain our God-given power, so His name may be glorified. "And they overcame him by the blood of the Lamb, and by the word of their testimony; and they loved not their lives unto death." - Revelation 12:11. End of Sidebar.

Pain is distressing and unpleasant but for most people, without it, you may never come to your purpose! There is a cost to be paid for living out loud one's God-given purpose. The anointing and calling on your life MUST cost you something otherwise it is not worth living. There certainly was a great cost for our Salvation and reconciliation with the Father - that cost was the Cross at Calvary.

For God so loved the world that He gave His only begotten Son, that whosoever believes in Him should not perish but have everlasting life.

- John 3:16

— ∞ —

SENTIMENTS

Broken for the Master's Use: The 828 Woman provides incredible and heavy insight into the mind of author, Pastor Teresa Dangwa aka Mummy Dearest. Painfully honest, without being poignant, this powerful introduction offers an amazing guide and helper, particularly for diaspora women everywhere, but also for anyone who doesn't quite see the point of life's hardships. *Broken for the Master's Use: The 828 Woman* shows that while unique to each person, life's hardships are prevalent in everyone's life. Life is a journey. It is quite easy to get sidetracked along the way and forget that there's always a bigger plan with God. This particular journey is a true and strong testament to that, and still, leaves you feeling that Pastor Dangwa's journey is really just beginning. – Nyasha C. E. Dangwa

– ∞ –

On behalf of the Gyrlfriend Collective/MMC Publishing, we are excited to bring to you *Broken for the Master's Use: The 828 Woman*, written by the dynamic Pastor Teresa Dangwa, affectionately known as The Diaspora Pastor, or Pastor Tee. This book, as well as Pastor Tee's life is built upon *Romans 8:28 (KJV), "And we know that all things work together for good to them that love God, to them who are the called according to his purpose."* In *Broken for the Master's Use: The 828 Woman*, Pastor Tee illustrates the principles of faith, forgiveness, resilience and obedience through carefully crafted depictions of her own life's story. With humor and grace, she brings Romans 8:28 to life through her transparency and animated storytelling. With the greatest humility, Pastor Tee reveals the ups and downs that come with being a devote Christ-follower. She exposes the reality of what it means to trust God completely – even when it seems the entire world is against you.

While acknowledging and remaining true to her religious and spiritual foundation, Pastor Tee invites you into her world and forces you to face your own truths – all the while, making you laugh, and sometimes cry, at the beauty of God's grace. If you are currently or have ever gone through anything that made you question your worth or purpose in life, then this book is for you! *Broken for the Master's Use: The 828 Woman* teaches us Pastor Tee's creed that "Nothing is Wasted" and all things do, in fact, work for our good!

Thank you, Pastor Tee, for trusting The Gyrlfriend Collective/MMC Publishing with your incredible story! - Dr. Blades

— ∞ —

ACKNOWLEDGEMENTS

IN THIS BOOK, I write about my life experiences. Since no one does life in a vacuum, mine – like everyone else – was surrounded by people. Every person I write about had a role to play in my life – for some their role is still playing out. Some of the people brought sunshine, some brought incredible autumn winds and others brought the much-dreaded avalanches. I appreciate every experience and am especially grateful for the winds and the avalanches because without them, I would not be the 828 Woman that I am today. As much a role as some played, in a few cases, I have changed the names of some people to protect the privacy of others'.

I am indebted to my extended family without whose support, I would not have finished this book in the time in which I did. The numerous cups of tea, the chocolates snuck into my bedroom away from Nyasha's watchful eye, the scones baked, the dinners heated numerous times, reminders to get some sleep, I mean the list goes on. I am grateful to my Publishing Team: Makaita Taruvinga for listening to my concept for the book then prayerfully creating a masterpiece inspired by the Holy Spirit. You brought another dimension of the meaning of the same Spirit that brought Christ from the dead, is the same Spirit that resides in you and me. Gyrlfriend Collective/MMC Publishing for stepping up to the plate, literally last minute and saved the day.

And, last but not least, lots of gratitude to Errol for keeping me entertained and Nyasha for popping your head often to ensure I was resting. You two are my sources of daily inspiration.

I am blessed beyond measure…my cup runneth over!

Here are some of the statements people used to describe me in the past:

"You are it".

"You are an enigma."

"Your personality is too much".

"You're too loud"

"You will never be anything"

"You're bossy"

I am looking forward to seeing what you will add to this list as the reader. Better yet, what are some of the statements people have said about you that have shaped how you present yourself to the world?

CHAPTER ONE
Hijacked Innocence & Love

"Though they intended evil against you and devised a plot, they will not succeed." Psalm 21:11

— ∞ —

MY EDUCATION AND CAREER HAS NOT ALWAYS followed the traditional path. As you will read in the next chapter, being denied education twice in my formative years created an unhealthy relationship with education in general for me. During the times that I was in school, I dreaded end-of-term exams because I was never a good test-taker. I still am not. My nerves get the best of me to the point that even the stuff I would have retained seemed to disappear during test taking.

Growing up under British rule in then Rhodesia now Zimbabwe, it was drilled into us that there is only one way to success and economic freedom and that was through traditional education. When a girl failed in school, the only thing to do was hope that she would get married into a good family or else go to the family's rural home and help her grandparents to till the land. OK, maybe you could get a job stacking items in a grocery store or hardware store.

Moreover, you may even work menial jobs in factories or other companies.

The importance of education was drilled in every kid as they grew up. For me, education was important, but in hindsight, being denied access at an early age messed up my psyche. I never did see a counselor or therapist for these things until I came to the US.

<u>Sidebar: Yes, I am a believer, a follower of Jesus Christ, born again and sanctified who sought the services of a Therapist to deal with my demons. It is a lie from hell that discourages Christ Followers from seeking the services of a mental health practitioner when needed. Of course, one prays that when you do seek these services find a Therapist/professional who is also a Believer. End of Sidebar.</u>

Here is what my therapist and I concluded. It wasn't that I was dumb (as I heard from most people around me, including some teachers and my father mostly); it was the fact that something in my spirit was broken the first time my parents let me stay home while all my siblings continued with school. (Keep reading and you will see the events that transpired and led to the decision of me staying at home at the age of 14). I went through the motions of attending school, but subconsciously I had already convinced myself that education was not that important. Because if it was, surely my parents would have ensured it wasn't interrupted in the same way they didn't interrupt my siblings' education. My self-esteem was ruined because those younger than me, my siblings, were not only good at school but at least one of them finished school earlier than me, even though I was older. My parents had to change my birth certificate to reflect a younger age for me to assimilate better after having missed school for a while. Adjusting of birth certificates was norm in Zimbabwe, especially because many schools were shut down during the liberation war and most kids my generation missed school. So now I am a girl who celebrates her birthday with two birth years (1966 and 1968). On the surface, it may seem harmless but when it comes to age related health challenges and eligibility of screenings it has proved to be a challenge. But for His grace.

Let's talk about school interruptions for a moment because they have their place in my thinking and values formation.

Sidebar: There were (and still are today) many children whose education was interrupted for a number of reasons. Some of those reasons include parents' death or loss of income, war, poverty, illness, lack of appreciation of its importance by parents or guardians, unavailability of nearby schools, cultural norms and beliefs as well as wicked stepparents. The last two are huge barriers in advancing the lives of children. Can you believe that even on the 21st Century there are still some cultures that believe it is better to educate a boy-child than a girl-child? It breaks my heart to know that there are still cultures who have not come to the realization - that is backed by research - of how educating a girl-child not only changes that child's life but also communities at large. We still have some communities in Zimbabwe who are marrying off their children a way of overcoming poverty.

> *Women by nature are nurturers, so when you educate a girl, you know your community will be nurtured. End of Sidebar.*

Even with the interruptions I experienced, I am proud to say that God opened windows for me to receive formal education up to graduate level. Perhaps one of the most formal educational accomplishments for me is the degree I obtained from Springfield College, in Massachusetts, May 2006. This accomplishment came at a cost. It was a weekend BS Human Services program (1st two weekends of each month). It was introduced to me by a good friend and Chaplin, Bruce Tamlyn of Silver Bay, YMCA. One could graduate in 16 months with no interruptions but it took me close to 6 years to complete this program due to financial challenges. As an immigrant with no status at the time, I did not qualify for any grants or financial aid, so I would work one semester then break the next semester to work for the following semester's fees. Because I resided in Albany, NY, which was about 2 hours away, it was not cost effective for me to drive back and forth every day that we had class. I would drive on Saturday morning, attend class all day, spend the night and then attend class all day Sunday. Except for rare expressions of goodwill from one or two people I met along the way, I spent my nights in the car. During warm nights it was easier, but the winters can be brutal on this side of the world. I would sleep bundled in my blankets with my car heater running to stay warm. I used to park on college campus and alternate with the local Wal-Mart parking lot especially on nights when the campus security were on my case. I know the angels were surrounding me always because I never got mugged or had anything bad happen to me during those nights. In the morning, I would be the first to be in class after freshening up in the campus bathroom. I persevered and graduated with a 3.6 GPA. None of my classmates, professors, and family knew of my predicament because I was determined to be the one to wear the biggest smile, to have the most positive attitude and participated in class like one who had slept in a 5-star hotel.

Sidebar: Sometimes it is good to confuse the heck out of the devil...where he thinks you will cry and mourn, choose to smile and be present with a bigger attitude. It builds character. Like James 1:2-4 says, "Count it all joy, my brothers, when you meet trials of various kinds, for you

<u>know that the testing of your faith produces steadfastness. And let steadfastness have its full effect, that you may be perfect and complete, lacking in nothing."</u> End of Sidebar.

Bondolfi Mission

IN THE 70s AND 80s (could be before that but I was too young to remember), there was a surge of parents who began to see value in sending their children away to boarding schools. My parents were not immune to this surge. The benefits of boarding school vary based on family dynamics; quality of education; safety in times of war -Church affiliated schools were not impacted to the same magnitude as day schools, especially in rural areas; because the environment is set up for study. The hope was that children concentrate on studying and not be caught up in the challenges of everyday life. Many years later, I too sent my son to boarding school. I was here in the US and he was in Zimbabwe. Boarding school provided some stability, at least for those 9 months a year when school was in session. It was also fiscally sound to do so too for me.

My brother Russell, my little sister Perpetua and I, were sent to Bondolfi Mission in a place called Masvingo, Zimbabwe for our primary education. My youngest sister, Janet, joined us a few years later. Primary education in Zimbabwe is Grades 1 through 7. In 1975, when we first went to boarding school, Russel was in grade 4, Perpetua was in grade 2, and I was in Grade 3. As far as I know, for my generation, we were the only family in my clan that was attending boarding school at the time. So in that regard, my parents were trailblazers.

It was such an exciting time and was also scary too to be so far from mum at such a young age. However, it was exciting, nevertheless. Going to boarding school meant new clothes, new shoes- at least 2 pairs, toiletries, and the famous "tuck" meaning special grocery goodies - biscuits (which my American family refer to as cookies); ketchup; peanut butter; sugar; powdered milk, etc. Each of us had 2 pieces of luggage with our names printed on them with paint for easy identification. We had a metal trunk for our clothes and a big metal tuck box for food stuff. Mum always prepared each of us an extra "lunch box" with baked goods she would have lovingly baked the night before we were to leave.

Bondolfi Mission, like most boarding schools in Zimbabwe, was a Christian school. It was run by the Catholic diocese. As far as I knew, neither my mum nor my dad were Catholics so the decision to send us there was purely by reputation from friends whose children attended the same school. As I said, being in boarding school at such a young age was both scary and exciting. It forced me to mature fast.

After all, I had a responsibility to watch over my little sister and sometimes my big brother too. Bondolfi Mission was a huge place. It did not just have the primary school; it also had a teacher's college, a home economics skills training of sorts, and a Convent. The mission grounds had a massive amount of land for farming our staple food (maize/corn) as well as vegetables and farm animals like cows, pigs, chicken, sheep, etc. Now, come to think of it, I don't recall ever eating chicken at boarding school. It was served mostly to the priests, nuns, and the teachers in training. Our meals were substandard, to say the least.

We ate mostly greens or cabbage that were so bland. We had a nickname for it, Jovochovo. Jovochovo were these overly cooked vegetables with no meat and very little oil and a hint of tomatoes. Sometimes, we would see snails in the vegetables, a sign that the vegetables had not been washed thoroughly before preparing. We also had beans, which we called Ndumba. Ndumba were equally nastily prepared and you were also guaranteed to see little worms floating. The Ndumba was always infested with zvipfukuto (weevils).

Our vegetable garden was managed by one of the Catholic Brothers who had been nicknamed Musvubu. I am not sure exactly what the name means, but it had to do with his meanness. Musvubu was so mean that we would be working in the garden with him and if he caught us eating even a single carrot we would receive a serious lashing. In retrospect, I realize that we developed bad habits such as stealing from a very young age because of the things we were denied. We would find ourselves jumping the fence in and out of the garden to steal vegetables to cook. I guess as long as we went to confession and did our Hail Marys, all was well with the world. Unfortunately, we would extend the stealing from beyond the vegetable garden. So, if one ran out of soap for instance, they would steal it from fellow students. Then of course, because they grew into habits, we didn't leave them at the school during the break, we took them home. If we didn't have money for candy, we would steal Mum's change. Of course, when caught, Mum dished out her own special version of Hail Mary aka shamhu, or the belt, mugoti or wooden spoon.

Every weekend, in boarding school, we were allowed to make our own food over open fires behind our dormitories. It is a miracle how our dormitories and the surrounding areas never caught on fire. We would buy meat at the nearest butcher and steal vegetables from Musvubu's garden.

Before Zimbabwe gained Independence from Britain, Masvingo was called Fort Victoria. Ndumba Dzatibaya, literally translated, means "too much beans". Our substandard meals were so bad that we, the school kids, had changed the school address to reflect that:

Bondolfi Mission	Jovochovo Mission
P. Bag 9050	P. Bag Ndumba Dzatibaya
Fort Victoria	Fort Musvubu

A Dark Hole in a Safe Place

CATHOLIC BOARDING SCHOOLS (and most mission schools for that matter) were regarded as some of the safest places a parent could send their child. Naturally, our parents sent us to these schools to shield us from the raging civil and guerilla war that was going on in our nation. Our parents did not know that we were at risk and needed protecting from the very same people they entrusted with their prized 'possessions'. The first time I was molested was at Bondolfi Mission. Of course, I didn't know at the time that it was called molestation. I sensed it was wrong, but at that age, what do you know about telling an adult what they are doing is wrong? As a matter of fact, in a twisted kind of way, you somehow get convinced that you are special. You believe the adult is treating you this way because they care. Listen, who am I kidding, when you are nine, ten, and even 18 years old, you don't have the capacity to sit and dissect whatever situation you are in and come up with, "Oh, I am being abused". Where I come from, adults have such authority that chances are, if I reported it, I would have been the one to be punished and even committed for having an overactive mind that tells lies.

When we took our trunks and tuck boxes to boarding schools, we were always given locks and keys to protect our stuff. Sometimes we would lose our keys and had to carry them to the Head Priest's office for him to unlock them for us. This would happen on weekends and sometimes we would have a few kids lined up outside Father Bauer's office. It was during these trips that we would be called in one by one, never more than two.

Sometimes my sister and I would go in together, sometimes not. At times, I would have gone with a friend and we would go in together or in turns. Father Bauer would call us in and we would be greeted with a smile and a "happy to see you" type of greeting. Of course, it turned out he was happy for a totally different reason than us. In his strong Italian accent (not that I knew accents back then, as kids we just thought he sounded funny), he would attempt to speak to us in Shona, our mother tongue. He then noted, the obvious about us needing our trunks opened and he would ask us to place the trunk on a bench.

<u>Sidebar: Now it is important that I mention that I am narrating my experience alone because I have no proof that it was happening to other kids as well because we never discussed our visits to Father Bauer's office except in innocent chit-chat and almost always in relation to how tasty Father Bauer's cookies were and how we hoped to get more next time. End of Sidebar.</u>

Father Bauer's office was connected to a long building, that might have been L-shaped, right behind the church. The building, I assume, had other offices because we would see people go in and out from the main entrance. We rarely used the main entrance to enter the building. The living quarters for the nuns, brothers and priests and the Convent were on the other side of the church. As far as I can remember, Father Bauer's office was the only one that had a private door that went outside. When you were inside the office, you could see another door. I assume it connected to the rest of the building. We never went through there. In fact, it was so rare I have no recollection of ever entering through that main door. His office always looked a mess and sometimes he would have us attempt to clean it up which was normal, in the same way we would help our teachers tidy up their desks. After placing the trunk on the bench, Father Bauer would then call me to come around his desk to where he was sitting on an overstuffed swiveling chair. He would lift me up and sit me on his lap or have me stand in between his legs. Keep in mind that I was in boarding school between the ages of 9 to 13.

I believe Father Bauer died when I was 12 or 13 so what I now know as abuse went on for at least 3-4 years. Father Bauer would reach out for his "special cookies" from Rome and give me one or two. While I was nibbling away on these cookies, he would have his hands all over my body touching me in all kinds of inappropriate ways. Of course, at the time, I didn't know it was inappropriate. African parents back then didn't talk to children about the bees and the birds or inappropriate touching (truth be told most of them still don't). As far as our parents knew, perverts didn't exist. Besides, Catholic or any other mission school was considered the safest place one could send their kids. Of course, back then, as I stated earlier, the concern was not having a safe environment from perverts, but from the war and other life distractions our parents didn't want us to worry about. Zimbabwe, formerly Rhodesia, at the time was at war with Britain in what is now known as the Second Chimurenga. Chimurenga means revolutionary struggle. It was after this Chimurenga that we gained Independence from Britain in 1980.

After Father Bauer was done helping himself to my innocent body, always being careful not to go too far (the perv had a conscience – go figure), he would then give me more cookies, sit me down and get on with opening the trunk. I am not sure if his kind of perversion was limited to touching, or if maybe he felt a natural wince coming from my tiny body in resistance, or the fear of being caught that made him not downright rape me. That is one of the many questions I will pose to Jesus when I shall behold Him face to face, just out of curiosity.

Father Bauer would give the "catholic blessing", i.e. draw the sign of a cross on my forehead, say a prayer, and send me on my way. I would innocently take the prayer and cookies and make my way back to the dormitory, happy to have access to the contents of my trunk. My poor Mum. I don't know how many times she had to purchase locks for us over those years.

Sometimes, we didn't go to Father Bauer's office for the trunks. You could just be passing by and he would open his door and call you in for the "special cookies". None of my friends talked about what happened to them behind the closed doors of Father Bauer's office, just as I didn't tell them about my experience. I don't think the omission of such discussions was intentional, it just didn't happen. I don't know if the nuns knew what was going on and chose to turn a blind eye. I don't know if anyone ever went to the Headmaster or our Boarding Mistress to say anything, but it was never announced. I don't even know if it happened to both boys and girls. All I know is, we always knew when one has been to Father Bauer's office, because they would come to the dormitories with the 'special cookies" from

Rome and they would be the envy for whatever time period it took them to finish their cookies - which we all always consumed leisurely to savor the experience. To this day, my sister and I have never talked about it. It wasn't that Father Bauer even bothered to tell me not to tell. It happened so matter-of-factly that it seemed normal.

The Transition: Rhodesia to Zimbabwe

GROWING UP, I WAS AWARE that there was a war going on around us, but it had not impacted my immediate family directly, at least as far as I knew; until it did in 1976. Being in boarding school and residing in the city, we were shielded from the wrath of the war which was largely impacting those in rural areas. Our cousins who lived in the rural areas would tell us stories of soldiers and terrorists coming into villages and terrorizing villagers. The terrorists were referred as such by the Colonialists and the government back then, but they were in reality the Black Zimbabwean freedom fighters.

> Sidebar: Isn't it interesting how humans like to change the narrative to suit their agenda? It reminds me of how when we were growing up we had foreign teachers coming for a short

while - with some eventually choosing to remain permanently. These foreign teachers were known as "Expatriates or Expat". But now that I am here in a foreign land, giving of my talent just like the expatriates yet I am called an "Immigrant". Or how Europeans went to Asia, Africa and other "poor" continents to share the gospel were called (and still are called) "Missionaries" while a pastor who brings the Gospel to the West is called...well you guessed it, "An Immigrant". End of Sidebar.

Then War Hit Home

BEFORE SEPTEMBER 11TH happened in the US, bombings and terrorist attacks were happening all over the world every day. In South Africa, there was Apartheid, in Mozambique there was Frelimo and in my native land there was Chimurenga War. For generations who did not live through a war in their backyard, these hits were abstract, hard to fully grasp because you just cannot imagine such a thing. We, in the US, believed that we were safe; we had all the intelligence needed to prevent such a thing happening on our home turf - after all, our nation is a superpower. Who would dare? When you hear it happening in other nations, as "a good Christian", you say a prayer for "the poor people" and you may throw in some gratitude for being in a safe nation and you adjust your blankets and go right to sleep. September 11th shook that narrative and some of us lived to tell the story. When such tragedies happen, you cannot say for sure how you will react, feel, or be. Some perspectives change for the better and some, well - you read the news so you have an idea.

May 29, 1974 the effects of war changed my family's lives forever. I don't recall if it was on the same date or soon after that while we were in class when my siblings and I were asked to present at Mr. Ponde's office. Mr. Ponde, our headmaster, was a tall gentle giant, whose presence could be intimidating if not for his kind and compassionate natural demeanor. He dished out punishment like any other headmaster but never from a place of anger. Mr Ponde sat Russell, Perpetua and I down and informed us that our father had just been arrested and was now a political prisoner for suspicion that he was a terrorist or somehow involved in the war. I don't know that we heard anything else he said beyond, "father was arrested". We all began to cry and he calmed us down and assured us that we were going to be okay. Then, shortly after that, he asked for the school to gather for a special assembly. He asked us to come to the podium and made the announcement of my father's arrest in which he was sure to inform everyone that a war was going on in our nation and my father had become a political prisoner. At the time, I don't believe the gravity of what was happening to my family was something I fully comprehended. I don't think my siblings did either. We had been upgraded to "special" now - kinda like "touch not the anointed ones" type of special, lol. I remember one of our teachers later getting into trouble for lashing one of us. Corporal punishment in a Zimbabwean classroom is norm so to be the only three students in the whole school to be exempt from it was pretty cool. The fact that Daddy could possibly perish as a political prisoner was really of no consequence (unintentional) to our innocent little minds at the time - the "benefits" to us were what mattered.

Mr. Ponde then proceeded to ask everyone to treat us with kindness and not cause us any undue distress. It was a somber moment but we felt really special. It didn't last long though because some kids started teasing us that our father was arrested after stealing a suitcase of clothes at a local department store. We cried all the way to Mr. Ponde's office. Those students were called to the office and received a generous helping of lashes and that effectively put a stop to any teasing throughout the whole school. If we were real estate property, I would say, our value went up a few notches.

It also became the time when I ceased to be bullied and called *Ngidhi*. *Ngidhi* means "the one who smells". (Okay, I am being kind to self - it really means, "the one who stinks"). A fellow classmate with initials KJ, had nicknamed me that because rumor had gone around that I was a chronic bed-wetter. So, my father going to detention brought with it an end to the terror I suffered under KJ and, subsequently, other schoolmates. I wish I could say that was also the same year I stopped wetting myself at night. It was going to be a few more years before that happened. Thank God for deliverance!

It wasn't until a year later that we were allowed to visit our father at HwaHwa Detention Center in Gweru. Until then, only my mother was allowed to visit him. We arrived there very early. My Mum's best friend, Mrs. Musekiwa was with us together with her children. Her husband had also been arrested at the same time as my father. She had a car so we all crammed into it and got to the Detention Center early. We parked at the gate. My Mum and Aunty had prepared a meal for us so they set up at the tables, right there in the presence of our enemies and we ate, albeit outside the gate.

At some point, for what seemed like hours, we heard a gallop, click-clack, click-clack, clickety-click-clack. At this point, we were standing right in front of the gate among other people who had come to visit their loved ones. Approaching us was a white prison guard in uniform riding on a horse. He summoned us to gather and then proceeded to give some speech. I guess some rules and expected conduct, but only the grownups were paying attention. To us kids, it felt like an adventurous field trip. (Oh, to be innocent again). He asked us to enter the gate and I remember him on his horse galloping around us up and down like we were a head of unruly cattle. We were walking. No civilian cars, at least for us Black people were allowed beyond the gate. As we walked on that semi-gravel road with my four siblings in tow, I remember thinking *what a long walk*. Tinashe, my youngest brother at the time was merely a toddler so chances are he was on mother's back.

We were all anxious to get there but were also aware that running was not allowed so we walked as fast as our little feet could carry us. Eventually, we arrived. The first thing we saw were men behind a huge security fence, standing as far as the fence came to the road. They too were waiting in anticipation as much as we were. You would know that people had recognized their relative by the way some wailed a name or began to cry or ran to the fence to try and make contact really quick before the guards noticed. In that crowd of people behind the fence, we couldn't see our father until Mum pointed him to us. Before we too could make human contact through the fence, we were summoned to a huge holding room with tables and chairs, nothing on the walls, dull painting- not welcoming at all.

After each family had settled at our respective tables, the political prisoners were ushered into the room. More screeching, wailing, screaming and crying as families connected with loved ones. Finally, there entered my father. My Mum pointed him out and we ran to him. Then, I stopped in my tracks. *That wasn't my father. This thin, sickly looking man was not my father. My father was a giant, strong and overly confident man. This man had a face that resembled my father, but he certainly wasn't my father. How did he become like this?* My Mum must have sensed my hesitation and she encouraged us all to sit down and said, "Endai munomhoresa Baba" ("Go and say hello to your father"). I sheepishly offered my greetings, still not sure if I should touch him. I am sure he asked me about school, about my friends, my likes, whether or not I was behaving well; but I cannot tell you that I remember anything. The only thing I remember from that day is the watch on my father.

My father, like most fathers back then, had this stainless steel, stretch silver, manly Seiko watch. He had it on but he was not wearing it the normal way - tightly knit on his left wrist. My father's watch was loosely on his upper arm, placed as far up his arm as he could get it. He had it on like that because he was too skinny to fit it anywhere else. That picture of my once strong, giant confident father wearing his watch on his upper arm, will never be erased from my heart and memory. I used to cry just thinking about it, but now it just makes me temporarily sad. On that day, my hatred for the White man was born.

Later in life, I attended what were named Group A schools; schools that used to be predominantly White and were now taking in Black people - post-independence. I tolerated the White kids who were my classmates, but something unhealthy in my heart was always there. I resented the White people for putting my father in prison and later after I learnt of the torture my father suffered while in prison, it just fueled and almost justified that hate and resentment.

It was not until a little over 20 years ago that I began to rid myself of the hate that ate me inside for the White man. I interacted with them for whatever was needed to be accomplished but I just could not understand how they held themselves superior to other races. Another question for my one-on-one face to face conversation with Christ. Thank God for deliverance. Ironically, later in life, there have been some amazing White people who have been great resources, support, and encouragement in my journey. Go figure…God and His sense of humor!

This visit was to be repeated every 3 months during school break. My mum's household became a single parent household before we knew what that term was called. Even though my mum was a single parent, she did not change our lives. We continued to go to the same boarding school, have the same lifestyle and some. She did her best to ensure we did not feel the void of not having our father around. Being in boarding school turned out to be a blessing in disguise in that we missed him in the same way we missed our Mum. I would be remiss if I didn't give credit to my uncles and aunts (my parents' siblings) for watching over my Mum and us during these times. We really did not lack for anything. As a matter of fact, my Mum became an entrepreneur before that word came into existence. Sometime during their early marriage, my father had invested in my Mum's dressmaking training school. She used to make our clothes and other people's as well, but now after my father who was the main breadwinner was no longer home, she no longer did this as a hobby. She grew her business to the point of hiring some young ladies to sell the clothes she was making throughout the country. We grew up with at least four maids in our home at any given time, housemaids and the ones she sent out to sell her products.

She travelled wherever she could sell her clothes and made sure we were well provided for. My Mum was doing so well that when my Dad came back, years later, we were still residing in the same house and our family was intact. Most men who had been political prisoners at the same time with my Dad came home to find disintegrated families. Some wives could not take care of their children, some got remarried elsewhere, some just lost hope because no one knew if their husbands were ever going to return home alive. It wasn't that my Mum, my Aunty, and other women who kept their families intact loved their husbands more - not in the least. It is just that living in uncertainty was too heavy a burden for some to carry. My Mum and Aunty Mai Musekiwa were the only two households that I know of that survived. I truly believe that they, like Winnie Mandela, were completely sold to the liberation struggle. So, waiting patiently for when their husbands would one day come home was their way of participating in the liberation struggles. They are the unsung heroes who fought in silence but with resolve and unmatched resilience. They, like other women across the world, deserve a Veterans' Wives in the Struggle Day.

My father was released on April 18, 1978 - 4 long years after his arrest. I believe the British at this point had realized they were fighting a losing battle. The freedom fighters were not backing down. Ian Smith, Prime Minister of Rhodesia (now Zimbabwe) was grasping at straws through what became known as the *Internal Settlement* signed by the nationalist leaders of the day, Bishop Abel Muzorewa, Chief Jeremiah Chirau and Ndabaningi Sithole. Later the following year, Bishop Muzorewa became the 1st Black Prime Minister of Zimbabwe Rhodesia. In 1980, the *Lancaster Agreement* made it possible for the majority Black people to vote and Bishop Muzorewa was replaced by Robert Mugabe and the Republic of Zimbabwe was born on April 18, 1980.

Upon my father's release he came out guns blazing, even more energized to fight for the independence of our country. Ironically, Zimbabwe's Independence Day falls on my father's political prison release date, April 18. More of God's humor displayed. Many political meetings were to be had in our home in preparation for a year of campaigning. My father added his name to the ballot to become an MP (Member of Parliament) for Matabeleland North. Unfortunately, that was not the plan God had for him for he lost to his opposition. However, that did not stop my father from being ecstatic when his party, ZANU PF, won the overall votes. I remember when my father found out the results, he was with his fellow party members who had been campaigning with him. They gathered at a local playground next to our house which had become one of the favored venues for their political meetings. My father climbed on top of the car he had been given by the party and started chanting ZANU PF slogans with his fist lifted and the crowd responding:

Father: Viva ZANU!!

Crowd: Viva!!

Father: Pamberi na Comrade Robert Mugabe!!!

Crowd: Pamberi!!

Father: Abasha Chikonyongwe (Chikonyongo was the nickname of President António de Spínola of Portugal who was fighting Samora Machel, a friend of ZANU so an archenemy of any freedom Comrades became our enemy too).

Crowd: Abasha!!

Then he went into a freedom song with his fist up in the air and the crowd erupting in response and doing the toyi toyi freedom dance:

Father: Mabhunu sorry yayaya sorry maruza.

Crowd: Sorry yayaya!!

It was an exhilarating time even for us as kids. Of course, as children we didn't fully comprehend the magnitude of the tide that had just shifted in our nation. Black majority rule was apparently a big deal. We had brought Britain to its knees. We were a new nation full of promise and potential. There was a celebratory atmosphere across the country.

Even though we had won our Independence, there was some unfinished business between the two main parties, ZANU PF and ZAPU PF which divided the nation into North vs. South. ZANU PF was largely ruled and known to belong to the Shona people who resided mostly in the North of the country. ZAPU PF, on the other hand, was for the Ndebele people, largely residing in the South. These are not the only two tribes of Zimbabwe, they just happen to be the two main ones. In order to win the liberation war and gain Independence, the two, equally strong tribes, had to unite to fight against the mutual enemy, the White Britons. Then in 1981, soon after the war was won for the nation, the tribal disagreements that had been put on hold to fight a mutual enemy, White Rule, and for the sake of gaining Independence began to fester and eventually came to a boiling point. Bulawayo (capital city of the South) became the epicenter of one of the darkest seasons of the new nation. Entumbane Uprising started in the South and later became a full-blown civil war that is now known as Gukurahundi. During this civil war, a lot of the Ndebele people were massacred under the command and leadership of Prime Minister Robert Mugabe. It is reported that over 20,000 people lost their lives in a matter of days. My family was impacted particularly by the Entumbane Uprising because we were northerners residing in the South. Some Southerners did not appreciate my father's campaign and support of ZANU PF. Thus, my father came to realize that we were in danger and he moved us, the children, to Harare while he and my Mum stayed in Bulawayo. This is what led to me being pulled out of school for the first time.

Bullets Flying

Another date that is etched in my heart is July 1979. The war in Zimbabwe was raging and fixing to reach its peak at least for my siblings and I. Remember I mentioned earlier that my siblings and I were shielded from all the activities of the liberation struggle. July 1979 the war came to our Mission Boarding School doorstep. It started the day before when soldiers came through our school. I remember them coming looking for our teacher, Mr. Chibaguza claiming he had been helping the "terrorists". There was commotion on the school grounds and we were told to remain in our classrooms.

Then we saw it. One of the soldiers' trucks was openly parading a dead body. I had never seen a dead body prior to that point. Of course, as school kids, curiosity was normal, we were snickering and debating whether or not the person was dead. Then some people claimed it was Mr. Chibaguza, our dear teacher who walked with a limp. To-date I don't know if that was his body but some time much later, maybe months later, we heard news that he had been killed.

That night we went to bed with a weirdness in the atmosphere. We were awoken in the middle of the night by sounds some of us could not recognize. Some of us had never heard what bullets sounded like until that night. Those who knew the sound, came running through our dormitories screaming, "Mabara! Mabara!" (Bullets! Bullets!).

Our dormitories were divided by grade level, young ones slept on one side of the building and the older ones on the other with shared bathrooms and dining room in the middle. Someone told us to move to the bathroom area because of its long concrete walls, we would be safe there. I, however, needed to find my sisters, Perpetua and Janet who were on the younger girls' side. Someone had announced earlier for us to crawl through to the bathroom to avoid being hit by flying bullets. I went to get my sister Perpetua first and asked her to crawl close to me and left her in one of the bathroom stalls. I went back for Janet and as we were turning a corner on our knees, she somehow hurt her knee and she could not move. She started to cry and I managed to carry her on my back as we crawled to safety. I found Perpetua and we all huddled in the bathroom stall for what seemed like forever.

In the morning the Headmistress came in and gathered all of us, told us to pack all our belongings because we were going home. Bondolfi Mission had become a battleground and the school had been given a few hours to shut down. We ran and quickly gathered our trunks in the trunk room, packed as much as we could and we went outside to await further instructions. By the time we got to where others were gathering, there were so many buses in the school ground it was like a parking garage. We were told to get in on any bus going the direction of our homes. With Janet on my back, while carrying her trunk and mine (one on my head and the other in one hand) and Perpetua in tow carrying her trunk, we looked for our bus, Alec Stewart, and sure enough it was there. Russell was walking around looking for us and we connected, the school was closed with no open date. We left Bondolfi, never to return again.

An Encounter with a Snake

MAININI MIDDLE was one of my favorite aunts growing up. Her name was Mildred, Middie for short. Mainini, loosely translated in Shona, means "small Mother" on account of her being my Mum's little sister. Mainini Middie was a fireball, beautiful with dark flawless skin. She was tall and skinny. She was the first woman I thought defined beauty. She always looked like someone out of a movie, like she didn't belong with us, but in the suburbs somewhere. Of course, my Mum, was beautiful (and still is) but she was Mum. I never thought of my Mum or defined her as anything other than my Mum. Of course, now I see life differently and the definition of beauty has changed over the years. Beauty, to me, is beyond the facial features or the symmetrical structure of one's body or the measured strut of their step. Nor is it defined by the heavy or no makeup on face or the quality of clothes one wears or bags one carries on their shoulder. Rather it is more of one's inner-self, the character with which they carry themselves; the respect by which they treat both themselves and others. Don't get me wrong Mainini Middie, like all of my aunts and uncles back then, was kind, funny, witty and extremely generous.

She was into fashion and she loved to stretch the envelope a little. When she and my Sisi Jennifer met…well, let's just say together, they were a riot. Sisi Jennifer is my first cousin on my father's side. In my culture, we really don't have the word cousin per se. Our cousins are either our brothers or our sisters and are not treated any different from one's siblings. Sisi Jenny, as we affectionately called her, and Mainini Middie were about the same age, if not the same age. They were thick as thieves and a hot mess.

Back then I don't remember them being gainfully employed, but they always had money and nice things. Fashion was a shared passion between them. I have a very distinct memory of the two of them sneaking out at night in knee-high black leather boots with their pants tucked neatly inside their boots. They looked like horse riders - without the horses of course. Unfortunately for them, they got caught by my father as they snuck back in during the early hours of the morning. That was a Saturday night. They both got good hiding from my Dad. I remember them being forced to take us to church the following day and had to hide their eyes behind dark shades. I don't know if they were hiding scars of my father's beating or their hangover - we may never know because Mainini Middie took their secret to the grave and Sisi Jenny is not going to spill the beans.

Over the years, every time these two came to visit us, they brought us gifts. It is one of these gifts from Mainini Middie that led me to my encounter with an S-N-A-K-E and instilling a serious dislike of them. I remember exactly what the gift looked like and how it quickly became my favorite top. It was called "bob tube" back then – a ribbed mock neck halter top, except with halter straps that I would tie in the back of my neck and let them hang in my bare back.

One day, while we temporarily resided at a relative's home, my top disappeared. I mean for months my Mum and I would look for it and it was nowhere to be found. There is no place we didn't search - under wardrobes, beds, cabinets in every room, except one. The main bedroom was always locked. It was the norm and we had no need for going in there anyway, so it wasn't something to write home about-at least until this fateful day. The relative, who shared the main bedroom with her husband, on this day, forgot to lock the door. When I noticed that, it simultaneously hit me that it was the only room we had not locked. Knowing that we were not allowed to venture in that room, I looked around to make sure there was no one and I went in there in search for my top. I remember the room feeling heavy on my spirit, but I was too young to pay much attention to it. The room had a smell. It wasn't stinky nor was it pleasant – just a different smell. I was on a mission and nothing was going to stop me from completing it, unless my Mum, who was cooking in the kitchen, found me or my siblings playing outside. There was a dirty linen hamper made out of bamboo similar to willow in the corner with lots of dirty clothes in it. I emptied it and methodically returned them one by one as I looked for my top. I closed the hamper. I moved on to the wardrobe and still no top. There were suitcases on top of the wardrobe, I grabbed the only chair in the room and climbed on it, brought the suitcases down, and searched in there, still to no avail. Under the wardrobe where shoes were stored, I moved the shoes and still no top. I even looked in the chest of drawers. My top was nowhere to be found.

Okay, at least I looked, I consoled myself as I turned around to walk towards the door.

Oh wait! What is that peeking under the bed?"

I don't know why it had not dawned on me to search under the bed. As I looked intently, I saw it, the straps of my top! I started to pull it as I was leaning on the side of the bed. The top felt tight like it was caught in something.

Oh, it must be caught on the spring wires under the bed, I told myself as I got ready to kneel next to the bed to see what was going on.

Back then beds were not box bottoms. The part where the mattress sat was made of steel with some coiled-up springs. I figured that was where my top was caught, so I would need to kneel to unhook it. As I knelt, I kept tugging at it and pulling it peradventure it may loosen up. It didn't budge. I finally knelt down and there it was! A python coiled up in a woven African basket we call 'rusero'. Its head was lifted and for a minute I froze as I knelt looking straight into the eyes of the S-N-A-K-E, its tongue salivating. I clearly had startled it. It too seemed to freeze in that moment with its eyes directly at par with mine. As we sized each other up, I noticed that its body was filled up on the rusero and cuddled on top of my bob-tube top. To this day, I don't know what came over me, but I was not leaving that room without my top. I pulled my top a few times and I managed to free it as the python hissed and was yet still seemingly frozen in time. As I pulled my top, the S-N-A-K-E tried to attack. I don't know how I wasn't bitten. OH, BUT GOD!!! Even back then God had His hand on my life. I dashed for the door and bolted out like lightning. I slammed the door behind me and screamed, "I found my top! I found my top!" I almost ran my Mum over as she tried to inquire where it was. I said, "In the bedroom" and I went into our bedroom, happy to be reunited with my top. My Mum, who was busy preparing dinner, acknowledged that she was relieved that I had found it and went on about her business. In retrospect, my behavior after that didn't make sense. I took off whatever I was wearing and put on my beloved top. It didn't seem to bother me that it was under the python hidden under the bed in my relative's bedroom. Nor did it cross my mind to tell anyone about my encounter with the python in a rusero under the bed in the same house that we slept in every day. I put it on and went straight to play with my siblings outside. "Wariwana! Wariwana!" ("You found it! You found it!"), they chanted in unison. In that moment, the python in the rusero under my relative's bed became a non-entity. We went back to playing our game, like it was normal to find one's top under a coiled-up python in a rusero.

That evening my relatives arrived home from work and as they parked their car, it dawned on me that I was going to be in trouble. This woman didn't like me to begin with. Even at that age I knew that she disliked me with a passion for no apparent reason, at least to me. She pitted me against one of my little sisters, whom she favored. I had long gotten used to her disapproval of my existence. She began to berate my poor Mum for having an unruly child who had disrespected her by going into her bedroom in her absence. Although even in her presence, that bedroom was a no-go zone.

It is at that moment that my Mum realized that when I said I found it in the bedroom I wasn't referring to any of the spare bedrooms. Mum began to plead on my behalf and the woman insisted she wanted me disciplined and thrown out of the house. Over the next few days, my Dad received numerous calls on the phone. He lived away from us at the time. My relative insisted that my Dad come and discipline me – a rule my Dad had instituted that no one was allowed to discipline his kids, not even the teachers or headmasters in our schools. Of course, with relatives sometimes that rule was broken, but not this time. This was serious. By discipline, I mean corporal punishment. Africans believe sparing the rod does spoil a child, derived from *Proverbs 13:24, "Whoever spares the rod hates their children but the one who loves their children is careful to discipline them."*

Sidebar: It seems a significant number of parents did not get the memo on the thin line between sparing the rod and abuse, so they opted for an unrealistic blanket of no rod. The challenge with this school of thought is that we now have parents struggling to effectively nurture their children. They have instead opted for being friends with their children and left the parenting to nature and our future is not looking good. End of Sidebar.

For a long time, since that time in my early teens, I have always had an unhealthy relationship with any S-N-A-K-E. I purposefully spelt it out because there was a time when I couldn't say snake without getting palpitations and semi-anxiety attacks. It's kinda like the S-P-I-D-E-R which I don't like for the simple reason that a) it has more legs than I care to count; b) it can invade my space at will and c) I read somewhere that they crawl into our mouths while we sleep (Okay this last one I have since learnt is a myth, but that knowledge came late after the former had taken root). The struggle was real BUT GOD, thank God for deliverance! I digress.

Just to be clear, for my religious brethren, no, my unhealthy relationship with the S-N-A-K-E is not because of the role it played in the downfall of humankind in the Garden of Eden, at least not directly. I have not always been spiritual. My relationship with the S-N-A-K-E was distorted way before I grasped the realities of the Word of God.

You see, I grew up with a recurring dream in which I was chased by a snake. It would chase me in and out of buildings, up and down streets, in the forest, etc. Within the dream, I would start jumping from tree to tree and still this snake would be on my heels. At some point in the dream, the snake would be so close, but not quite catching me because when it was about to catch me, a small still voice would say, "It's time for you to fly". Then I would run, kind of like the way a bird does when you are chasing it on the ground. My grandson loves to chase birds whenever he sees them in the park or in our backyard. At first the bird will almost toy with him as it runs a little and comes to a halt hoping to be left alone, then, it runs a little as he runs after it. At some point, when it realizes how persistent he is, the bird picks up speed and eventually flies away.

Just like the airplane at takeoff, it starts by rolling on the tarmac and majestically scrolls as it slowly but surely picks up speed. Then just as you are getting used to the rhythm of its strut, it speeds up like lightening and kisses the tarmac goodbye and goes straight into the sky. That is the same type of momentum I have in my dream once I hear the small still voice and I literally start to fly. At first, I am flying just a little above the trees, even landing at some trees and the snake will still be in pursuit. Like my grandson with the bird, I too seem to be toying with it, although the sense I feel is that of fear of it catching up with me. It starts jumping from tree to tree trying to catch me. When I am flying above a tree, it would try to stretch itself as if to hook me down. However, I note that no matter how much it is elongated, its tail never leaves the tree. I get the sense that it needs something to hold it, that it cannot operate without its tail connecting to the Earth. It is only now, as I mature in the Lord, that I see the significance of that tail remaining on the ground. Consider the way the eagle swoops onto the ground for its prey. When it sees a snake, it doesn't land on the ground to fight the snake so it can have its meal.

The eagle recognizes that in order to conquer the snake, it needs to bring the snake outside of its comfort zone (the ground/earth) into unfamiliar territory, the air. Once the eagle has the snake in its claws, it flies as high as possible then in releases the snake and before the snake hits the ground, the eagle comes and scoops it back up. The eagle has this release and catch before it drops game with the snake, only the snake is not in on the rules of engagement because it is still trying to figure out where it is and what is going on. It is in this helpless state that the eagle eventually decides the meal is ready to be consumed. Game over! So likewise, as long as I am flying, the snake cannot catch up with me. I continue to fly until the small still voice says, "**You're safe now, it's time to land**". I won and lived to fight another day. This went on for years until 2017 when I asked the Holy Spirit for permission to face this snake. Then I had three more dreams of snakes that changed the trajectory of my relationship with the snake.

Dream #1

I was preaching at a congregation, but we were outside like in the bleachers of a football field and I sensed that the snake was around. I then started subtly asking people to get ready to run because a snake was about to attack us. It wasn't really going directly for the people but it was coming for them through me. In my dream I somehow knew that I was ready to fight it. It started advancing towards where we were gathered except this time it was underground. I kept telling people that a snake was coming to attack us but because they were not seeing it above ground, they didn't believe me.

Sidebar: Sometimes in life God will reveal to you some things and when you try to share with others, it can be frustrating when they don't see what you see. It is also easy to make judgements on people when their revelation is not as clear as yours or when they are not spiritually mature. It's important to remember that we all mature at different times and levels and our journeys are as unique as our fingerprints. End of Sidebar.

As the snake advanced it seemed to grow bigger and bigger and the ground started to crack. Foundations of buildings started to be destroyed. I knew instantly that it was coming for me, so I shouted at people to run. I too started to run. Then I remembered that I had said I wanted to fight it. I turned around and started fighting it with my Bible in one hand and my bare fist on the other one. Every time I stroked it with my Bible, it felt like I was hitting it with a knife or sword. This experience reminded me of what the Apostle Paul says in *Ephesians 6:17* which states, *"Take the helmet of salvation and the sword of the Spirit, which is the Word of God"*.

Somehow, in the dream, I knew that I needed to destroy its head. The more I cut it the bigger it became. At some point, I struck it and the head got separated from the rest of the body. Before the body finally lay still, it shook the earth so much it cracked even more where people could fall into the cracks. Even after it was dead the cracks kept going and splitting almost like the earth had been hit by an earthquake. I started to run and told people we needed to leave the place where we were attending service because the ground had been destroyed and it will be falling in soon. We began to run leaving the ground cracking behind us. As we ran, I looked back and noticed that the head was running after me even though it was detached from the body. The closer it got to me, the bigger it became, I turned in anger and with every strength that I could muster, I lifted my Bible and in one swift move I cut it into two pieces with the top of the mouth as one piece and the bottom of the mouth as the other piece.

> Sidebar: Genesis 2:15 says, "And I will put enmity between you and the woman and between your offspring and hers; he will crush your head and you will strike his heel". This is an interesting scripture because I believe it gives us a glimpse of the mind of God in His desire to reconcile with us and foretells the endgame of the devil as mentioned in Revelation 20:10, "And the devil, who deceived them, was thrown into the lake of fire and brimstone, where the beast and the false prophet are and shall be tormented day and night forever and ever". Crushing the snake's head in my dream is confirmation of His Word and promise to us that the devil shall forever be underneath us. All he can do is bruise or strike

<u>our heel but we have been given dominion over him and the power to crush his head. End of Sidebar.</u>

<u>Dream #2</u>

Somehow, I found myself in a dessert praying. As I prayed I felt the urge to get up and go. I realized that I seemed to go deeper into the dessert rather than out. Then, all of a sudden, I was surrounded by snakes everywhere. I remember saying to myself in the dream, *I just need to avoid locking eyes with them and I will get through this.*

<u>*Sidebar: In every dream I have had, I am aware within the dream that I only need to avoid making eye contact and I will be OK. But once that eye contact is made somehow that is when the snakes start to pursue me. Sometimes I think it is because that first encounter with the python under the bed in a rusero, I "challenged it" by looking it in the eye and fighting it for my top. I may never know why on this side of eternity. End of Sidebar.*</u>

So, in this dream I tell myself *Don't make eye contact. Don't make eye contact.* But there are so many snakes some of them are falling out of trees that look incredibly barren. Very dry trees with no leaves. I notice I am stepping over some of them but as long as I don't make eye contact I am cool. The ones on trees began to fall on me and I would flick them off my head, my shoulders, my arms and my feet. Then, I notice that the more snakes I flick off me, the calmer and more unafraid I become.

I continued to walk and the dessert doesn't seem to come to an end. All the time, I am hearing from a distance- yet loud enough for me to hear a very still, but strong, voice continuously recite Isaiah 43:19, *"Behold, I am doing a new thing! Now it springs forth, do you not perceive it? I am making a way in the wilderness and streams in the wastelands"*.

Keep walking, don't make eye contact, I keep telling myself. It seemed I was walking for a very long time and then all of a sudden, those snakes began to retreat and become less and less. I realized that the voice reciting Isaiah 43:19 had become louder and louder the further away I moved from the snakes. I got to a spot where there were no more snakes and I heard a voice say, **"Turn around and**

look at them". I hesitantly looked back at the snakes and at that moment I noticed that all the snakes were blind. That is why I didn't get to make eye contact with them. They were just walking aimlessly. The Voice and I started laughing hysterically. I woke up laughing so hard my belly hurt. *Psalm 23:4* in motion. *"Yea, though I walk through the valley of the shadow of death, I will fear no evil: for thou art with me; thy rod and thy staff they comfort me"*.

<u>Dream #3</u>

I dreamt I was in a room that resembled a church that was filled with believers. I recognized some of their faces and others were unfamiliar. People were busy having discussions in small groups. Some groups were sitting down and others were sitting on couches and chairs. I recognized the pastor of the church standing and chatting with a group that was directly in front of me but on the other side of the room. Then, I noticed a little hole in the center of the floor and said to myself, *that's odd, that hole needs to be sealed, urgently.* But it seems no one was paying much attention to it. So, I continued chatting with others, but my eyes kept looking at that hole.

My spirit was not settled and I was trying to get the attention of the pastor for the group without alarming everyone else. He was looking at me from across the room, but he was ignoring my warning. He almost seemed annoyed that I was trying to get his attention. He continued to chat with those near him. I tried to get others' attention and still no joy. All the while the corner of my eye was still focusing on the hole.

Then, sure enough, I saw just the top of the head of a snake popping out. I told people, now even more urgently and loudly, but they were too engrossed in conversation as if their ears were closed from what I was saying. I found it odd that when I was chit-chatting with them earlier, they could hear me just fine and yet now it seemed they had developed some condition that prevented them from hearing when I spoke about the snake specifically. I noticed that the snake would pop its head out like it was scanning the room, then it would disappear into the hole. It did this several times and at some point, it became aware that I was the only one that could see it, because at one point we locked eyes and it went back underground. Then, at some point, as it was popping its head through the hole, it began to bring up more of its body to where I saw more of the snake with each appearance. It was as though the snake was aware that everyone else in the room was not paying attention to its presence. It did this quite a number of times and sure enough, at the end, it was completely out. I began to signal to the pastor again (as if I needed to get him to act first before I did). Not sure why, since he wasn't heeding my warnings.

The snake then came out completely and began to slither its way around the people. Again, I tried to warn people but no one was paying attention to what I was saying. So, the snake began to slither its way through the people and around the furniture in the room. As it moved around, it kept looking my way. At one time, it began to slither under my chair trying to avoid eye contact with me, but somehow, I could see it through the chair. I sensed that I was no longer seeing it with naked eyes because how could I possibly see it through the chair I was sitting on? You see, all the time it was slithering around the room, we would lock eyes and then it would change direction trying to avoid me. So, when it came under the chair I was sitting on, it thought that I couldn't see it.

Then, it began to advance to a toddler who was sitting on the floor almost like in the center of the room, but in direct eye view with me. Then, I started warning people that the snake was about to bite the baby, but still they continued like they couldn't hear me. The snake slithered towards the baby. I made a fist and hit its head and kept pressing it against the floor. I just kept grinding its head to the floor. I was using my left hand and remember telling myself that left is not as strong as right. As soon as I put my fist on it, it began to vomit venom which was coming out like a spray. It was only when that venom started to spray on people that people began to scream, "Nyoka! Nyoka!" (Snake! Snake!) At that point, everyone began to come behind me, afraid of the snake.

I continued to grind it into the ground until I felt a strong presence beside me. Then, I heard a voice of a man say "Wayiuraya" (You killed it). When I looked, I noticed that he seemed like a huge giant and yet, very gentle. I also realized that this presence had not been in the room prior to this moment but I was familiar with it. I have been in His presence before. I couldn't seem to see where he ended because he was so tall and yet still felt like His face was right next to mine. I was in the presence of Jesus. He then lifted the snake from the ground and said, **"See, you killed it; now let's go and bury it."** He and I walked out of the house and I woke up right as we finished burying the snake. No one else seemed to have felt Jesus' presence, it felt as though everyone was frozen in time. They were there in body but completely oblivious of His presence.

CHAPTER TWO

Disowned, Rejected and Abandoned

"For my father and my mother have forsaken me but the Lord will take me up. Teach me Your way O Lord and lead me in a level path because of my foes. Do not deliver me over the desires of my adversaries for false witnesses have risen against me and as such they breathe out violence. I would have despaired unless I had believed that I would see the goodness of God in the land of the living. Wait for the Lord; be strong and let your heart take courage. Yes, wait for the Lord." Psalm 27:10-14

— ∞ —

EVERYONE HAS A FEW DATES ETCHED IN THEIR brain and hearts that they will always remember. There are the obvious dates like birthdays, anniversaries and holidays. Then there are dates that other people remember on our behalf like the day we took our first step, the day of our recorded or witnessed 1st step or first word, the 1st day of kindergarten or, "crèche", as it was called in my birth country, Zimbabwe. Then, there are those dates you want to forget, but won't. In some instances, you not only remember the date, but the weekday, the weather, the smells and even the outfit you wore.

I, too, have such dates in my mind, but the one I want to talk about is Sunday, November 16, 1986. In Zimbabwe, like most British colonies, one's educational and/or career fate was decided by whether or not you pass the exams for a certain grade. For instance, you could not proceed to Grade 2 unless you have mastered Grade 1, nor could you proceed to Form 1 if you had not mastered Grade 7. Even the school you went to for Form 1 (8th Grade in the American system) was determined not only by social class, but by how well you had passed or failed the Grade 7 exam.

The next level of national standardized tests that determine one's fate was Form 2. From that point on, it was "the test of all tests", Form 4 or "Ordinary Level". This test was important because it pretty much sealed who you will be when you grow up. Doing well in Form 4, back then, determined one's next steps. It determined whether or not you would proceed with traditional education. i.e. Form 5 and 6, which hopefully would lead to you getting into college or university. Passing your Form 4 exams also opened doors for access to Teachers' Colleges, Nursing Colleges, and Tertiary Colleges.

Repeating a grade did not always mean you were unable to master that particular level. Sometimes it was for reasons beyond your control. I know a few people who repeated these grade milestones before they could proceed to the next grade due to not mastering the current grade. But then there were some like my brother, Russell, who repeated Grade 7 because that year there was a serious outbreak of measles and it got him really bad. They had to send him home to be treated. It was so bad that the bus that used to ferry us to and from Bulawayo to Bondolfi Mission in Masvingo quarantined him. Alec Stewart Bus was the only bus line at the time that I know of, that had 1st class and 2nd class.

Sidebar: First class was the section soon after the driver's seat and took up a 1/3 of the bus size. It was reserved only for whites and sometimes coloreds, if there were spare seats. The 2nd class was the other 2/3 and was for the Blacks. But the day the bus picked my brother from the school, they asked everyone to sit in the 2nd class so Russell could sit in the 1st and not contaminate others. He felt really special because 1st class got

> treated to tea and biscuits all the way. I know because on rare occasions when no Whites or few Whites were traveling, we were allowed to ride 1st class. There were only 3 families from Bulawayo at our school and we all fit nicely in 1st class. End of Sidebar.

I too was one of the repeat offenders, except for me, it wasn't because I had not mastered grade 7, but because of the transition the nation was in as we gained Independence from the British rule. Education in Zimbabwe was tough; my goodness it was tough. In every grade, you are pushed to be better than the next person, never better than who you were yesterday. The system is set up in such a way that after all tests are in, the teacher then adds up the cumulative to get your average score and then based on that you are graded against your classmates.

It is also set up for unhealthy and sometimes unrealistic competitiveness. So, for demonstration's sake imagine this scenario: You're a Grade 5 pupil in a class of 43 with one teacher and no teacher assistant. As a matter of fact, teacher assistant is not a thing in Zimbabwe. At that age (10 years old), you are limited to about 4 subjects (English, Mathematics, Content and a Vernacular

Language). Your grades are scored in percentage. Schools in Africa have three terms a year, each three months long, and you are tested at the end of each term. So, let's say this particular term you did better than last year and got 25/50 (50%) in English; 32/60 (53%) in Mathematics; 27/50 (54%) in Content and 20/50 (40%) in Vernacular Language. Your total score average is 49%.

Your teacher then averages each student and lists them chronologically. These results were sometimes posted for all your classmates to see. Some schools would even put them against your schoolmates in the same grade level for the whole school to see. Naturally, there were students who did much better and had 100% average and better than your 49% and others who struggled and had lower scores than 49%. Out of the 43, your average ranks you at 31, meaning there are 30 students who ranked better than you. Sadly, as parents, the system has conditioned them to see anything less than a top 10 ranking as failure. Most parents reacted to "failure" in brutal ways which included serious lashing. As if the pain of a lash somehow caused your brain to function smarter. In retrospect you almost want to go back to all those adults and say, something my kids and I like to say when we think what one of us is doing or saying has not been given due thinking through. We say, "Let's just think about this for a quick minute". This causes someone to consciously consider the possibility of what they said which, in most cases, is highly unlikely.

Sidebar: Unlike here in the US, perhaps your parent(s) would ground you for the first week of summer, if that, and provide tutoring services in hopes that next year you will do better. For us, you will get a good lashing, uncles and aunts may join, and even grandparents too. Discipline in most African culture is a community thing. One doesn't have to be your relative to discipline you if they catch you misbehaving. Then after the lashing, it would be assumed that you just needed to study more during the school breaks while others had fun outside. Funny enough, you would do this "study" unsupervised except for the occasional check-in to see you were searing where you were supposed to be. It kinda begs the question, "If you couldn't master the concepts with a teacher breathing down your neck, how would you master it on your own? Once in a while your smarter siblings may show you a thing or two but it was sometimes done begrudgingly because you would have been preventing them from playing with their friends outside. No adult that I know of ever took the time to figure out how their child learned. Some kids are visual learners, some hear a concept and their brain just gets it; others have to repeat it over and over to retain it, and for others their left brain and their right brains are kinda switched so they will view things from a completely different perspective. Our teaching and testing methods do not take into account all these variables. In the US, they will provide "special accommodations" if you need it so that you are not judged by the same measuring method as your friend "Joey" or "Lisa". So as one who has "failed", you were continuously reminded of your "dumbness" every time you mess up

> anything. You could miss a spot while cleaning the floor or mistakenly add extra salt in a dish you are preparing and the next thing you hear from the adults, and even from your "smarter" siblings/cousins, "Ndosaka usingagone kuchikoro" (That is why you are dumb in school). Believe me, you hear this enough times, you begin to believe it and less and less even, your expectations of self are to fail. I should know, I lived it. All my siblings were smarter than me, so I never quite measured up. End of Sidebar.

With each subject, the score on your report card is accompanied by the teacher's comments as well as the Headmaster's comments. Now, again in retrospect, it never quite made sense to have the Headmaster's comments because they never knew you personally unless you were either a really smart kid or a troublemaker who had been to the Headmaster's office numerous times for discipline. The comments sometimes were encouraging, but at times would be a bit emotionally scarring. Some scars can live with you throughout adulthood.

Sidebar: Interestingly, when I went to England in the early 90s, I noted a contrasting approach to education from that in Zimbabwe, even though the Zimbabwean system was supposedly a mirror of the British system. Students were not considered failures when they somehow did not perform well in class or in their grade level or even college level, they were provided other opportunities to learn differently and could still pursue successful careers. For instance, when I went to England, my initial desire was to study nursing. Because I had not successfully completed my O' Levels (equivalent to high school), I was redirected to doing what was called, "Access to Nursing" back then. Not sure if it still exists. This was a year of study that focused on entry into healthcare and taught in a way that was made easier to understand sciences. Of course, I switched halfway through after recognizing I did not have

> the grace for nursing. I went on to seek to study computers and still didn't have enough O' Level subjects to go straight into University so I was enrolled at Acton College to study Access to Computer Studies for a year then enrolled into Thames Valley University in Ealing. End of Sidebar.

— ∞ —

This part of my journey starts on Friday before the November 16th that I mentioned earlier. The following Tuesday, November 18th was Day 1 of my O' Levels Exams. A few months prior to this date, my aunt who was a teacher, Tete Rosie, had moved into our neighborhood. She had lived with us for a little bit while she looked for her own place which she had found a few weeks prior to November 16th. Tete Rosie's brother, Rodwell Samkange, was married to my first cousin, Sis Joyce. In our culture, Tete Rosie and her brother receive the same reverence bestowed to a son-in-law. A "son-in-law" in the form of a woman - in other words she received the same reverenced bestowed to her brother who is the son-in-law. Her relationship with my father is one of deep respect and reverence so much that you hardly saw them sitting in the same room together as per custom norms.

As a matter of fact, when my aunt was in the kitchen, which was connected to the backdoor, my Father would turn around and use the front door to come into the house. One has to know this culture in order to fully understand and appreciate it. They don't hang out, per se, as he would say with her brother. So when Tete Rosie moved to her new home, my father was not privy to where it was located at the time. The right protocol would have been for her to invite both my Mum and Dad after she had settled. However, being that it had only been a couple weeks since she moved out, my Father didn't know where her new home was yet. He may have known the vicinity or the street from general talk, but up until that November 16th he didn't know where it was.

A Big Misunderstanding

TETE ROSIE, was still a young lady at the time she moved to our neighborhood and I want to believe she was already engaged to be married to her current husband. Her fiancé lived in Harare, the Capital of Zimbabwe, which was about 120 km from Chinhoyi, our home town. Tete Rosie would generally leave Chinhoyi on Fridays soon after class to go and visit her fiancé. Before she left for that weekend, as she had become accustomed to do, she brought her spare keys to my Mum asking her to allow me to go and clean her cottage for her in her absence. I would generally do it on Saturdays after my chores at home. This was a courtesy gesture most young kids do for relatives and family friends.

<u>Sidebar: In the West, you call it child labor, the majority of the world calls it teaching responsibility - when done right, of course. End of Sidebar.</u>

So, this particular weekend was no different except instead of Saturday I was going Sunday because I had spent that Saturday studying for my school exams. Possibly, unbeknownst to my Dad and common practice, my Mum and I agreed that I would clean Tete Rosie's cottage early on Sunday on my way to church.

Sunday, I woke up earlier than usual and headed to Aunt Rose's cottage which wasn't too far from my house. It was a beautiful, sunny Sunday and I was feeling pretty in my Sunday best since I was going to go directly to church after cleaning Tete Rosie's cottage. I was also feeling really happy inside. Partly because Tete Rosie had favored me to do some chores at her home in her absence and partly because I was feeling really good about the upcoming exam. I felt like I had studied hard and was confident that I would pass. Also, Sunday services at church were always something to look forward to. I had been born again about 2 years earlier and was enjoying this new found faith in a Pentecostal church.

So here I was with my jovial-self, going to the cottage, and I ran into my brother, Russell's friend, Patrick Moon who happened to also attend church with his family at my church. We exchanged pleasantries as we walked towards Tete Rosie's cottage, Patrick informed me that he was coming from purchasing the Sunday paper to search for a job. He explained that he was going to read it in the park next to the church as he waits for the church service to start. I offered for him to keep me company while I did my chores and we would walk together to church. He agreed.

We arrived at Tete Rosie's one-roomed cottage. I asked him to stand outside while I cleaned the room because there was hardly much room for two people to maneuver comfortably. As you entered the door there was a small area dedicated to the "kitchen" to the left, then immediately you saw the double bed that stood like an overstaffed two-seater in the middle of the room with one end tightly against the wall. As your body was completely in the room and looked on your right, on the other side of the bed was a wardrobe *or were they just suitcases on top of each other?*, I don't recall. I remember for sure the bed and the makeshift "kitchen". Right behind the door was a window which I opened immediately when I entered the room to let some fresh air in. When I was finished scrubbing the floors, dusting and making the bed, I went outside to the "sink" to wash the dishes. All the while as we chatted about church and upcoming exams, he was telling me how hard it was in the real world because he was not able to secure a job yet since he had flunked his O' Levels.

He was considering repeating that grade or embarking on a correspondence program (self-guided study) and taking the subjects he didn't do well in so he could supplement his grades. Every good job, at the time, was asking for a minimum of 5 O' Levels, including

English, with a grade C or better. He didn't have that. He really wanted to be a police officer like his parents, but he didn't have the grades to get into the Academy. We encouraged each other and chatted about who knows what.

I had taken the dishes outside to wash them as we chatted outside since there was no sink in the room. When I was done washing the dishes, I invited him to come in and sit at the only place available, the bed. I knelt on the floor next to the makeshift shelf Tete Rosie had created to store her dishes. The shelf had several old newspapers on the 'base' which was the floor. I had thrown out the old newspapers that were no longer clean and replaced them with newer old newspapers. The shelf was made from some 4 by 6 or so plywood which sat on two big cedar bricks, one on each side. I started drying the dishes and placing them neatly on the shelf. Unbeknownst to us, Mr. Mukombe – an elder in the community – had seen us go into my aunt's cottage and concluded two things a) that this was Patrick's place and b) that Patrick and I were up to no good. The elder purposed in his heart to go and tell a sinister story to my father.

Because my father was not aware of a) the arrangement between Mum, Tete Rosie and myself and b) Tete Rose's address, he, as usual, got all fired up and ready to kill someone. Had he taken a minute to speak to my Mum, perhaps the misunderstanding would have been cleared before it escalated in the manner it did. Instead, my father and Mr. Mukombe, whom we call uncle out of respect, got in Mr. Makumbe's police car and came over to the cottage. He was a police officer whose rank awarded him a company car. Whatever this man had said to my father, my father believed it and he came with guns blazing.

Now, the cottage where Tete Rosie lived was located in somewhat of a cul-de-sac. One would not see what was happening there unless one was next door or in the neighboring houses. We used the back gate to enter the premises from a foot-street, in other words, no road, and therefore, no cars. Later on, we tried to figure out how this man had seen us in the first place because where we were was nowhere near his house. It turned out he had a girlfriend next door to Tete Rosie's cottage. He was not supposed to have a girlfriend because he was a respected married man. Because he was where he shouldn't have been and because the guilty are always afraid, he made an assumption that we had seen him or his car when we arrived and was afraid that we may run and tell his business, so he decided to cover his sins, so to speak, by making up a story about Patrick and I. We also found out much later that there was also a much more sinister and serious reason why he had made up such a story. Keep reading you will find out soon. You will see why he chose to run with the issue to my father instead of calling Patrick's father whom he worked closely with at the local police station.

I was just about to get off the floor as I was telling Patrick I had one more thing to do – wash the dish towel - and we will be on our way to church. He started to put the newspaper together because he had spread it on the bed while he circled possible job opportunities. Then we heard some commotion outside. The hairs at the back of my neck were on overdrive. We looked at each other and without uttering a word, Patrick got up to look through the window and he announced matter-of-factly that it was my father. I knew immediately that wasn't a good sign.

Knowing my father, I panicked and knew first I needed to close and lock the door. I quickly got up, ran for the door, pushed it shut with a loud bang, and locked it. I don't know how I beat Patrick to the door; he was closer and was starting to want to go and meet my father. A very innocent move that could have ended up tragically had I not intervened. Of all the children in my father's house, I had witnessed that when it came to me, my father immediately acted or lashed out first. This was even before he sought to understand the story. I grew up feeling like he never loved me. I was the one who got the most beatings out of 6 siblings, so I expected him to beat the daylight out of both Patrick and me.

My father came to the window and he demanded that I opened the door. I refused. Patrick wanted to open the door, but I refused. I did not have time to explain to him the type of father that I had. I knew right away that my father was not coming in peace. I wasn't concerned about myself; I was used to his beatings. I was concerned about what he would do to Patrick. You see, my father once he has something in his head there is no talking him down. He is as stubborn as I am, or rather, I am as stubborn as he is.

It took me less than a minute to see that my father clearly had a misunderstanding of what was going on at my Aunt's house. He was beyond furious – he was out for blood. I mean my father was fuming! This is before he even asked me anything. He had gotten wind of me being at a certain address with a boy and that was enough for him to grab an axe and come charging to where I was. If nothing else, the sight of the axe in his hand was enough message to keep that door in between us locked. So, you see I knew my father he was going to hurt somebody and then ask questions later.

I tried so many times to impress upon my father that there was nothing that was going on here. But the way in which he was speaking, it was clear that somebody had informed him of my whereabouts and also that I was with a man. My father was not hearing any of it. He was furious. I mean, the way he was mad you would think that he found us naked and doing the deed. I was a virgin and determined to preserve myself for marriage at the time. I was a high scholar for crying out loud.

The back and forth went on for what seemed like forever until "someone" came by. It was Mr. Mukombe. Not knowing he is the one who had set this whole thing in motion I was glad he was there and I started to plead with him to take my father away as I assured him nothing was going on in the cottage. Mr. Mukombe, after asking my father to move away from the cottage per my request, convinced me to open the door and I wanted some assurance that my father was not going to hit Patrick.

I knew that Mr. Mukombe drove a police car so I asked him if he had his car to which he acknowledged. I asked him to tell my father to go and wait in the car which apparently, they had parked outside the front gate in the hope to catch us compromised and unaware. My father reluctantly agreed. When my father was in the car, I opened the door and we tried to explain to Mr. Mukombe that I think my father had misunderstood the situation. My father then ordered both Patrick and myself to go into the back of the van of the police car. My father ordered him to drive to Patrick's house. Which it turned out he knew without being given direction. Remember Patrick's parents were police officers.

When we arrived at the house there was nobody there except for the maid and everyone else had gone to church. My father turned back at me and ordered me to stay there until he came back. He and Mr. Mukombe then drove off while Patrick, the maid and I stayed at the house. You know, as a kid I didn't think much of it, I just said okay and while figuring he's going to come back in the evening and or whenever he comes back and pick me up. Evening came and Patrick's mom and his siblings came back from church. She already knew me from church so we informed her about the situation that had transpired earlier. Even she assured us that my father was just angry and had acted in the heat-of-the-moment. "Don't you worry when he comes back, we'll sort this out and you will go home". She proceeded to call her husband who had at the time been transferred from Chinhoyi to another town called Marondera, 190 km away.

My father arrived just as we finished dinner. He proceeded to have a conversation with Patrick's mom. Patrick's mom tried to let my father know that he had misunderstood the situation. She even tried to vouch for me since we went to church together, but my father had already made up his mind. In an effort to try and resolve the situation, Patrick's mom called her husband on the phone so he could reason with my father. My father was relentless. He was not budging. He then said his goodbye, but before he walked out the door he made an announcement that would make my life a living hell.

"She", he started, deliberately avoiding mentioning my name, "is no longer my child. You and your husband have won yourself a daughter-in-law for free." He went on to tell her that he was leaving me in their hands and that I was forbidden to come back home. Then, he stormed out before I tried to persuade him to change his mind.

After my father left, Patrick's mom tried to not show the obvious concern and disbelief that was in her face and tried instead to comfort me by saying she needed to sleep over the matter, my father would be back. I couldn't even cry in disbelief. I felt like someone had taken a dagger and pierced through my heart. She then prepared for me to spend the night in the servants' cottage where their maid resided. Just before we went to bed, the phone rang. It was Patrick's father. He asked to speak to me. After pleasantries, he asked me to narrate what had transpired prior to us getting to his house which I did and I showed him that there was nothing going on between his son and myself. I also informed him that I knew Patrick from him being my big brother's friend. They had both attended the same school, Nemakonde Secondary School. Patrick's father then encouraged me and comforted me the same way the mother had the night before. "You know us parents sometimes we misread situations that will calm down later so don't worry; you'll be going home tomorrow. Just spend the night and your father and I will talk about it again tomorrow".

You see, that is how parents who love their children react. They seek to understand then they take the time to consider the least harmful way to resolve the issue like "go to your room", "you are grounded for a month", "no basketball this week", "no TV", okay… not the last one, we didn't have a TV in my Mum's house. I bought my family their first TV after I moved to England a few years later. Radio was where our news came from, or did we have a black and white TV? Eish, I don't recall. I remember we had to go next door whenever we wanted to watch an episode of whatever shows were trending back then.

Monday, we waited all day with no show from my father. Patrick's parents then decided to send mutual friends whom he thought my father would respect and heed to his advice. But before Mr. & Mrs. Gonzo went to meet with my parents, I was summoned for an interview which felt more like an interrogation. I went there with Patrick's Mother. I was grilled to ascertain my character. "Was I a loose girl? Did I like boys a lot? How were my grades in school? Did my teachers like me?" Patrick's mother turned out to be a blessing during this grilling session because she vouched for my character based on seeing me in church. Being that she was a police officer as well, her opinion mattered and it carried weight. She told how she had seen other girls in the church doing questionable things but never this young girl. "Ari kupomerwa mhosva isiri yake" (She is being wrongly accused). *Finally,* I thought to myself, *an adult with sense, now go and talk to my parents so I can go home. I have an exam tomorrow.* With that, and as if to read my mind, they got into their car and left. Patrick's mom and I walked home confident that all would be well. Mr. & Mrs. Gonzo lived down the street from the Moon home.

It was now past dinner time, it had gotten dark, and for what seemed like hours later, there was a honk at the gate. The Gonzos were back. The gardener went to open the gate, they drove in and parked in the gravel driveway behind Mrs. Moon's car. They were greeted at the door by the maid and after pleasantries were exchanged everyone was asked to leave the living room except for Mrs. Moon and myself.

They started to narrate how they were received pleasantly at my father's house. I am sure they gave a bullet-by-bullet narration but all I heard was "Dangwa is not budging". What? Okay, now it was beginning to sink in that I was in serious trouble. As if to sense my dejected spirit, Mrs. Gonzo then said something that threw me off completely. They had presented an opportunity for a way out to my father but first the Gonzos needed to know: Had I slept with boys, (euphemism for having premarital sex)? Was I a virgin? Screech...*isn't sleeping with boys the same process as losing one's virginity? What is wrong with these adults? I am a tomboy, yes, but my goodness, why in the world would I sleep with boys?* I was having conversations with myself at the same time as the grilling. "Of course not, I have not slept with boys. I am a virgin", I defended my honor.

Why is this happening? I am just a kid for crying out loud.

Mrs. Gonzo's next question was what threw me off to the next season of a badly written sitcom. "Would you be okay to be taken to a doctor to prove that you are still a virgin?" *Wait there is such a thing? Wouldn't this test damage my hymen?* I'm confused, but at this point, I was open to anything to go back home. "Yes, please take me to the doctor, right now," I said out loud. There was a visible sigh of relief from all the adults in the room. So that was their grand plan for getting me out of this mess. That was what they had presented to my father as a resolution, and my father, after much convincing had reluctantly agreed, the Gonzos reported. *Hooray, I am going home,* I rejoiced silently. In retrospect, I get that they needed to ensure they were going to face my father with facts and that they were confident in refuting every scenario he may present to them. My Dad was being radical in his wrongness so they decided to think outside the box. Which was radically cool, had this not been happening to me. My response and agreement to get the virginity test eerily brought a relaxed mood in a tension-filled atmosphere. The Gonzos left after promising to take my response back to my father in person the following day. They were confident that this would resolve this whole mess. I went to bed hopeful too.

True to their word, the Gonzos went to my parents' house to present this new update to my father. Sadly, they returned dejected and having washed their hands off my case. They narrated how when they informed my father that I was open to virginity testing, he had shown disappointment as if he expected me to refuse that test so he could be vindicated of his behavior. Apparently, he told them he was no longer interested in proving my virginity and reiterated to them that I was no longer his daughter and therefore, never to be welcomed at his house. He went on to tell them that they could tell the Moon that they could do whatever they wanted with me. *Wow! Just Wow*, like my grandson says when he is exaggerating his disbelief on something. So just like that I was no longer anybody, I became a thing, a possession. The Moons continued to be gracious to me. Their father came back home that weekend and assured me that my father would come back to his senses. Sadly that never happened. Tuesday, November 18th was the day that I was to start writing my exams and in order to do that I needed to have a uniform. Remember, I only had the clothes on my back when I was told not to come back home. Mrs. Moon was concerned about me missing my exams so we devised a plan for me to go to one of my best friends' house, Tarisai Kungwengwe, who was the same size as me, to see if she could lend me one of her extra uniforms. She had to sneak it out of her house because apparently word had traveled within the community that I had been caught with a guy and was now betrothed to him and her parents did not want her associating with me anymore. Other rumors ran that I was found pregnant and was chased to the guy who was responsible for the pregnancy. Which, had it been the case, would have been well within my parents' right to do because culture allows it and eventually the two families come together and some type of settlement is discussed. Some end up getting married and others deny the pregnancy and they are charged "damages" (a certain amount of money which may include livestock in which you are acknowledging you messed up someone's daughter).

Patrick had been asked by his mom to accompany me to Tarisai's house because by the time we came up with that plan, it was already dark. As we walked, we tried to assure each other that this was going to be cleared out soon. I was grateful for the uniform and walked back to Patrick's house in the dark. In Zimbabwe, school children wear uniforms. One cannot attend school or write an exam without one. I also needed school shoes but that was an easy fix. When we got home, Patrick's mom gave me some bandages which I wrapped around my leg, like one who is too hurt to wear the standard school shoes. It worked. I presented to the exam room and took my exams.

Later on, in the afternoon, one of my sisters came to the house and gave me a letter from my father as well as a few clothes. Basically, the letter was talking about his disappointment and how he has now disowned me. He went on to reiterate what had become his mantra over the past few days that he no longer had six children, rather he now had five. I was the excluded child. He went on to write that I was not to come back to the house and that I was now married to the young man I was "caught with". He did not want to hear from me ever again in his life. The letter continued to threaten me that if I were to go to any of his relatives, he was going to kill any relative that takes me in or accommodates me. If I were to go to any of my mother's relatives, he was going to divorce my mom. He also went on to bar me from any communications with my siblings. I was to ignore them when I bumped into them, otherwise, if he knew I had spoken to them, he was going to punish them. I knew what that meant. I grew up with a father who didn't discipline, he beat the living daylights out of us and I got the brunt of his rage most of the time. I will never know the real reason my father hated me so much. I have my own theories of why I got most beatings. I knew my father was furious, but in retrospect, I cannot imagine how he justified putting such a weight on my young shoulders. In any event, knowing my father, I believed every word he had written and so I stayed away. I was a child left with no parental covering and, in essence, my father had started a spiritual disturbance that was to haunt me for years to come. Even though my sister brought me the letter and a few dresses, they did not bring me my uniform so I still needed to use Tarisai's uniform and walk around school with a bandage on my leg to avoid being expected to wear school shoes. Something transpired between the first 2 days of exam season because I ended up missing several exam dates. It could be I was emotionally drained; we will never know. All I know is I missed a few exams. During exams, classes are no longer held so daily attendance is not required so it's easy not to notice that someone is missing. After days missing in action, my friends began to notice and they put it upon themselves to come looking for me. There is nothing like good girlfriends. We were young but we loved each other and got in trouble for each other. Great friendships are tested in the deep of a storm so the fastest way to separate types of friendships or to test them out, let trouble knock on your door. As one might expect, stories like this travel fast like wildfire. By the time it has circulated to my classmates and the school, the story had evolved to, "Teresa eloped". Of course, none of my friends and teachers believed it. Everyone who knew me knew that I had my vices – talking smack, being a tomboy and being the mischievous; but sleeping with boys was not one of them. One of my favorite teachers, Ms. Joyce Mururi, heard the rumors and sent my friends, Tarisai Kungwengwe and Joyce Mangwiro, to come and get me. Her house was on the school grounds, Patrick's house was about ¼ of a block away. Tarisai and Joyce were among the friends who stood by me as much as they could. I will never forget the kindness they extended to me during that season.

Ms. Mururi was not only my geography teacher; she was also my Girl Guide (Girl Scout) leader. She was the kindest and most compassionate person I had the privilege of knowing. Sadly, she passed away before I had a chance to fully express my appreciation to her in my adulthood. Mai Mururi, as she was affectionately called, deposited so much value and spoke greatness into my life. At the time of her counsel, I didn't fully comprehend what turned out to be a prophecy for my life. One of the things she kept saying to me was, "Your life will be great, you will impact many lives and you are going to go back to your father one day and he will welcome you with open arms". She went on to say that my father was one day going to speak of me with pride. I let her know about the challenges I had including not having my exam preparation notes and school shoes. She promised to help me study every day before each exam. I was to go to her house after the school day for those not writing exams. She also gave me more bandages to wrap around my foot like I was hurt which would explain to the teachers why I wasn't wearing my school shoes as before. Sure enough it worked and I was able to sit for the remainder of my exams. She became my first angel on assignment and destiny helper of many I would meet along the way as you will see throughout my story. Telling my story and mentioning their names is my way of expressing gratitude. I really believe the people we meet along the way; those who give us a helping hand, a push, an encouraging word, are the owners of that part of our encounter as much as it is ours. My destiny helpers, I salute you, wherever you are. Sadly, a couple of years ago when I was looking for her, I learnt that Ms. Mururi had passed away before I could personally express my gratitude for her compassion and encouragement in a time of significant challenge in my life.

The Marondera Experience

SCHOOLS CLOSED for the Christmas Holiday and for those of us not pursuing further education, this was the end of the formal education. Back then, we never had graduation ceremonies. After one's last exam, one was proverbially released into the world to go and see what we could do with our lives. I was still residing at Patrick's house with everyone still believing my father would come back for me. He never did. I got clothes from well-wishers. Mrs. Mururi bought me underwear and packs of sanitary pads, soap, deodorant and a bath towel. I still remember when she called me to her house to what turned out to be my last ever conversation with her. "Don't forget everything I said, one day you will make a difference in many people's lives and your father will be proud of you". Mrs. Moon came back from work with some news one day. She called Patrick and I so we could all go to the Gonzos' house. We walked over, not knowing what she had to share, but always hopeful for being taken back home. All these meetings, as far as I was concerned became routine of being informed of a strategy to get my father to change his mind and allow me back into his home. The Gonzos were expecting us. We were politely offered tea that we all politely declined – following Mrs. Moon's lead. After the peasantries, Mrs. Moon started to narrate the latest she had heard at her job. As she narrated we were all mad, disgusted and in a state of unbelief.

Apparently, the reason I was in this predicament was not only because Mr. Mukombe thought Patrick and I had seen him at his girlfriend's house and was afraid we would tell. That was the least of his worries. Mr. Mukombe upon seeing us, had seized the moment to cook up a story that he believed would discredit Mr. Moon. Why? Because Mr. Moon had just been promoted to Police Commissioner in Marondera and Mr. Mukombe thought he was the one who deserved that position. Somehow, in his twisted mind, he thought that the mess would reach the powers that be in the police force and discredit Mr. Moon which will mean he, Mr. Mukombe, would get the promotion instead. All this had nothing to do with me. Patrick and I became pawns in his sick revenge for losing a promotion to Patrick's father.

Mrs. Moon and the Gonzos informed us that they had already presented this new info to my father who was equally shocked at this evil plot. They presented that given my father's reaction to this news, they didn't think that my father was aware of Mr. Mukombe's evil plot. Here is the puzzling part, even with this new revelation, my father refused to reconsider his stance and take me back. The conclusion, after at least an hour of further discussion, was that my father was too proud to admit that he, as smart as he is, was duped by another man to the point of destroying his family. It was easier for him to continue to disown me than to admit to the world that he had messed up. My father too had become a pawn in Mr. Mukombe's plot and I was paying the price.

Then, 24 hours later, on that 1st Saturday after school was over, a police lorry (cargo truck) came to pick up all things from Patrick's house because the family was moving to Marondera to join Patrick's father who had already gone before his family following the coveted promotion to Police Commissioner. Patrick's mum called me aside after all things had been loaded on the truck and informed me that her husband had told her to leave me behind. She tried to convince me that it was the only way my father would take me back. I asked if she would accompany me to my father's house and leave me there but she refused for fear of my father's retaliation. Mind you, many community elders, some friends and relatives had tried to convince my father that he had overreacted, but he stood his ground. Some community leaders, as well as my relatives, had asked me numerous times on various occasions if I would agree to a "virginity test" by a doctor. A test to see if my hymen was still intact. My response was the same every time, "Take me to the doctor now". Up until my 24th birthday, I was still trying to convince my father I was still a virgin. After that last attempt, I came to terms with the fact that my father would never take me to get that test. Here is my theory. My father didn't take me because deep down he knew the truth but was too prideful to admit his wrongdoing. Needless to say, I begged and cried for Patrick's mum to take me with her. She advised everyone, including Patrick, to get on the truck and I realized I was being left behind. I ran in front of the truck and refused to move. I begged them to run me over and leave me dead than to just abandon me there. They tried to move me but I wouldn't budge. Some policemen who had come to help with the move tried to move me but it didn't work because they would lift me, put me on the ground, get on the truck and I would get up from the ground and run back to the front of the truck. I climbed on to the grill (didn't know the name of it then) but I held on to it like my life depended on it, well… it kinda did. Leaving me behind was not an option for me. The whole time I was crying so loud the neighbors came to watch. I didn't care. I just couldn't be left behind. Mr. & Mrs. Gonzo were summoned and they were trying to convince me to stay behind arguing once my father knew I was destitute, he would take me back.

When I inquired from these elders if they would take me in to stay with them, they too, were afraid of my father. So after more than two hours of negotiating, they finally gave in and asked me to get in the truck. I was still crying for a while as the truck made its way to Marondera, a place I had never been – 190 km away.

If these things were not happening to me, I would have a hard time believing this story myself.

I should have stayed behind and allowed fate to take its course because Marondera was not as safe as I thought it would be. First, I started being segregated, treated like a servant and not being allowed to attend Home Group which was midweek Bible study at the house. Sad thing is while the whole family was in the living room praying and studying the Word of God, the maid and I were preparing dinner in the kitchen. We would then be asked to bring the food in the dining room so the guests would join us for dinner. The guests were usually the pastor and his wife or a few other people from the church. I was to eat in the kitchen like the maid while everyone else was enjoying their dinner, watching TV and having happy conversations. Then the next thing to be denied was going to attend church. The maid had weekends off so I needed to be home doing chores and preparing food for the family while they were at church. I don't know what the pastors were told about my absence, all I know is that I often wondered if they didn't care that I was no longer attending church with the family. All I know is no one came to look for me. Mind you, these pastors were no strangers to me. I had met them numerous times at camp meetings that we used to attend 3 times a year (Easter, Heroes and Christmas holidays) while I was in high school. I couldn't do anything without Mr. & Mrs. Moon's permission. I was completely at their mercy. I continued to behave like I was their child because I didn't know any better. Clearly to them that relationship had shifted into something else that neither of us could define because it fell outside the cultural norms. Late December, a few weeks after we arrived, I asked for permission to look for a job which, surprisingly, I was granted by Patrick's father. This was a complete miracle and I didn't know it then but something was shifting in the atmosphere in my favor. Even though I was not allowed to attend church or home group, I never stopped believing in God. I prayed for my father to come and get me. I prayed to be delivered out of whatever stronghold I had supposedly committed to be in this situation. When I was granted permission to search for a job I was so happy because I thought this could get me away from home for at least 8 hours and I saw it as a way out of this rut that I was in.

Sidebar: I cannot help but think, now in retrospect, that my father had inherently sold me into slavery unintentionally and absent the price/cost. I was enslaved without knowing that I was. I was treated as a slave because I couldn't do anything without Patrick's parents' say-so. I couldn't live. I couldn't protest when I was not able to go to church like everyone else. By all definitions, I was a slave, which is ironic given my father fought for the Independence of black people from the white Britons. He is so committed to the deliverance of people from political slavery that his nickname is Countryman. Even now, in his late 70s, he is a patriot to the core. Thank God for deliverance. End of Sidebar.

So Patrick and I, still behaving like brother and sister, started going through the daily newspapers together looking for employment. I may not have realized it at the time, but in retrospect, I know that God's hand was on me. I applied for only one job that I saw in the paper one day and sure enough I received a letter in the mail to come for an interview by a local Pharmacy for a Pharmacy Assistant position. I walked in, introduced myself and was asked to wait. The place was spotless, white walls with some informational posters plastered on all walls. Not completely covering the entire wall but very tastefully placed. I remember the huge windows in the front of the store. I was feeling myself working here. I even started practicing my greetings to my imaginary customers in my head. At the same time, saying a prayer for favor from God. Sure enough I found favor not only with God but with the man who interviewed me. After what seemed like forever, I was ushered into the office. I was interviewed by the owner, Dr. Kutoka, who turned out to be another angel on assignment and destiny helper. I had sent in my application, even though the ad in the paper called for "at least 5 O Levels" (similar to a high school diploma). During the interview Dr. Kutoka asked to see my school certificate and I told him I didn't have it. I told him I was not able to complete my exams due to a family issue, without elaborating on the details. It didn't seem to faze him at all because he offered me the job on the spot on account of my "good spoken English". He asked me when I was available to start. I told him I could start right away and he joked that I would need a uniform first. I told him I didn't have money to buy a uniform. He introduced me to Priscilla, his Senior Pharmacy Assistant, and asked her to give me money from the petty cash for my uniform and gave me directions to where I could purchase the uniform. "Senior" was my addition to distinguish her position from mine although she always made sure to humbly point out that we were at the same level. I was to start the following day. I couldn't wait to get out of that place, not because I wasn't excited about the offer, to the contrary I was ecstatic! But there was a more pressing matter that needed releasing immediately away from the presence of my new boss and his assistant. I needed to step out and get a good cry. My body could no longer contain the lump that was massively lodged on my throat. It felt like I was having an anxiety attack, not that I would have identified it as such back then because I didn't know what an anxiety attack was. As excited as I was, with my heart thumping like it was going to leave my chest, the urge to cry was much more overwhelming. I walked to the edge of the building. The walk only lasted the length of those big windows in the front of the store which were a point of admiration a few minutes before my interview but now they seemed to be a barrier. *"If I can only get to the edge where they cannot see me,"* I thought to myself. Finally, I arrived to the "safe zone" and the waterworks just poured out. You know the freedom and gratitude your bladder feels after releasing the pee you have been suppressing for a while? Now transfer that feeling to the throat. That is exactly how I felt, complete exhilaration of sorts. I must have cried loud enough for passersby to notice because they kept asking if I was okay. All I could say between sobs was, "Ndawana basa", "I got a job". Heck I am tearing up just thinking of that day. Thank you, Lord. You are hearing my prayers after all!!

Upon releasing my emotions, I cleaned up my face just as Patrick was coming from across the street. I don't know to this day if he saw me trotting from the Pharmacy or if he had witnessed me sobbing. Maybe he did and decided to give me a minute thinking I had not gotten a job, but then again as Africans there really isn't such a thing as "giving someone space" or "privacy". The whole community is in your business and not always in a helpful way. Patrick and I had some kind of exchange and I told him I had gotten the job. He was genuinely happy for me and even offered to buy me a drink (Stoney Ginger Beer to be exact) and box of choice assorted biscuits to celebrate. We walked to a local park and sat down as we shared this moment of excitement while eating and drinking. In that moment, we could see light at the end of a very dark and windy tunnel.

We then walked over to the store where I needed to purchase my uniform. It was very exciting. At these shared moments, as brother and sister, we enjoyed each other's company, goofed around as we walked home. It still brings a smile to my heart when I think about it 32 years later. Sadly, that euphoria didn't last long.

The news of my new job was celebrated by Patrick, his brothers, sisters, Uncle Joe and the maid. Patrick's parents were indifferent; a response I would soon be acquainted with. It was when I received that first paycheck that Patrick changed. You see, he had graduated about two years prior to me but because he didn't do well in his final exams, he had a hard time finding a job. His father started demanding not only that I give Patrick all my money but also he started forcing Patrick to sleep with me and make me pregnant. His argument was that without a pregnancy, he couldn't claim me as his daughter-in-law. At first when Patrick told me he, like me, saw how absurd that was and we ignored his father's request for a little while.

<u>Sidebar: Let me put into context where Patrick's father was coming from before you judge him</u>

<u>too harshly. He too, was put in a predicament and didn't really have a handbook of how to deal with it particularly when all cultural conflict resolution observance seemed to fall on deaf ears on my father's part. End of Sidebar.</u>

In my culture, there are several ways one can get married. These are traditions that have been observed from the beginning of time that have been eroded by the introduction of Western culture. African traditions are complex to the outsiders. Notice I said complex not inferior as some may want to present. These traditions are rooted in systems that ensure that our communities not only thrive but that individuals take responsibility for the greater good. I cannot possibly address these traditions in detail without writing a few other books within my book so I am going to give a brief and simplistic overview on various ways in which marriages can be established within the Zimbabwean culture, particularly, the Shona culture. This is just so you can get an appreciation of where Patrick's father was coming from. Please note I may not translate certain identifiers or statements in this section because there really is no English or Western version for some of our culture:

a) Typical - Boy meets girl. After courting for a while and with the approval of girl's aunt (Dad's sister) they inform the elders and arrangements are made for the two families to meet - always through representation and not directly to the girl's parents until certain protocols are observed. Dowry is charged by the girl's parents for the boy to pay. Usually dowry is not paid in one seating. It may take months or even years to pay off. As long as part of the designated dowry is paid, girl and boy are considered traditional and officially married. They can ask for a blessing to do a white wedding celebration but that is really just an outward showing to the clan at large as well as the world of what is now official.

b) Kutema Hugariri - this is like the complex biblical story of Jacob, Leah and Rachel told in Genesis 27-29. Jacob, after taking the blessing meant for His brother Esau ran in fear of his life. He ends up at his uncle Laban's home who graciously takes him in. As life happens, Jacob fell in love with one of Laban's daughters, Rachel. Jacob agrees to work for Laban for seven years in exchange for Rachel's hand in marriage. The story goes on to say that after the agreed upon seven years, Laban deceitfully presented his older daughter Leah to Jacob instead. Even though Jacob reluctantly took Leah, his heart was sold out to Rachel so he ended up working another seven years for her.

In our culture, a man who finds himself unable to pay the dowry for his wife, volunteers to till the land for his chosen in-laws for a specified amount of time or for a crop yield. Once he has met the agreed upon terms he is given his chosen woman as his wife.

c) Kugara kana Kugarwa Nhaka - this is similar to the story of Tamar, Er and Onan in Genesis 38. Judah's son Er was married to Tamar. God killed Er because of his wickedness. Judah, following Levirate law/union, he asked his second son, Onan to take Tamar as a wife in order to continue Er's bloodline. Of course, it doesn't go as planned because Onan in his own wickedness chooses to release his seed into the ground prior to being with Tamar just so he doesn't make her pregnant. God kills him for it.

In my culture, when a man dies, it is the responsibility of the man's brothers to take care of the widow and her children. So, a ceremony is set after a certain amount of time has passed upon the death of the man. At the ceremony a 'husband' is either chosen by the widow or one of the brothers offers to take responsibility. For the most part, the idea was to ensure that the quality of life for the widow and her children does not shift too much for the worst. Some individuals end up living as man and wife to the fullest extent but others choose to take on responsibility without the matrimonial benefits.

d) Kuzvarira kana Kuzvarirwa - this was generally practiced by poor families who upon realizing they cannot afford their meager livelihood, would pledge their young girl to a rich family. The rich family would then assume financial responsibility over the little girl's family by providing food, crops, and other basic supplies. The girl will continue to reside at her parents' home until she is mature. Upon set time, the families would meet and do the 'handover' of the now mature girl, to her husband. Financial assistance continues to come to the girl's family, especially if their economic status has not been upgraded over the years. If it has upgraded, their in-laws continue to bring small tokens of assistance.

e) Kutiza kana Kutizisa Mukombo - This can be initiated by either boy or girl. Two discuss the best way to approach upon realizing the girl is with child. If girl is to initiate here is how it goes down. She approaches boy's people to inform them of the situation and starts residing at the home of boy's parents (or other relatives). Boy's parents through designated family representations send word to girl's family basically acknowledging that their daughter is safe with them. Because when she goes to boy's home after falling pregnant, she generally does so in secret and hopefully before her parents find out she is pregnant. Otherwise, she risks being chased away from her parents' home and/or beaten by her parents for bringing shame to the family. A date is set and both families gather, a token of wrongdoing on the boy's part is charged by the girl's parents. Thus is called "damages". This amount may reduce depending on whether or not boy wants to acknowledge the pregnancy and take girl as his wife. If he denies the pregnancy, because some people want to do the deed but do not want the responsibility that comes with it, he can be charged an arm and a leg to compensate for the fact that he would have deflowered their daughter rendering her a challenge to marry off in the future.

It is this last version that Patrick's father was trying to "customize" to try and fit our circumstances. There was no guarantee that my father would have honored this arrangement. For all we know, I could have ended up pregnant and still unwelcome by my father. Or worse, that would have vindicated him.

Soon, the pressure from his parents became too much for Patrick and he began to drink alcohol. He would come home drunk and became abusive to me. At first it was emotional and mental abuse then it escalated to physical abuse. Although one may argue the escalation was at emotional and mental abuse. The physical just took another form of what had already escalated. I asked for permission to find my own place and Patrick's father said he needed a letter from my father absolving him of any responsibility. I wrote my father numerous times begging him to release me but he never responded. I went to visit one of my father's brothers in Harare (Babamunini Elias) to see if he would inquire on my behalf. He politely declined on account of my father's eminent retaliation. I was stuck with this strange family who were becoming increasingly hostile. I must say the hostility came from the parents; the other kids were too young to know what was going on except for the twin brothers. They were in high school at the time and they knew what was going on but felt powerless to do anything about it. They were just kids themselves.

My highlight and safe haven became my job. Priscilla and I became friends almost instantaneously. I started sharing with her my situation especially after she noticed bruises on me from being beaten by Patrick. In the meantime, Patrick was still struggling to get a job. Even his father couldn't get him into the police academy on account of having failed his O Levels. Patrick made an art out of stalking me. He would pass by my job several times throughout the day and every time he saw me serving a male customer, I knew I would get a good beating when I got out of work. He would get into these jealous fits that scared the life out of me because prior to being in this predicament I had not experienced such violence. It became a routine that he would walk me to work each morning, pace up and down the street at my job all day, go drinking when he was tired of pacing, and come back to stalk me some more until my work day was done. He would come to the door and walk me back home. Even though I was somewhat independent, I was still not permitted to go to church. I literally had no rights whatsoever. Many nights, I cried myself to sleep thinking of how I was where I was and nobody from the church seemed to care. In the instances I would run into the pastor or any of the church elders, they would say they couldn't help me because their hands were tied as they needed to respect the Moon family's wishes. I believe I, like many other people in similar situations, was suffering needless abuse because church folk were more concerned about being politically correct. Lord, help us, because that hasn't changed even to this day.

Even though all my money was being taken by Patrick, with his father's blessings, I enjoyed waking up to be at work 6 days a week (we worked half a day on Saturdays). I felt free in Dr. Kutoka's office, the pharmacist who took a chance on me in spite of my not having my O' Level diploma. He said he "was impressed by my command of English" but I know it was the hand of God. Those words would be an ever-present phrase that would follow me throughout my career and life, "you have such a great command of English". It opened up many opportunities over the years. I now have a deeper understanding of *Psalm 18:16, "A man's gift makes room him and leads him before important people".*

My numerous attempts to get out of Patrick's house were met with equally measured resolve to keep me in bondage. The reasons were always something they knew was unattainable. Their favorite was that they needed a letter from my father releasing them from any responsibility and giving me permission to move. They essentially needed my emancipation letter. I wrote my father numerous letters which were equally ignored. I went to visit one of my uncles, Babamunini Nathan, whom I thought would be sympathetic and have the skillset to speak to my father being that he was a social worker by profession. Babamunini Nathan wouldn't touch my case with a ten-foot pole again for fear of my father's threats and possible retaliation. It's crazy to think now, in hindsight, that all these adults believed my father's threats. They were more afraid of my father's retaliation than they were concerned about the well-being of a mere teenager. The important thing to note is that I didn't blame my aunts and uncles or any of my relatives for not coming to my rescue. Even back then, I understood that their hands were tied. Nobody was willing to cross my father. So, I remained a slave in a country that had fought so hard to eradicate slavery.

I have to say, even with all the pressure Patrick was getting from his father to take money and make me pregnant, something in him would not allow him to cross that line of forcing me to have sex with him. He would tell me what his father instructed. I would be called to his mother's office to be told the same thing about getting pregnant to establish the official in-law relationship. In their minds, and to be fair, they didn't know how else to get out of this situation my father had put them in. I believe it was one of the reasons that caused Patrick to drink because he didn't know how to stand up to his father and yet at the same time, he knew having sex with me was crossing the line. For that I will always be grateful. Even though he abused me emotionally, physically, mentally and fiscally, I will always have a level of respect for not crossing that line of forcing me into sex. When things were good between us, Patrick and I would on occasion discuss ways of getting out of the situation we were in, including possibility of getting married, to which we always agreed that we were both too young to have such a responsibility and that kids needed stability and better income. We had a working understanding. So, for that I will always be grateful and hold great respect him.

CHAPTER THREE

The Escape

"For He will command angels concerning you to guard you in all your ways" Psalm 91:11 & Luke 4:10

— ∞ —

"See, I am sending an angel ahead of you to guard you along the way and bring you to the place I have prepared" Exodus 23:20

"The steps of a good man are ordered by the Lord and He delighteth in his way" Psalm 37:23

— ∞ —

Anonymous:

"The hardest choice is to risk everything."

"The greatest tragedy in life is not death, it is a life without purpose."

"The only power they have over you is the power that you give them."

— ∞ —

THE PRESENCE OF ANGELS SHOULD NOT ALARM US AS children of god because if you believe the Word in its entirety then we ought to believe what it says about angels. In *Matthew 18:10,* Jesus tells us that we each have a guardian angel assigned to us. Here is what it says, *"See that you do not despise one of these little ones. For I tell you that their angels in heaven always see the face of my*

Father in heaven". Angels have always had a role in the history of mankind to help fulfill the purpose of God. Throughout the Word of God we read about encounters with angels. Angels appear to man in three forms, in a dream a vision or physical appearance. Let me give a few examples of angels appearing to man in the Word:

Genesis 28:12-17, "And he had a dream in which he saw a stairway resting on the earth, with its top reaching to heaven, and the angels of God were ascending and descending on it. There above it stood the Lord, and he said: "I am the Lord, the God of your father Abraham and the God of Isaac. I will give you and your descendants the land on which you are lying. Your descendants will be like the dust of the earth, and you will spread out to the west and to the east, to the north and to the south. All people on earth will be blessed through you and your offspring. I am with you and will watch over you wherever you go, and I will bring you back to this land. I will not leave you until I have done what I have promised you." When Jacob awoke from his sleep, he thought, "Surely the Lord is in this place, and I was not aware of it." He was afraid and said, "How awesome is this place! This is none other than the house of God; this is the gate of heaven."

Verse 19 goes on to say that Jacob named that place Bethel.

God to Moses - *Exodus 23:20-21, "Behold, I send an angel before you, to keep you in the way, and to bring you into the place which I have prepared. Beware of him and obey his voice, provoke him not; for he will not pardon your transgressions, for My name is written in him."*

Acts 8:26-27, "And *the angel of the Lord spoke to Philip, saying, Arise and go toward the South on the road that goes to Jerusalem…And he arose and went".*

One of the most fascinating stories in the Word of God is told of Daniel who went on a 21-day fast to seek the face of God and direction for the children of Israel, at a time when God had turned His back on them for worshipping other gods and idols as well as disregarding specific instructions that God had given them. It is from this story most believers who do 21-Day fasts get their inspiration. *Daniel 10:10-14* says, *"A hand touched me and set me trembling on my hands and knees. He said, "Daniel, you who are highly esteemed, consider carefully the words I am about to speak to you, and stand up, for I have now been sent to you." And when he said this to me, I stood up trembling. Then he continued, "Do not be afraid, Daniel. Since the first day that you set your mind to gain understanding and to humble yourself before your God, your words were heard, and I have come in response to them. But the prince of the Persian kingdom resisted me twenty-one days. Then Michael, one of the chief princes, came to help me, because I was detained there with the king of Persia. Now I have come to explain to you what will happen to your people in the future, for the vision concerns a time yet to come."*

Angels on Assignment

IN MY PERSONAL LIFE I have had encounters with angels. One that I want to share appeared one Christmas season. At one job I used to work many moons ago, several people in my department were being let go and being the head of the department, I was responsible for informing people of who was being let go, who was staying, as well as some changes that needed to happen for the department to function effectively. Unbeknownst to me, there some people who had gotten together to plot my demise. A couple days before the holidays, I had felt a presence in my bedroom. It was so strong it woke me. I felt scared but not afraid. With the scary, there was a sense of peace. I got up and sat on my bed and looked at the right side of my bed, right next to my headboard and I saw this being that was in a form a man wearing armor like one going to war in the old days. He stood there as a giant. I couldn't see how far his height went but I sensed the seriousness on his face. He was looking directly in front of him. He reminded me of the soldiers that guard Buckingham Palace in England. The guards are there for one thing only and he will not let even an annoyingly buzzing fly deter him from his mission. I looked at him again and my mind drifted to Ephesians 6:13-17. I went back to lie down and as soon as I closed my eyes I heard God whisper to my spirit, "**I have assigned a warrior to you**", then I fell asleep. I woke up the following day and continued to hand out letters of dismissal to people. I felt really bad that the holidays were around the corner and here I am being bearer of bad news. But it needed to be done. It was part of that fine print on everyone's job description that we all like to ignore that reads, "And all other responsibilities as directed by your supervisor." We commit to it because if we don't, we may lose the opportunity. We then pray and hope that we never have to actually fire someone because it is not easy to take someone's livelihood from underneath them, especially where you know children are involved.

Naturally, I had become an enemy to those who were getting the pink slip and not necessarily a friend to those who were staying - a few maybe. When it was time to close for the holidays, I left my office and walked to my car as usual. I got in the car and felt a little uneasy driving. I thought I heard an unfamiliar sound but I was focused on picking up my kids and us hitting the road. We drove all the way to Maryland because I had taken some time off to spend some time with my family at my best friend Iris' home for the holidays. Iris's house was about 4.5 hours (a little over 250 miles) from my house. As I was driving, even on the highway, I felt the uneasiness and the foreign sound. My kids heard the noise too but we figured it was an old Volvo, we would take it to the mechanic when we got back. We arrived at Iris' house safe. That night I slept in Morgan's room (Iris' first born) as was tradition whenever I visited. As soon as I closed my eyes, I heard the Spirit of the Lord whisper again, "**I have assigned a warrior to you**". Immediately I felt that same presence again. I looked and sure enough the warrior was standing in the same way he had at home. I fell asleep. In the morning, Calvin, Iris' husband, said to me, "What was going on in your room last night?" I said, "What do you mean?" Not wanting to say anything first in case I freaked him out, lol. He said he got up to go to the bathroom and he sensed the presence from my room and believes he saw a different kind of light through the bottom of the door. Morgan's bedroom and her parents' bedroom are right next to each other. I went on to tell him my experience of the last few days.

We spent all our time at Iris' home and didn't have the need to drive our car around. If we needed to go anywhere, Iris would take us around. We had a great Christmas and New Year and we made our way back home.

As we drove, my son noted the sound again and I promised to take care of it as soon as we got home because this time it was more pronounced. The following day, I decided to stop by a local mechanic who advised me to leave the car. I called a friend to pick me up and went to work expecting the mechanic to call me. Sure enough, he called me and asked me where I had gone again, because I had told him about the trip to Maryland. He asked if he could send me some pictures on the phone and I agreed. He sent them and he began to walk me through what I was looking at. Apparently, someone had cut my brake fluid with a sharp knife because it was cut nice and clean. I said this is an old car so is it possible it is wear and tear and he said it wasn't possible. He said, "Someone intentionally cut your brake line; you and your family were intended for death". He went on to tell me that with the distance I drove, I should not have any brake fluid in my car at all and yet there was still a little bit in there. He kept saying, "I am telling you it's a miracle". I agreed with him. We discussed a plan of action and he offered to call the police but since there are no cameras in the old building of our office there was no proving who did it. I, myself, did not fully comprehended what he was trying to educate me on regarding brake fluids and breaks; so I went to show my boss the pictures and we agreed it was tough to prove.

Fast forward to about a month later. We had settled, everyone there knew they were not getting fired -at least not this round- so people were a bit more relaxed. One of my staff walked into my office and asks to speak with me. I obliged. She proceeded to tell me that she wanted to confess something. I encouraged her to go right ahead. She told me how she and other people in the office had sought the services of a witch to bewitch me and how one of them had cut my brake line. She asked me if I had noticed that a group of them had started wearing these special beads as bracelets to which I said I hadn't. She said that they were given these beads by the witch who instructed them to always make sure that when they speak to me the "eyes" on the beads are pointed at me. I have to say I was taken aback because these kinds of things you usually hear associated with

African culture. Now that I am mature in Christ, I am aware that just as God is not governed by earthly boundaries, neither is the devil. Spirits of darkness have no respect for the first world; the Devil is an equal opportunity being. She said that the only reason she was telling me was that she believed that the God I worship is more powerful than their witchcraft because I was meant to die as I drove my car. She and her friends were not expecting me to come back to work. She asked me to pray with her and right there we prayed and I forgave her and her friends. Only God!!! From that point on, I don't always see my warrior but I know he is there, standing on guard – my very own angel on assignment.

If this wasn't happening to me, even I wouldn't believe it!

I also have some individuals I like to see as my angels on assignment who present in human form, flesh and blood. These are individuals who I have met along the way who have guided, protected, loved and supported me in my journey. Throughout the book, you will come across them as I mention them at the point that they appeared in my life and the role they each played. We all have these angels around us. I pray that you take the time to appreciate them where you can.

Easter, for Christ Followers, is a pretty significant holiday because it represents the sacrifice our Lord and Savior Jesus Christ gave us at Calvary. For me, 1987 marked the turnaround of my situation. Wednesday was the day we were scheduled to work half a day to close shop for the 5-day holiday. My morning started like any other. Patrick was walking me to work and he was showing what I came to term "payday jitters" where he would attempt to be nice knowing I was giving him my pay at the end of the day. The day before as he walked me to work we had an argument about the way he was carelessly using money and it had resulted in a lashing. I got to work with a bloodstained uniform which caused Priscilla to tell Dr. Kutoka my ordeal.

He called me in his office and I had no choice but to give him the full story of why I was in the situation I was. Dr. Kutoka, naturally, was shocked and disappointed. He, like most people who hear my story, couldn't understand why my father would take such a stand. He was also convinced that if I went home and spoke to my father in person and explain to my father the conditions under which I was living, he would, at the very least, give me the "letter of emancipation" so to speak. He went on to point out that since we had

5 days of the Easter holiday, it was plenty of time to travel to Chinhoyi, talk to my parents and come back to work. So we made a plan.

Wednesday, April 15, 1987

I went to work as usual, with Patrick in tow. It wasn't going to be a full day, but I didn't tell Patrick. Dr. Kutoka went to the bank that morning and gave us our pay. Those days, we received our pay in cash. He was now aware that Patrick "patrols" the front of the store. When the time came, he became our lookout while Priscilla and I left through the back door and ran to the bus terminal. We arrived as a bus to Harare was loading people. We went in, Priscilla with her weekend bag and I just my handbag. We managed to find seats towards the back of the bus and just as we thought we had gotten away, the conductor let one more passenger onto the bus. It was Patrick. Back then, people boarded the bus and while the bus was in motion the conductor would make his way from the front of the bus collecting fare for the ride. Since Patrick was one of the people in the front, naturally he was among the first people to be asked for fare. Unbeknownst to me, Patrick had told the conductor that I had his fare. So, when the conductor inquired upon arriving where we were seated, I told him we didn't have his fare that we were not traveling together.

Naturally, the conductor shouted back to Patrick that if he came back to the front and he didn't have his fare ready, he was going to leave him at the upcoming stop which was a police roadblock. Police roadblock were often set up along highways to inspect busses for their road safety worthiness and also to ensure the bus had not taken on more passengers than it was legally allowed to. All safety precautions – annoying to most travelers eager to get to their destinations because sometimes the police made everyone come off the bus with their luggage only to reload after clearance– were a necessary evil for our safety. Patrick started making his way towards the back. Somehow, I knew that he was only interested in the money. I quickly gave Priscilla all my money and instructed her to not release it no matter what. By the time Patrick got to where we were seating, I was ready for him.

He got to where I was and I could smell alcohol on his breath. He asked me to pay for his fare and I told him I didn't have any money. He insisted that I should be able to pay since I got paid that day. I proceeded to let him know that Dr. Kutoka had missed the bank so we will be getting paid after the holidays. He didn't believe me because he started searching my handbag and my pockets. When he didn't find any, he became agitated and within seconds, he had lifted me from my seat and ripped my uniform open. He put his hands inside my bra, yanked my breasts out accusing me of hiding the money in my bra. Of course, he couldn't find any and before I could button myself up I felt an incredible pain that pierced through my whole head. As I fumbled to catch my breath, I felt another blow, then I realized I was being head-butted. I don't know how many blows I got in my head but I began to see stars and the next thing I know I was being fanned outside the bus. When I came to, the conductor gave me $5.60 and told me he had to reimburse me for the bus fare since they couldn't wait any longer. I then noticed that we had actually stopped at the roadblock and there were police around. Once the bus left, policemen started asking both Patrick and I what had happened. Patrick gave them his version and I mine. The police worked under Patrick's father so one of them offered to drive us home. When we got back home, the policemen narrated to Patrick's family what had happened. After the police officers left, Patrick told his parents that I was running away. At this point my head was pounding and swollen. I was excused from their presence with a serious scolding. I went to assist the maid with the chores of the evening and she, feeling sorry for me, asked me to go lie down. I remember that I was falling asleep when I was yanked out of bed and got punched, kicked and head-butted over and over. There were people in the house but no one came to my rescue. I kept going in and out of consciousness. I was only saved after his twin brothers returned from school and they pulled him off me. "Mukoma, munouraya Maiguru". ("Brother, you will kill our sister-in-law"). Yes, at some point after I arrived in Marondera, I transitioned from being a sister, in their eyes to a sister-in-law, largely out of respect.

<u>Sidebar: If I hadn't been before, I sure was more determined than ever to escape this situation. End of Sidebar.</u>

When we were growing up in boarding school, we always marveled at how much swelling happens when someone had been beaten by a swarm of bees or wasps. When I woke up the following morning my head was like a watermelon, just like those people we used to make fun of after they had been beaten by bees or wasps while in the forest looking for wild fruits. I could hardly see as my eyes were almost buried; but I was going to get out of there one way or the other. I felt like Esther in *Esther 4:16*, when she said "...*if I perish, I perish.*" I woke before dawn, took my shoes and enough clothes that fit in a little plastic bag. I opened the door very slowly, while everyone was still asleep. I ran and threw the shoes and plastic bag over the fence. Our gate used to squeak a lot when it was being opened, so I didn't want to wake anyone. I went back to the house and took my wrappers - one for my head and the other for around my waist. I then took the broom that we used to sweep the yard and I went to work. I swept the whole yard as I slowly but purposefully made my way towards the gate. It was our practice to also sweep the space just outside our yards. I tried to open the gate as slowly as possible to avoid the squeak. As soon as I was clear, I went to retrieve my bag of clothes and shoes. As I bent over to pick the bag up, I suddenly felt I wasn't alone. Sure enough, my worst fear, Patrick, was standing in front of me ready to give me a slap across my face. I stumbled and fell. He dragged me back into the yard, kicking and screaming. The whole house was awakened by the commotion and Patrick told them he caught me trying to run away. Once again, his twin brothers came to my rescue and saved me from another beating. I remember hearing one of them begging, just like the night before, "Mukoma Patrick, muchauraya Maiguru". Loosely translated, "Brother Patrick, you are going to kill our sister-in-law". He let me go and things calmed down. The maid had gone away for the long weekend so I started preparing breakfast for everyone.

At some point during the day, as I was nursing my wounds, Patrick came to where I was seated under a tree and started inquiring about my pay. When I did not respond, he started apologizing for hurting me. I saw my window of opportunity right there and I told him that I had given Priscilla the money. Now the conversation that transpired could only have been inspired by the Holy Spirit because I have no idea how it flowed out of me effortlessly. I went on to tell him that the journey he interrupted last night was for us, him and I. That brisk fateful November day when they wanted to leave me in Chinhoyi and I hung onto the truck, I had learnt something new that had not been shared before. As we were driving along the highway someone mentioned that the policemen who were driving the lorry had been instructed to make a detour in Chitungwiza-St. Mary's to Patrick's mother's house. Patrick's mother? *So, who was that woman in the little car that went ahead of us to Marondera with all the little kids?* On that day, I learnt that Patrick, his twin brothers and one of the little girls had their own biological mother who had been Mr. Moon's first wife. This is one of the beauties of our culture, "step-parents, step-children, step-siblings" are terms we don't use in the same way as it is in the Western world. I am not saying there are no abuses that transpire between the former wife's children and the latter. Back then they were rare. Most blended families made it work and strangers may never know the difference. Such was the Moon family.

I told him I was on my way to his biological mother's house in St. Mary's. He looked confused. I went on to explain to him that I had noticed that every time I gave him my pay, he squandered it on alcohol. So, I was on my way to give his mum the money so she can keep it for us until we had enough for him to go back to school to learn a trade. I told him that I knew that he was under pressure from his father to start a family, but I was afraid that doing so while he was unemployed was not a good idea. He started crying and at this point I knew I had the upper hand. For the first time, I actually sensed I could get out of this situation alive. He then promised to take the money to his mother upon Priscilla's return from the holiday. I then told him I was afraid that Priscilla may use the money if she were to get to her home and found a need that may force her to use the money. I pointed out how challenging it would be to pay back that money and we would most likely get it not as a lump sum but in insignificant installments. We weighed various options and finally he decided he was going to use the refund I had gotten from the bus fare from the previous night and travel to Harare, find Priscilla and retrieve the money. I pointed out given what Priscilla had witnessed on the bus I didn't think she would give him the money. He asked his uncle, Joe (his father's brother who lived with us at the house), to loan him some money but uncle didn't have any. His hope was for us to travel together. Finally, I convinced him that I should go as quickly as possible to reduce the chances of Priscilla using the money she had. To my relief, he agreed. His greed for that money got the better of him and it worked in my favor. He even planned how we would leave the house without his parents suspecting anything. Very early in the morning of Friday April 16, 1987, was to be the last day I ever laid my eyes on Patrick. We sneaked out of the house, with him as my lookout, and he accompanied me to the bus station as he held my paper bag of clothes. I got on the bus and waved goodbye. By this time my whole head was swollen beyond recognition. I was like one who had been stung by the biggest swarm of bees you can think of. I was in pain. But I was free! I purposed in my heart that no matter what my father was going to say, I was not returning to Marondera.

God Orders My Steps

WHEN I GOT TO HARARE, with no money on me, I got off at the intersection of Seke Road and I believe Mutare Road. That corner was called "Coca Cola" back then because a huge Coke plant was located right there. Being that I had used up all the money I had; I began to walk towards the city center with a destination in mind. Sisi Joyce, the oldest girl among the Dangwa clan, lived with her husband and family at Harwell Court on North Avenue just before one gets to Parirenyatwa Hospital. Sisi Joyce was the same cousin who was married to Tete Rosie's brother, Rodwell Samkange.

I was walking a long time but I didn't feel the distance. I was free! I could hardly see where I was walking due to the swelling. But I was free! Eventually I arrived. I was knocking on her apartment door a few minutes when her neighbor from across the hallway saw me. She asked me who I was looking for and who I was. This woman had seen me many times visiting my sister over the years, she knew who I was but even as she came closer, she still couldn't recognize me. I told her who I was and naturally she inquired about my swollen head. I didn't want to get into it so I just told her I was attacked by a swarm of bees. She then remembered me and informed me that my sister and her family had gone to the rural areas for the holidays. Visiting family during national holidays was a norm for most families, so it wasn't surprising. As I was walking to my sister's house earlier, I had not considered that possibility. *Now what?* I told my sister's neighbor that I didn't have money to go home so asked if she could loan me some money, I was sure my sister, Joyce, would pay her upon her return. She gave me $20 and we parted ways.

Next order of business…find Priscilla.

I needed to find Priscilla if it was the last thing I did. But there was a challenge. I didn't know her address. All I knew was that she lived in Seke. I remembered a conversation we had at work one time about going to church and she had told me that she really couldn't get away from going to church because they practically lived next to a Roman Catholic Church. Her mum was Catholic. So now I had 2 vital pieces of information. I set up to travel to Seke, a place I had never been, except for that detour to Marondera. On that day, we were at the back of an enclosed lorry, had no idea how we got there, what the address was, just that we got to Patrick's biological mum's house, she made us lunch and took it on to eat as we proceeded to Marondera. My plan was to visit every Catholic Church and inquire around it if they knew a Priscilla who worked in Marondera. I couldn't even remember her last name. I was pretty messed up. Now, if you're a

Zimbabwean and are familiar with Seke you know that was a tall order and a seemingly impossible task. Seke was divided into various sections all of them densely populated. But this did not deter me. I owed it to my freedom to at least try. I went to the terminal to catch a ride out of Harare city center, Seke is about 20 miles from there. I arrived at the first section and just kept going from one section to another with just two questions: 1) Where can I find the local Catholic Church? And once I arrived at the church, I would ask anyone the 2nd question 2) Do you know Priscilla whose parents live around here and she works in Marondera?

At some point, I realized that I couldn't keep getting on the Kombis to travel from one section to another as not only were my funds depleting but soon it would be dark. Kombis are the main modes of transportation in Zimbabwe. They are overused vans that stop anywhere along a specific route and let people on and off upon request, unlike buses that have designated bus stops and are owned by the government. Kombis are privately-owned passenger vans. As I stood at a crossroads, considering whether to get one last Kombi then walk the rest of the way, I asked a man I ran into to let me know where the nearest Catholic Church was from where we were. You see, it never dawned on me that I would not find Priscilla that day; I just figured it was only a matter of time. I never stopped praying and believing in my spirit. I alternated between praying and entering into negotiating sessions with God. The man I asked for directions pointed me to the nearest Catholic church to where I was. I thanked him and as I was walking away from him, he was getting back on his bicycle when he turned around after moving a few feet and called for my attention. "I just remembered that even if you go to that location, you will not find anyone. Because it's Easter, all Catholics are meeting at Unit K. You're better off going there instead". I inquired how I could get to Unit K and he advised me to get a Kombi because it was a long way. I told him I didn't really have money for the Kombi and asked if he could direct me how to get there on foot. He said it would take me at least an hour and a half if I took a shortcut but it wasn't safe after sunset. He gave me the directions and I started running across the semi-wooded area. At 19 years old my stamina was great because I ran cross-country and long-distance track in high school, therefore, I was used to running long distances. No matter what, I was going to get there. There are several things that could have happened to me as I ran through the wooded area - none of them pleasant. But I did not care. I didn't have the luxury to consider the danger. I just couldn't afford wasting time and risking sunset. So, I ran like Forest in Forest Gump, the movie.

As I got out of the wooded area I could see houses and I kept going because the man had said as soon as I got past the first set of homes, I wouldn't miss the church because I would start seeing Catholics in their uniforms. Sure enough, I saw a sea of people and I walked towards it. As I entered the church grounds, I was suddenly overwhelmed by the sheer number of people and thought, *Where do I start? Who do I ask?* I could hear music in the church and there were many women all over the grounds in pockets cooking meals and just being jovial.

As I stood there 'sizing up' each woman trying to decide who to ask first, I finally decided on one woman who looked kind. As I approached her, after I greeted her, I asked her, "Do you know Mai Priscilla..." and before I finished my question she said, "Teresa Dangwa, I was expecting you. Priscilla told me you would come; I am her mum". I just fell into her arms and cried...no, sobbed like a baby in distress. All I could say over and over was, "Thank you Jesus". Only God could orchestrate this encounter. The first and only person I approached happened to be the mother of my friend and colleague, Priscilla with no last name. How awesome is that!! How incredible is the God that I serve!!! She let me cry for a bit as she hugged me then I realized she too was crying.

If this wasn't happening to me, I too would be wide-eyed like you are right now!

Time stood still, surrounded by a sea of people but yet just two individuals reeling in emotions embracing one another. Not saying anything to each other but each of us recognizing the significance of this moment. She led me through the crowd to the other entrance on the opposite side from where I entered. We passed a couple of houses and we arrived at her house. As we entered the gate, Priscilla's mum made a loud announcement as we entered the house. Priscilla came from around the corner and we just cried and embraced. After we caught our breath, I noticed a whole spread of baked goods and a handwritten sign that read, "Welcome Teresa". Priscilla's mum told me that that's all her daughter did all day, bake, pray, cry and asked her mum to pray some more expecting me to show up. They both couldn't believe how swollen my head was. I asked if I could rest a while then go to Chinhoyi to my parents when I looked better. Priscilla's mum was not having it; clearly her daughter had given her the scoop. She explained that she really believed that if I went home in this swollen state. my father would have compassion and release me. While I ate the baked goods, my dear friend had prepared, Priscilla took my plastic bag that had my clothes in it and put them in a nice weekend bag. Then she did something that will forever be etched in my heart. She brought out the most beautiful two-piece light green skirt suit I'd ever seen. She had it specially ordered from South Africa for her Easter Sunday and she had not even worn it. She handed it to me saying, "If you got home dressed nice, your father has no choice but to take you back or at least give you the letter you need to live independently". No matter how much I resisted, she and her mother insisted. Needless to say, I lost the argument. Priscilla's mother prayed for me and bid us farewell to go back to church. We proceeded with a mini party as we hung out a little bit. Priscilla prepared for me to take a shower so I can go home as fresh as possible. I was ready to go and face my fate at my father's house.

Stubborn is as Stubborn Does

TO GET TO CHINHOYI I had to go back into the city, take another kombi to another suburb called Greencroft where I was to hitchhike from there to go to Chinhoyi. Hitchhiking is dangerous, especially in the

West - almost unheard of in the US, but a norm in Zimbabwe and most African countries. Chinhoyi was about 75 miles from Harare. In Shona/Ndebele custom, when you are in trouble, especially with your parents, you don't dare go confront your parents on your own. Depending on the amount of trouble you are in, you either send someone, like an advance team, to soften your parents, or you are accompanied by someone who then speaks on your behalf. The "someone" you choose to be your advocate is not just chosen haphazardly. Some thought and wisdom have to be exercised. It has to be a relative or a very close friend of your father that he respects. The relative cannot just be anyone either, it has to be one whose relationship your father values and respects. That individual is usually your father's nephew or uncle as in his mother's brother. Being that my kind of trouble was significant, I had to be very wise and strategic. So, I chose his nephew who lived not too far from my parents' home. When I arrived at Kamera's home, neither he nor his family recognized me due to the swelling. In hindsight, it was good that I was unrecognizable because it meant I could still pull off the element of surprise on my father. Even though I recognized some people I ran into as I walked to Kamera's house, no one could tell who I was, which became a blessing in disguise in itself so I was spared the need to explain my story to every curious George along the way. After some crying, a meal and a good night's rest, Kamera and his wife went to my parents to beg my father to forgive me and take me back. Before they left, I informed them that I was still a virgin and that my father could get me tested if he liked. Every year for many years to come after that, I kept asking for that virginity test to prove to my father that I was still "pure". But he was never interested. Anyhow, on this Easter Saturday, we all decided it was best I remained at Kamera's house until the "negotiations" were over.

It seemed like they were gone forever. When they eventually came back, they had my mum in tow. She only took one look at me and broke down. We both cried uncontrollably for a while. After we had calmed down a bit, Kamera broke the news that my father had refused to take me back, nor was he interested in writing my letter of emancipation. I was devastated. It's like my heart just shattered into thousands of pieces. All my hope just drained out of me. They had also come back with another message reiterating his original threats of killing his relatives or divorcing my mother as well as the fact that I was no longer his daughter. Kamera and his wife reported that they literally had to beg him to let my Mum come to see me. I was also informed that I couldn't stay at Kamera's house, not even for another night.

My Mum helplessly walked me to the bus station. She returned home thinking I was going back to Patrick's place in Marondera. I knew I would rather die than go back to Marondera. I went to another of my father's friends whom he respected because his wife shared the same totem as his mum, so they were like "parents" to my father. He reverenced them very much. Because of that connection, we grew up treating them as another set of grandparents. Most people in the community didn't know we were not really related. When I got there and narrated my situation, they came up with a different plan. This couple, Mr. & Mrs. Chisepo, had a rural home in an area called Guruve which was about 130 miles from Chinhoyi. But I wasn't going to their homestead; rather, I was going to live with my real uncle. Apparently, my father had an uncle from his mother's side (my grandmother), Charles Utete who happened to be a Mudumeni (Agricultural Officer) in Guruve. Sekuru and Mbuya Chisepo (Grandpa and Grandma) put me on the bus and said they will call Sekuru Charles ahead of my arrival. We made a covenant that we would not tell a soul where I was.

I arrived in Guruve, yet another area I had never been. It was more rural than Marondera and Chinhoyi. Uncle Charles' office was easy to find. It was just as the Chisepos had advised. Sekuru (this word is used for both uncles, on the maternal side, and grandfather) Charles welcomed me like a long-lost dear friend and assured me that all was going to work out eventually. He took me home and introduced me to his wife, a teacher. Her welcome was equally as warm. It turned out Ambuya, term for this type of Aunty, was a teacher away from home who only came home during weekends. So, during the week it was going to be just Sekuru and me. Months went by with no word from anyone.

So, what happened to Patrick?

THE FOLLOWING WAS WHAT other people, including my sister, Janet, narrated to me as events that happened soon after that Easter weekend.

After Patrick left me on the bus on that Easter Friday, he went looking for money to follow me to Harare. You see, back then, not every household had a house phone and cell phones were nonexistent. So, the only other way to communicate was by letter, telex, telegram, public payphones or in person. For Patrick, it was important that he got my salary in his hands. He always thought he could manipulate his biological mother. I understand he got the money a day or two after I left. He went directly to his mother's home in St. Mary's which interestingly was not far from Seke where I was, at Priscilla's home. When he got there, he was told I never got there. The truth of the matter is I couldn't have gone anyway because I didn't know her address, nor did I know her name. We had only gone there once. That was the day we moved from Chinhoyi the previous year on our way to Marondera on board that big police lorry. We stopped there for maybe an hour and that was it. I understand he tried to find Priscilla's house but failed. He didn't know any of the information I had about Priscilla. The next, natural, place to go and find me was Chinhoyi. Of course, he couldn't go to my parents' house directly, at least not if he wanted to live and tell the story. My sister, Janet, later told me that she had ran into him in our neighborhood. Apparently, sometime between leaving his mother's house and going to Chinhoyi, he had stopped to purchase a knife. He then showed Janet the knife as he narrated how I had tricked him. He told Janet that he had purchased it specially to kill me with it. I also heard from some church folk that he had gone to the church offices in both Harare and Chinhoyi telling whoever would listen that he was going to find me and kill me even if it took him his entire life.

It turns out he hung around my parents' street for days just going up and down thinking he may see me. He just wasn't believing my sister who was telling him I never came home. I don't know how long he hung around there but one day he was either just gone or he wasn't seen.

I heard through the grapevine that he went back to Marondera later and harassed Priscilla and Dr. Kutoka a bit but both of them were tough cookies.

I don't know how long he searched but about 3 months after, Sekuru Charles was listening to the radio and he heard an announcement during the news that my father was trying to locate me. Back then, the radio used to do a public service announcement around news time in which people called in to report lost or missing loved ones; death announcements; lost national IDs or school/college certificates, etc. I guess my father had heard word that Patrick was looking for me to kill me. Now there was panic because no one knew where I was. Sekuru Charles decided we were going to let my father stew a little bit. The announcement would come out often and we would just ignore it. The Chisepos kept us in the loop too whenever they came to visit. Their reports were that my father was worried that Patrick may have carried out his threats. I never heard from Patrick again. I found out a few years ago that he had passed away. I can only hope that he found peace in the end.

The Stubbornness Runs Deep But This Time It Met Its Match

AFTER ANOTHER 2 MONTHS of my "disappearance announcement", Sekuru Charles thought it was time to put my father out of his misery. We made a trip to Chinhoyi. When we arrived Sekuru Charles insisted that I walk in with him into the house. As we entered the house, my father saw me and immediately that worry turned to wrath and ordered me to leave his house. After back and forth with his uncle, I was asked to step outside. My father screamed after me that he didn't want me in the yard. So, I left and went to sit on the garbage can just outside the gate. I didn't have leprosy as in the 4 lepers in 2 Kings 7 but I sure felt like I did. I could see my siblings peering through the windows looking at me but unable to come to me in fear of my father's wrath. To be discarded or shunned by those who are supposed to love and care for you is a horrible place to be.

Discussions went on for what seemed like a lifetime. Eventually I saw my uncle coming out and going to the car. He summoned for me to come over and asked me to get in the car. My father, who had walked my uncle to the car, didn't even look at me. We drove off and my uncle explained that my father was not shifting his position. He assured me it was going to be okay. I remember as we drove back to Guruve my uncle kept giving me encouragement that one day I will have a great future that God will use all this trouble to propel me to greatness. Neither of us realized at the time that he was speaking Romans 8:28 into my life. That coupled with Ms. Mururi's words of encouragement a year before would be the hope I held on to. Romans 8:28 would become an anchor in my life to this day.

Uncle Charles and I were to make two more trips to my father's house to see if he had changed his mind. The second time was no different from the first time. The third time started as usual but this time my uncle insisted on me coming with him in the house. My father started to protest but my uncle was not budging. I don't know if it was the sternness in his voice or the "enough with this nonsense" look on his face that made my father not argue. Whatever it was, here I was sitting on the floor of my father's living room, feeling worse than a stranger. I sat closer to the door in case I needed to bolt.

My Mum, always hospitable, started to prepare some food but my uncle interrupted her and asked her to come and sit down because he needed to talk to both of them together. The following dialogue transpired, after the pleasantries, in Shona but I am going to write in English without the Shona version. Sekuru Charles, sat up straight with a face and attitude that meant business and addressed them with their totems.

"Sinyoro naGambiza," he started. "You both know why I'm here". He didn't wait for any verbal acknowledgment. "I've been coming here for a while now and still getting the same response from you, Nephew", he said as he addressed my Father specifically.

Silence.

"Each time I've come here, you have indicated that this child is not yours. Correct?" he again addressed my father directly. With unresolved anger and absolute resolve in his decision, my Father responded, "Hongu, ndakamuramba kare" (Yes, I made my decision a long time ago, she doesn't belong to me).

"You still stand by that?" my uncle inquired almost offering my father a way out and for my father to take back his words.

"Yes Sekuru (Uncle)," my father answered unmoved.

"Gambiza, mainzwaka nyaya iyo?" (You heard that right?), Sekuru Charles said turning to my Mum. Sekuru wasn't trying to get her to agree or to disagree with my father's take on the matter. Uncle knew better than to question my father's status as the patriot authority in line with our custom. He was merely seeking a witness to what my father had said. My Mum, with all humbleness she could muster and being careful not to seem like she was challenging my father, said - almost inaudible acknowledges him, "Ndazvinzwa Sekuru" (Yes Uncle, I heard). Over time my mother has become recipient of the rhetoric of my father's rage. Not physically or anything like that (not to my knowledge anyway, except at least 3 times that I can recall). But his words. She knew there was nothing that could persuade her husband to change his mind. Not from lack of trying, but my father was as stubborn and prideful as they get.

"Very well then", Sekuru continued in total surrender. "If that is the case, please let me know who her people are so I can take her there because I cannot keep her with me now that we have established she is no kin of ours. I will not keep a stranger in my house lest something befalls her while she is in my custody".

My uncle was not playing my father's games anymore. Right there in that moment Sekuru evoked his right to use reverse psychology before it had a name. It was game over for my father.

We were all stunned. Did he just smoothly put my father in a corner with no apparent Exit sign? My Mum and I looked at each other inconspicuously, daring not to look at my father. We both looked down as my uncle repeated himself. My father, who has always prided himself in always having something to say, was equally stunned. This time with an unmistaken twinge of anger and frustration; but he knew better than to question the manner in which Sekuru Charles had chosen to end this fiasco.

"Who are her people?" My uncle asked pointing at me in case it wasn't clear to my father who he was referring to.

"What is that supposed to mean?" my father retorted with a measured tone.

"I am not leaving this place without an answer," said Uncle Charles. "This has gone on for too long. This child deserves to know who her people are so she can go".

My uncle is fully aware of my father's belief system as it is all our belief system. Within our culture, it is believed that when a stranger dies in one's custody, especially under circumstances where unpleasant words are exchanged, the deceased's spirit can and will haunt the clan and future generations until repentance and some form of remunerations are paid. So, to my father that question from my uncle about who my people were, was loaded. There is no deeper hurt than that of being abandoned and rejected by your parent or parents. It makes you lose your sense of belonging and identity. No matter the outcome of this conversation, I was always going to know I was not wanted. Needless to say, this line of questioning from Sekuru Charles ended the impasse and just like that, I was allowed to stay at my father's house.

CHAPTER FOUR

The Church - Sadly not Always a Safe Haven

But you will receive power when the Holy Spirit comes on you; and you will be my witnesses in Jerusalem, and in all Judea and Samaria, and to the ends of the earth." – Acts 1:8

And they devoted themselves to the apostles' teaching and to the fellowship, to the breaking of bread and the prayers. – Acts 2:24

Then Jesus came to them and said, "All authority in heaven and on earth has been given to me. 19 Therefore go and make disciples of all nations, baptizing them in the name of the Father and of the Son and of the Holy Spirit, 20 and teaching them to obey everything I have commanded you. And surely I am with you always, to the very end of the age." – Matthew 28:18-20

Religion that is pure and undefiled before God the Father is this: to visit orphans and widows in their affliction, and to keep oneself unstained from the world. – James 1:27

I BELIEVE IN ORDER TO FULLY UNDERSTAND THE purpose of the church the way God intended; one has to delve into the Book of Acts. It provides the foundation of what church is supposed to be. I also believe if church was to have a mission statement, it would be summed up in four scriptures, Acts 1:8; 2:42; Matthew 28:18-20 and James 1:27 - all quoted above. After I was born again in 1982, I have not seen myself doing anything else outside of church. Certain things no longer appeal to me. Of course, there are some areas where I am still a work in progress while I have matured in other areas. I don't always succeed but I try my best to follow the Word. Pentecostal or Charismatic Renewal, as my friend used to call it, brought with it a certain awareness of one's spirituality that calls for a deeper personal and collective accountability. It definitely has a different way of doing things than the traditional churches. I grew up a Catholic only because we went to a Catholic boarding school when we were younger. In my opinion, observation and experience, in the Catholic faith everything is so rigid and more about rules than about grace. The verses are only read by the priest, there is no requirement to bring a Bible or to open one. There are catechism booklets you study when you prepare to be confirmed and baptized. The priest is the go between and Mary has a much more significant role that she is not given in the Word of God. As a matter of fact, just before Christ was nailed to the cross, He ensures that He has left Mary in someone's capable hands, signifying her job/assignment was over. *John 19:25-29, "Now there stood by the cross of Jesus His mother, and His mother's sister, Mary the wife of Clopas, and Mary Magdalene. When Jesus therefore saw His mother, and the disciple whom He loved standing by, He said to His mother, "Woman, behold your son!" Then He said to the disciple, "Behold your mother!" And from that hour that disciple took her to his own home."* The Pentecostal on the other hand, I found was all about grace, memory verses, know the Word, there is only one mediator between us and God, that is Jesus Christ; being filled with the Holy Spirit with the evidence of speaking in tongues, casting out demons, giving more than just a few pennies in the offering basket, the three day dry fasting was a must so were all night prayers, Bible studies in home groups, etc. Clearly, I am oversimplifying things here but you catch my drift. The Pentecostal church I became a member of was serious about teaching the Word of God. I owe my unquenchable thirst for the Word to them. The leader, the Prophet, was (and I believe still is), an incredible teacher of the Word. So was the bishop, pastors and lay pastors. I am grateful for my knowledge and understanding of Salvation to three of those lay pastors.

So Many Bumps Under the Rugs

WHEN MY TWO SISTERS and I left the Catholic Church to follow the Pentecostal teachings and belief system, we had some cultural shocks of our own. For instance, once one was born again, one was discouraged from associating with non-believers to the point that even one's parents could be placed in that category. So you found most people would stop residing at their parents' homes and move in with the local pastor who then took on the role of your parents in all decisions including marriage and in some cases career choices. Some pastors as they got called into ministry they even took their college certificates to the fire in some misguided attempt of showing outwardly that they are committing to the ministry full time. My sisters and I did not have the luxury of choosing a "new family and parents" so to speak. My father, in his strictness was not hearing it. He would tell us we were free to join that church but we were to always come home. Unlike most of our friends and fellow church members, we never spent a night at the pastor's house unless it was the venue for the all-night prayer. In that regards we were quite fortunate because as people grew in the Lord some people realized or came to understand that *Exodus 20:12 and Ephesians 6:2* did not apply to so called "spiritual parents". Some people however realized it after it was too late and relationships with parents and other relatives had been ruined.

<u>Sidebar: In as much as the Word was taught in this new church, there were some behaviors that could pass for cult tendencies. Even to this day there are some church leaders who want to control every move of their congregants. One of the things I regret about joining this type of Pentecostal was the time that was stolen from us effectively barring us from spending time with family. Before joining the Pentecostal movement, my sisters and I spent time with our parents, aunts and other extended families. Sometimes we would go to our grandparents' home to be with our</u>

cousins and other relatives. But after joining, every significant public holiday was strongly encouraged to attend what were known as 'camp meetings'. Every quarter there was a camp meeting with the biggest one taking place over Christmas to New Year's, effectively cutting out time with family. Our non-believing relatives, including parents, were something to be disassociated from me. As if the blood of Jesus was so porous that the nonbelievers would somehow contaminate us. Kinda defeats some of the memory verses we used to be taught like being the salt and light of the earth (Matthew 5:13-16. So, if we isolated ourselves from the non-believers, how are we to spread the goodness and love of Christ? What good is our saltness and light then? How so removed we were from

<u>emulating Christ who was found among the sinners of sinners which always angst the Bible scholars and teachers of the day. End of Sidebar.</u>

The Devil You Know is Better than the One You Don't

AFTER MY FATHER REJECTED ME and I had escaped from Patrick and his family, I gravitated towards the pastors and some lay pastors and ended up residing and/or visiting for weekends at several of their homes at different times. I was very disappointed to learn that what these particular individuals preached at the pulpit was more often than not what they practiced at home. I was up for a rude awakening to the point that I decided during that time that marriage was not an option for me. I figured, if what I was experiencing or witnessing was the example and extent of Christ Followers' marriages, there really was no need to enter into a life commitment with anyone. My parents' marriage, though not based on Christ-centered values per se, was a much stronger example of a good marriage. My parents did not attend church while we were growing up – at least I don't have a recollection of us walking or driving together to go to church. It was always us kids. My father is a traditionalist who believes his ancestors are on the lookout for him and if anything is wrong, then there must be something the ancestors are not happy about. Therefore, one needs to do all they can to appease the ancestors with various rituals. What I will forever appreciate about my parents, especially my father, being that he is the head of our household, never and I mean NEVER forced us to follow or participate in his belief system. In fact, anytime he went to the rural areas for whatever ritual, he would take his wife and leave us at home in the city. My siblings and I grew up very shielded from it – at least the oldest four.

I used to call it the misfortune of residing in the church leadership's homes until I realized it was necessary for me to see those things. If nothing else, I was able to come to the conclusion that, unlike popular belief (and at times, these leaders present themselves), evangelists, pastors, lay pastors, bishops, prophets and their spouses are human beings seeking grace just like me. They too are fallible and far from perfect.

This may sound naïve, but when I started going to this particular church, which I believed was more enlightened in comparison to where I was coming from, Catholic, there were things I did not expect to learn or be exposed to in the church.

<u>Sidebar: If you are looking for names and obvious identifiers, sorry to disappoint you. The purpose of me sharing my experience and my truth is not to expose specific individuals (although if they do read this book, they will identify themselves and hope that they make it right with God for I have forgiven them all, completely). I am here to expose behaviors and a way of living that does not lineup with the Word of God when one professes to be a servant of God that is often taboo to speak about in Christian circles – unless you want to risk being branded as "a scatterer" or "a perverse generation" which was what I was called</u>

more times than I care to count. Now do yourself (and me) a favor, don't start folding your mouth upwards and fix your heart and mouth to say, "Now she thinks she is perfect – no one is perfect". Well, truth is you are right about one thing in your thought process. "no one is perfect", least of all me. Like Apostle Paul, I say, "This is a faithful saying, and worthy of all acceptation, that Christ Jesus came into the world to save sinners; of whom I am chief." (1 Timothy 1:15). After all, it is written that "There is none that is perfect, not even one". (Romans 3:10). So now my dear friend, I am in no way shape or form implying that I am perfect nor do I expect anyone to be perfect, far from it. We are all made perfect in Him. (2 Corinthians 12:9). End of Sidebar.

Sometimes we like to use Romans 3:10 as an excuse to do what we know we shouldn't be doing but want to do it anyway or to "cover" bad behavior for our loved ones. As believers, we should not excuse sin and "weaknesses" but we should bring it to light so it is dealt with. The church today, is full of so many bumps under their rugs, it is no wonder no one wants this Jesus that we are selling so to speak. The characteristics of a servant of God are clearly defined in no uncertain terms in the Word. First Timothy and Titus provide comprehensive and similar but not identical lists of those characteristics (1 Timothy 3:2-5; Titus 1:6-9 and also see 1 Peter 5:3).

The following are some of my personal experiences that expose the bumps under the church rugs that I hope will help someone who may be going through what I went through and have not found their voice to speak up; help someone who is looking to heal and find their purpose post trauma; help bring about healing for individuals as well as the church. I truly believe that once we bring these bumps from underneath the rug, we can see and expose the spirit that is behind it and the author of such weaknesses, the Devil. Honest discussions, forgiveness and healing transpires when exposure happens, rendering the sin and weakness powerless. As long as we don't talk about it in the church, we will continue to be bound in secrecy as we lead each other straight to hell. These events happened between 1988 and 2016.

<u>Experience One</u>:

I went to live with one family whose husband was a servant of God. I knew the husband first before the wife due to his role in the church so naturally, I was closer to him than the wife. She and I hardly interacted but she was kind to me, at least in the beginning. The husband would sneak into my room as the wife slept or was away attending some church meeting or choir practice. It is important to note that even though I was considered an adult at that time, I was a naïve, damaged and vulnerable young adult. My age merely tallied how long I had been here on earth. I was immature. I was still a very vulnerable young woman still seeking approval from my father so when these male leaders showed me a little bit of attention, I didn't stop to think of the ramifications of what they were doing. You see when you don't deal with 'daddy issues' effectively, they will come back to haunt you at some point in your life, adult or not.

At first when the elder touched me it was just a little brush here and there and dismissed as a mistake. Now in retrospect I see that it was to get me to a place where it seemed or felt normal or comfortable. Please understand this is merely an assumption on my part because I cannot speak intelligently to what one man's thoughts were or are, especially since it was never a discussion. Sure enough, over time the brushing became normalized. See when you play with fire long enough, it will burn you. At first the fire brings warmth but if you don't control the source of that fire, it will burn you. Before I go on, please don't think that I am not taking responsibility of my own actions. At the time, as a damaged individual, the electric cord wasn't reaching the outlet, if you know what I mean.

When you build a fire on a cold wintery day, at first it brings warmth but you sit in that place long enough, your body temperature begins to adapt to the temperature in the room. However, if you keep watching the news and the weather continues to report dropping temperatures, if you don't account for the adjustment in your own body, you keep adding more firewood and by the time you realize it, it is too hot. That's when you see some people opening windows to let the cool air in because they did not pay attention to their individual circumstances. Same with sexual advances, if you don't snip it right away, it begins to build up and the next thing you are unable to sleep without masturbation. Yes, I became addicted over years – long after I left that couple's home. The elder literally showed me how to touch myself until I climaxed. Now whether that was his fantasy of watching me do this to myself and drift off to sleep or he derived some satisfaction out of it or he went back to his room and finished off with the wife or had a one man party, I cannot tell you. I was knocked out! Some days, he would guide my hands to touch him but somehow it always felt weird for me – touching myself was one thing but feeling his manhood was a bit much.

<u>Sidebar: For parents who may be considering disowning your children or who have done it, I need you to know that that</u>

action is placing your child in a very vulnerable situation. Parents are our security blanket and when they disown us, they are living us open to the Devil's devious ways. When my father disowned me, I was left open. I had no parental covering because even after my father was strong armed into allowing me to come back home, he hardly acknowledged my presence. So as much as possible I visited home less and less and gravitated to the next best thing. It is no coincidence that Apostle Paul admonishes fathers in Ephesians 6:4, *"Fathers, do not provoke your children to anger, but bring them up in the discipline and instruction of the Lord."* and repeated again Colossians 3:21, *"Fathers, do not provoke your children, lest they become discouraged."*

Why fathers? Because they are the heads of households and therefore the ultimate responsibility of how their children are raised lies squarely on their shoulders.

The word provoke is an interesting one. It means to negatively stir up something or someone. In other Bible versions it uses the word exasperate, to cause them to be angry and become bitter or resentful. Then when you look at the word, discouraged it means to lose confidence or enthusiasm; to be disheartened; make despondent; dampen someone's hopes; to depress, to disappoint. An individual who has lost hope is easy prey for the devil. Just as God uses people for good, the devil too uses people – including pastors/servants of God - for bad. Maybe this man who taught me masturbation had his own distorted way of connecting and showing love, we may never know on this side of eternity. End of Sidebar.

Experience Two:

I grew up skinny. I was very active in school – basketball, cross-country, volleyball, tennis, you name it. I was even in some of those school sports teams. So when I dared to gain weight, unintentionally of course, an assumption was made by church leaders that I had become pregnant. So one of those three lay preachers I mentioned earlier was asked to confront me about it.

I arrived a little early at the venue where a midweek service was held and the lay preacher, let's call him Mr. LP for lay preacher (get it, lol), asked me to take a walk with him. Nothing unusual about that people would hang around awaiting the beginning of service. I guess the church leadership figured since him and I were close, it will be best addressed by him. So we took a walk and after the pleasantries this is how the conversation went, bear in mind it was happening in Shona so I am literally translating):

Mr. LP: So whose is it?

Me (clueless): Whose is what?

Mr. LP: Don't play with me. Whose is it?

Me (completely perplexed): Whose is what, Daddy? (all married men and women in the church were addressed as daddy and mama/mummy, respectively – don't worry, I was delivered from that nonsense)

Mr. LP: You don't play with me, the pregnancy, who is responsible?

Me (more perplexed): Who is pregnant?

Mr. LP (annoyed): Yours of course!

Me (even more perplexed): Me? Pregnant?

Mr. LP: Please don't play dumb with me, just tell me whose it is so we can figure out a plan.

Me: (Now extremely annoyed, especially since even at that time I was still trying to prove to my biological father that I was still a virgin so the thought of me having done the deed and now pregnant was preposterous) Whoever told you I was pregnant is the one responsible

Mr. LP (almost jumping out of his skin): Aah! Are you mad?

Me (not discerning where this was going): Of course I am not mad but whoever told you I was pregnant is the one who is responsible, I sarcastically responded.

Mr. LP (clearly confused and genuinely concerned): OK, here is what we will do. Please don't talk to anyone about this until I come back to you, OK? Please my daughter (pleadingly).

Me (nonchalantly): OK Daddy.

We walked back to the venue, him hurriedly and extremely concerned. Me, proud that I had told him a piece of my mind and not giving it much attention after that. A while later, unbeknownst to me, a quick hush-hush meeting was called and the result of that meeting, well let's just say, my smirk got wiped right out of my face. After the service, I was summoned by one of the senior pastors to his office in the back. Here is the translated version of the conversation (we will call this one SP, got it – Senior Pastor?)

SP (trying not to show his cards): Shalom

Me: Shalom Pastor, life to you

SP (eager to be done with pleasantries and uncomfortable at the same time): I receive life. So concerning the situation, we will take care of it. Please do not do anything haste or talk to anyone about this. Today, I want you to come and spend the night at my house then tomorrow you will come back here and we will sort this out. OK my daughter?

Me (unsure how to respond to that, yet another declaration): Ahmm…

SP: Don't worry it will all be sorted

Me (a bit more forceful): But I can't spend a night at your house, I have stuff to do tomorrow and then I am heading out of town to visit my mum

SP (seemingly not wanting to push the matter but still forceful): OK, can you come and see me here tomorrow on your way to hitchhike your ride home?

Me: OK

SP (as he uncomfortably shoved some dollars in my hand): Here get yourself a drink and see you tomorrow

Me: Thank you.

I walked out of there perplexed by this crazy conversation as well as the fact that a pastor had given me some money. That was a rare occurrence back then because pastors in full time ministry were always begging congregants for money. I was just a little confused because it was an awkward situation. Perhaps, he acted that way because it was an awkward exchange. Him telling me to get myself a drink was an attempted gesture to kindness. I went home that day and everything that transpired got swept away by my sleep. When I woke up the following day, I went about my business and didn't give SP's request much mind till I was getting ready to leave to visit my Mum. I passed through the office and went directly to the back. There were no cell phones in those days and outside of landlines, best and quickest way to get to anyone was in person.

SP: I am glad you came

Me: OK

SP: You said you are going home, right? OK, please take this package to the pastor's house in that area. Stop by on your way there because the package is very important.

Me: OK

I was annoyed that I had to stop there, my time was limited as it was since I needed to be back by Sunday. But sometimes, the need to belong or to be liked/loved causes us to be blind to some of the questionable behaviors of those you seek approval from.

Because I left late, I ended up arriving at this pastor's house very late and was forced to spend the night. The next day, Saturday, I woke up to the pastor (let's call this one Pastor Musa) already gone for some errands with instruction for me to wait for him. I waited all day and when he came back he called me to have what turned out to be a strange conversation.

Pastor Musa: Is it true what you told Mr. LP?

Me: Whatever he told you. Can I please be excused, I need to go and see my mum?

Pastor Musa: I just need you to say Yes or No and I will excuse you.

Me: Yes, it's true

I am thinking *I am merely confirming that I had a conversation with Mr. LP and why is everybody making a big fuss about it?* I left him with an expression that was between shocked and frustrated. It seemed like he wanted to ask more questions but wasn't sure if he was authorized to do so. I left for my Mum's house and got there after dinner time only to wake up and attend church and hit the road again. But before I left the church, the pastor approached me with a request for me to take a package back to SP. I told him I wasn't going to see him until midweek service and he insisted that I had to take it to him on Monday.

So Monday, I am back at the office and sitting in front of SP and he speaks.

SP: As I said we will take care of you. We have already spoken to Pastor Kool in So and So area, he is on board. He will take good care of you and we will have a quick wedding and you will be happy there.

Screeeeeeeeeeeeech!!!!

Me: What? Who said I wanted to get married? I am only 21 years old for Christ's sake!

SP (trying to control my alarmed voice): No, my daughter, don't worry, this is what is best for you and the church.

More Screeeeeeeeeeching!!!!

Me: No Pastor, I am not interested in marriage. Why would I want to get married to Pastor Kool?

I didn't wait to hear his response, I stormed out disgusted that they think I was old enough to want to get married. *What gave him that stupid idea? I still need to show my father I am a virgin. Why would they say such a thing?* My mind was going a hundred miles a minute. I stormed out of the building and ran from that place and went home.

<u>Sidebar: In retrospect, knowing now what I wasn't privy to then, I think they were</u>

<u>afraid of the ramifications of such a scandal so they needed to be strategic about where they placed me. It was important to place me with someone who would provide security and stability that they assumed I needed but most importantly it had to be with someone with whom they can control the narrative. End of Sidebar.</u>

During this incident I had changed residence and was living at another senior pastor's house. There were a lot of people who lived at this house including a dear friend of mine, Farai. Farai came looking for me that night and he started quizzing me about what had transpired. I told him the church leadership was trying to marry me off and I was not interested in getting married. He then went on to ask me what it is I had told Mr. LP. I was a bit startled as to how he knew about that conversation then I realized his nature of work with the church put him in a position to hear everything. As a matter of fact, he had been sent to talk some sense into me. He went on to ask me why I was having an affair with SSP (senior senior pastor).

Screeeeeeeeechest!!!!!!!!

Me: What are you talking about?

Farai: Well, did you tell Mr. LP that the person who told him about your pregnancy is the one responsible for it?

Me: Yes I did because I was annoyed.

Farai: Well, Mr. LP was sent to talk to you by SSP

Oh Holy Crap!!!!

I started to laugh hysterically and he was puzzled. In between laughs I told him I wasn't pregnant and of course I am not having an affair with SSP and he ought to know better than that. He is relieved and we laugh it off but he rushes, presumably to inform the powers that be that it was a false alarm.

Interestingly, no one ever came back to me to say sorry we made assumptions and that there was a breakdown of communication – not Mr. LP; not SP, not Pastor Musa, not Pastor Kool and certainly not SSP. To this date as I write this book, all these individuals are alive and none of them have said a word to me and have no expectation of hearing from them on this side of Heaven. The thing that breaks my heart is the realization that these servants of God put my integrity and faith to question with zero disregard as long as the SSP's secret was kept under wraps.

After the dust had settled and another friend and I were talking, we realized that this event was very telling of the nature of church we were involved in:

a) All these servants of God were aware that SSP was having affairs with women in the church and were willing to cover for him

b) Mr. LP and SP were running interference to control the potential disturbance if this was to come out, choosing to manipulate the narrative rather than addressing the root cause

c) Were all the weddings in the church genuine or were they arranged as cover up for the sins and weaknesses of some leaders?

d) Did SSP know these leaders were running interference on his behalf and how was his conscience leading him?

e) If SSP was innocent, why didn't they have the guts to confront him about my unintentional accusations?

f) If Pastor Kool, was truly on board, what kind of a man was he of wanting to take on someone else's pregnancy of a girl he never showed interest just to cover up another man's infidelity? Where was his integrity?

g) What else are these leaders doing to cover up sins for one another?

Amai Frank, my friend, and I had so many questions and naturally we began to dissect relationships and all weddings we had attended. All the rumors we had heard of girls getting pregnant and aborting, even a story about a young woman from Highfields (a township in Harare) who had died as a complication of an abortion from a pregnancy by SSP. Were they true? Did the parents of the young woman really bring the corpse to the church office until the church made a payment of a certain amount? OMG, this is crazy! I went on to tell my friend of the next experience I had that left me permanently scarred about marriages in the church. Well before I get into HoH's story let me share a quick one regarding Mr. LP:

<u>Experience Three</u>

Mr. LP invited me to visit his house one weekend. Naturally, just like Mr, Fantasy in the first experience, I was close to him due to his being one of the preachers who would be sent to preach in areas outside the main church in Harare. At the time I was doing my temporary teaching outside of Harare so I would come down most weekends and spend nights at various pastors' houses. It's important to note that the culture back then one didn't need to announce they were coming to the pastor's house. You would visit and if you decide to spend the night you were welcome, if you decided to move in permanently that was OK too. Rarely would you be asked if you had intentions of returning back home because one could very well be running away from perceived persecution for being a believer or a member of this church. The doctrine too was that no one else was on the right path all other churches were "in error". We even had t-shirts too (I was too poor to own one) but they existed that were printed, "XYZ is RIGHT".

Anyway, I arrived at Mr. LP's house late and joined the women in their bedroom. In the morning everyone woke up to do whatever and I continued to sleep. Mr. LP came into the room, presumably to say hello since I had not seen him the night before. I don't know how long he was standing next to my bed but I got startled by angry voices and I jumped out of my bed. Mr. LP was trying to calm his wife down as he tried to guide her out of the room. She was screaming at him and I was trying to understand what was going on. Mr. LP instructed me to go back to sleep and not to worry about anything. Well, there was no going back to sleep. I was wide awake. The commotion continued from their bedroom into the parking lot until the husband drove away.

I was still sitting on my bed in a daze still not sure of what was going on when Mrs. LP stormed into my room screaming and calling me names.

Me: Mama, what did I do?

Mrs. LP: Please don't play innocent you came here to seduce my husband what was he doing in the room while you were sleeping? Tell me what was he doing if it wasn't for your seduction?

Me: But you just said I was sleeping so how would I know what he was doing?

Mrs. LP: Don't be smart with me. Get up right now and get out of my house, you prostitute.

Me: Mama, why are you calling me prostitute? I haven't done anything.

Mrs. LP: You left your husband in Marondera whom you were betrothed to come here and mess up my marriage.

Clearly, her husband had confided in her about my story and now she was twisting it to make me seem like something I was not. I wasn't going to win this one. I was used to her kind. I knew that people whispered behind my back about my situation. Because my father had found me with a guy, people made assumptions about my character. She was no surprise to me.

Mrs. LP: Get out!

Me (crying and confused): I am leaving, let me take a shower and I will leave.

Mrs. LP: You're not leaving your dirt in my house get dressed and leave, now!

She stood right there and watched me as I uncomfortably undressed out of my nightgown and dressed into my clothes. I packed my stuff and left.

After church that Sunday, I was summoned to Mai Yonini's office and asked in front of 5 other women leaders, including Mrs. LP, if I had slept with Mr. LP and how long our affair had been going on. When I denied their charges, I was told I needed deliverance and their version of exorcism started. I was pushed to the ground and "demons" were cast out. "Out in the name of Jesus!" "You spirit of prostitution out!" "Satan, we cast you out in Jesus' name!" At some point someone burst out in tongues and as on cue they all started speaking in tongues. Every time I think of that incident, I wonder if they were addressing the devil in tongues, if so, were they aware that the devil doesn't understand tongues? Food for thought, *1 Corinthians 2:7-12 and 14:2*.

There was serious trouble in Mr. LP's marriage. There were not just serious trust issues and even as I write this, I am saddened by the fact that Mrs. LP felt the best way to deal with her husband's apparent infidelity issue was to attack me and subsequently other women too.

Sidebar: To the married women whose husbands tend to stray off the reservation – let's just say I am the other woman and you hear of our fling/affair and you and your girlfriends come and attack me. How does that resolve you marital issues? How many of us will you go around attacking? Do you know how many women by behaving like lunatics have driven their husbands straight into the loving and willing arms of the other woman? What is it you are afraid of in confronting your husband and living the other woman out of your mess? While you ponder on those questions, a word of advice – when you ask, "What are you doing with my husband?" what exactly are you expecting to hear? A denial or a confession? How is that going to resolve the root cause of your problem. Listen, if you can't trust the one who shares your bed every night, don't come to me with that nonsense because one day you will hear a response that sends you to the loony bin. Just saying. End of Sidebar

For a few weekends while I was in Harare after that, I don't know if Mr. LP was deliberately avoiding me out of guilt or shame because I didn't see him. When I eventually saw him, he "apologized" for his wife's behavior and the events that transpired. I wish he had quit right there while he was ahead, instead he went on to tell me how he really felt that he liked me and how he could get me my own flat (apartment) in town and it could be our own secret.

Listen, if this stuff hadn't happened to me, I too would be as stunned as you are right now.

His house is on fire and instead of saving those in his household he claims to love, he is busy casing out a secret lover and love nest.

When I told him how he, my "Daddy" sounded ridiculous, he went on to tell me that when it's just the two of us, it was OK for me to call him by his first name. Needless to say, I found myself missing Harare church services more and more and visiting other branches.

Many years later I was to be visited in England by both Mr. Fantasy and Mr. LP at different times. Every time anyone came from Zimbabwe, they would be given an opportunity to preach in the local branch whether it be in London, Birmingham or Manchester. So their visit was no different from any other. As always they preached up a storm, people gave their lives to Christ, they laid their hands on those who needed prayer. After all that, they still came to my apartment hoping to get some. They both came thinking they were going to find the same naïve and vulnerable young girl. But boy were they shocked when I showed them that those days were gone and I was not that girl anymore. I remember Mr. LP saying, "I am embarrassed to say I have had the longest crush on you and I always thought you and I would get together. But today, you showed me you are the better person, I am proud of you". We said our goodbyes and never to see them again, well until I came to the US. They tried to reach out and it didn't go as well as they hoped. As a matter of fact Mr. LP was visiting family in the US as I am writing this book and he deliberately booked a flight that gave him an overnight in New York. He reached out to me to inform me and looking for a place to spend the night. I informed him I didn't mind picking him up from the airport, bringing him home and then taking him back to the airport as long as he informed his wife the plan. He tried to convince me it wasn't necessary and I reminded him of the incident many years ago in Zimbabwe and that was the end of that. He chose to sleep at the airport rather than tell his wife where he was spending the night. So much for "let bygones be bygones".

Like I said, if it wasn't happening to me, I too would be wide-eyed like you are right now. Sometimes truth really is stranger than fiction.

The next experience permanently sealed my resolve to never get married and if it were to happen, NEVER to a Pastor.

Experience Four

I moved in to stay with one of the senior leaders in the church. Let's just say he was among the top 5 in the church hierarchy. He had an amazing anointing upon his life. He wasn't a preacher but a teacher of the Word. My goodness, I still remember some of his teachings. He once preached on "Jesus the same yesterday, today and forever" and I thought Jesus was going to come down that very day and take us home in a blaze of glory. His understanding of the Word was pretty deep. But he had a weakness.

When we resided in pastors' homes, we would have chores and if there were a significant number of people living there at the same time there would be a schedule of those chores. Who cleaned what room, who cooked what meal on what day, who washed the dishes on what days, who took care of the young kids, who washed the pastor and his wife's clothes, etc. Each person was responsible for washing their own clothes. For a small fee, I would offer to wash and iron the young men's clothes (sister had needs, monetary needs so don't judge). It was something to marvel how 'Mama' ran her house. The house had several rooms, the communal areas then bedrooms – main bedroom, children's bedrooms, the women and the men's bedrooms. Most people who resided at pastors' houses were single so made sleeping arrangements easier. Some people would be on shared beds and others would line up on the floor. During times when there were more people than the bedrooms could accommodate, some of us slept in the living room. We would be the ones to wake up early to clean the house before others woke up.

Then there was the pastor's study. It had one single bed, a desk, a chair and the closet. Only one woman slept in there. When I inquired from those who had been there the longest, I would be told, "Ndezvameso" (it's for the eyes only, mouth be quiet). I developed a friendship with Yolanda, the woman who slept in the pastor's study, at least I like to think so. Anyway, I ended up being the one who did her the favor of washing and ironing her clothes whenever I washed mine.

The pastor always worked late and always got home in the early hours of the morning. He traveled with his driver and sometimes other people too. I began to notice that whenever they got home, he would not eat the food that had been prepared by his wife, instead he would insist on freshly cooked food prepared by Yolanda. I remember the first time I observed the wife, a highly educated professional woman being excused from her duties, my heart broke. She had woken up with the intention of preparing her husband a fresh meal and serve him his dinner. He dismissed her by telling her that Yolanda will make him the food, she can go back to bed.

Many nights after the night crew had eaten their dinner Yolanda would go to bed and the HoH would also go in there "to study" sometimes for a little while and sometimes till dawn. Apparently the only one who seemed to be shocked or confused by this arrangement was me. Everyone else behaved as if it was normal. Sadly, the wife even had her sister and brother reside at the same place and they seemed to have accepted the fact that their brother-in-law was having an affair under their nose. I came to realize also that maybe these relatives and all the single people had nowhere else to go so rather than risk being thrown out on the street, they turned the other way. Poverty and ignorance are two things that shouldn't reside at any address at the same time. When you are poor, you will fall for anything for fear of being thrown out or denied access to whatever it is you need. Ignorance of the Word of God put you in a place of being thrown by every wind of doctrine.

One Sunday, 'Mama' had asked all the women to rush back home after service for a meeting about chores. I had never attended any of these before. As we left the church premises, I saw Yolanda and I told her of Mama's request. I will never forget her response, "Havasi kureva ini, ndezvenyu vamwe mese, kwete ini" (She doesn't mean me, it's for the rest of you). *Say what!!! Who disrespects the 2nd in Command in their house?* Naïve me, responded, "Hanzi vasikana vese (she said all the girls)". Again, Yolanda repeated that the message was not inclusive of her. If I hadn't caught on about this weird arrangement, it was made very clear on that day by her defiance that she, the mistress, had no respect or regard for the wife. I trotted to catch up with the others to go home. When we got home, the meeting proceeded without anyone bothered that Yolanda was absent. *What the heck!*

That Monday, I made my way to town on a mission. The big shots needed to know what I was observing at this leader's house. So I made my way to the office where "my demons were cast out" for allegedly seducing Mr. LP. I figured since she was the Big Mama, seemingly with zero tolerance for nonsense as exhibited at my exorcism, she would deal with this immediately. I narrated my reason for coming to her office and she immediately rebuked me for spreading rumors and accused me of being a scatterer. *Hezvo! Are you kidding me?* She went on to tell me that I was spreading untruths and I should go home, pack my bags and leave the house immediately. I told her I had nowhere else to go and that didn't seem to matter to her. I got out of there before I got prayed on and continued to reside at the HoH's home until I had other options. As I continued to observe all these bumps under the rugs, I made a conscious decision that I no longer wanted HoH or anyone else to lay their hands on my head to pray for me. I was not having any transference of spirits on my head. To this day, I am careful and very particular who prays over me. I no longer jump at every altar call unless the Holy Ghost releases me in my spirit. Imagine, a very senior leader in the church, not only had a weak waist (proven by them willing to marry me off when they believed he had made me pregnant) but had the audacity to have his mistress reside under the same roof with his wife. An open secret that no one dared discuss. Lord have mercy!

> Sidebar: With human nature, when we are accustomed to something, although deep down we know it is wrong or iffy, we don't leave that something because it is familiar. We don't leave because we convince ourselves that we can deal with it. You rationalize that the devil I know is better than the one that I don't. Then, the question of: if you knew all of those things, why do you stay? After my father disowned me, this became my family. You don't leave family. You just don't up and go. Sometimes, the up and going is nerve-wrecking. It is not easy to find a church home. It is tough, especially when you know where you are spiritually or you get a sense of where you need to be. Identifying a church home can be very tough. You just do not want to fall into anything. End of Sidebar.

My conclusion then became: if Church leaders' marriages are this way, what was the point of marrying? I have had the privilege to observe and even counsel pastors, wives and husbands who are in loveless marriages that are also emotionally, fiscally, physically, sexually and mentally unstable. We have pastors who have resorted to irresponsible fiscal management, drugs, gambling, pornography and prostitution to numb the feeling of failure. We have couples who continue to uphold the status quo, with no place to go when they hurt. Some get so overwhelmed by some of these demons, sadly they resort to suicide. For that reason the Lord deposited in my heart *the Diaspora Pastor* to provide a platform where all and more of these conversations happen openly with the hope of bringing healing to the leadership in the Body of Christ. I strongly believe the church is only as strong as their weakest leadership. As leaders, our homes need to be in order before we can effectively effect order in the church.

<u>Sidebar: It is important that we as believers are careful who and/or what we follow. It is important that we follow Jesus Christ. The pastor is important in our spiritual growth that is why God gave those five-fold ministries; however, it's much more important to also read the Word of God and be clear that you are following not a fallible human being but Christ. As believers, we should keep the right perspective and not place pastors and their spouses on pedestals that are reserved only for God. The dangers of following people instead of Christ is that when those people fall, which</u>

> they sometimes do, you too will fall and sometimes you cannot get up from that fall and you head straight to hell. Contrary to popular belief, pastors are not righteous; they are not immune to temptations. Remember God will not share His glory (Isaiah 42:8). Every human being has flaws. That is why we lean not on our own understanding but on Him (Proverbs 3:5-6). End of Sidebar.

Experience Five

When I moved to London and as soon as I had a good place to stay, I looked for a church. In my belief system, Sundays, at the very least, were designated days of worship and fellowship with brethren. So naturally it was important for me to have a church home. I began to attend various churches in my neighborhood in an effort to find something similar to what I was accustomed to and it just wasn't happening. So when I finally learnt of a Zimbabwean church in Seven Sisters Tottenham, North London, I was excited and eager to return to the familiar.

Church folk as a community, we can be self-contradictory. We will give you the biggest welcome when you walk into the church a new person and celebrate even more when you give your life to

Christ derived from Luke 15:10 which tells us that angels rejoice in the presence of God over one soul that repents. When you happen to be in a church with extra helpings of hospitality, they will give you a gift as a token of appreciation, pastor may take you to lunch or you may be invited to the pastor's house for dinner. Church folk, we ask all kinds of questions diplomatically to try and place you in some proverbial category. When you are not forthcoming with info, like in my case they made up stories because they felt they needed to know who I really am. Is she married? How come she doesn't have a ring? Is she divorced? Who was the husband? Does she work? What is her immigration status? We wonder how much she earns (well, we will see if she tithes that is if she is a tither)? Is her son black or colored? When did she come to the UK? Where does she live and with whom?

So after they made their assumptions and with half-truths here and there because some sisters come to visit you at home kunge rudo (as if they love you) when in reality, they were just spies for the local "Mama aka Mai Mufundisi aka First Lady." Now they know I am single, they have bumped into my White boss a couple of times, not knowing he is my boss and they have assumed he is my son's father ("But he looks like a married man because he is older," they would say), I am in a nice apartment, I am enrolled in college at Thames Valley University. With that data, they create a working profile of me to be used at the opportune time.

Women in the church were placed in groups of the precious stones in the Bibles (to this day, I have no idea what the criteria was for each stone). I am designated to the Sapphires and our color is royal blue. Each group takes turns to decorate the sanctuary (a community hall we used to rent at the time). So one would know which group had decorated based on the corresponding color scheme associated with the group. In my group, at the time, we had mostly students and only two working, Dori and myself. We were responsible for purchasing the drapery, the flowers and corresponding vases. It was always a competition of which group outshines which one. Something that can easily go south if unmanaged effectively. It turns out our group was the best at the time - no surprises there. So whenever the pastor and his wife knew we were having guest speakers sent from Harare, Zimbabwe, we would be asked to decorate. I happened to be the only single woman with a car at the time so it made sense for all of our stuff to be kept at my house. We will all gather on Saturdays to iron drapes and get ready whenever it was our weekend.

I began to notice a pattern that whenever the high ranking leadership was coming, my counterpart Dori would make up a reason why she should come to my apartment on a Saturday to pick up our materials and be at the church before I got there, even though she had no car or reliable transportation. One day I confronted her and she reluctantly informed me that it was instruction from 'Mama'. I called a couple of my friends and found out that 'Mama' had given instruction that I could not serve or prepare the sanctuary because I was a single mother and that she referred to my son as "an Ishmael". An Ishmael because they equated him with Hagar's son.

> Sidebar: Hagar was Sarah's slave whom Sarah had asked to have a child with Abraham in a momentary lapse of weakness after realizing she was old before God's promise to Abraham was fulfilled. God's promise to Abraham was that he was going to be a father of many nations and Sarah could not see how it would happen seeing that she was reaching menopause before bearing any children. End of Sidebar.

Are you kidding me? So you will use the materials of my sweat but I can't decorate the church, I wasn't holy enough? My grandson, Errol would say, "Wow Gogo, just Wow"!

My beautiful son, my gift from God (because after all it is God who gives seed), was "an Ishmael" in their eye for he was not "Isaac, mwana wechipikirwa" (Isaac, the son of the promise). And we wonder why church growth is not rising? We wonder why not too many are jumping on the Jesus wagon? Again, Wow Gogo, just Wow!

<u>Experience Six</u>

It is quite possible that the reason he resented me and found it necessary to lay his hands on me was because I took his virginity. OK, I didn't take it. In all fairness, I didn't know he was a virgin and I didn't take it, he was a willing participate as much as I was.

One day a pastor I respected and whose friendship I had enjoyed, approached me to help his "spiritual son" who had come into town and had nowhere to stay. Even though we were 6 years apart, me being the older, we were both consenting adults. But before I get to the consenting part I was asked to accommodate this young man by the church leaders. Right away, I should have ran. It is never a good idea to put two people whose hormones are on high alert to reside together without proper supervision.

The inevitable happened and we were in a relationship. Unfortunately, we were not going to fully enjoy the relationship because it was a secret. We would attend church like brother and sister but at home we were pretty much shacking up. Like most secret relationships, the dynamics can cause some serious issues when the heart is involved because the heart wants what the heart wants. Like Apostle, we found ourselves living the Romans 7:15-20, *"For I do not understand my own actions. For I do not do what I want, but I do the very thing I hate. Now if I do what I do not want, I agree with the law, that it is good. So now it is no longer I who do it, but sin that dwells within me. For I know that nothing good dwells in me, that is, in my flesh. For I have the desire to do what is right, but not the ability to carry it out. For I do not do the good I want, but the evil I do not want is what I keep on doing. Now if I do what I do not want, it is no longer I who do it, but sin that dwells within me".*

One of the challenges of being unequally yoked or being in secret relationships is that when you run into problems, you really don't have anywhere to go because those who can help you, are not supposed to know that your relationship has turned sexual. I remember how furious we would get with each other when we each were getting attention from the opposite sex respectively but could not confront it in public. He was embarrassed to be known as a young man who fell for a single mother. I wanted to tell my girlfriends about this incredible young man I was seeing but couldn't because he was uncomfortable about it. So it went on for a while.

Then one day those feelings of jealousy got the better of me and I took back my car that he was using. Unfortunately, on that day, he had promised to drive some church leaders to another city that was 4 hours away without asking me. I was mad that the elders would ask him, knowing very well that he was driving my car, and not have the courtesy to check with me if it was okay. So I was refusing to give him my car keys and Wham! Right across my face. I was so shocked he had raised his hand on me. That became the beginning of many more beatings. When Mr. Fantasy came to visit, I poured my heart out to him with the hope that he would help me resolve this instead he was so caught up in what he had hoped to get from me that he left without offering any solution except to say, the church leaders shouldn't have placed this young man at my home.

Sadly, I was to endure domestic violence for a while before I had the guts to move from that area. Now I read of women having lost their lives after having been killed by their husbands in fits of rage and I cannot stop to marvel at God's love and protection of me, even in my sinful state. Sending him to jail and having a protection order was not helpful because he would breach it and the situation became a YoYo with the police.

A lot of times we as adults assume that our children are not privy to adult activities happening in the home, especially domestic violence. I was one of those people. I assumed my son was young (he was ⅘ years old at the time) and was not comprehending what was going on. That is, until that one day when I was talking to my mother on the phone after I was in the US and she was my son's guardian in Zimbabwe.

Mum Dearest: Nhai mwanangu, anonzi uncle Chase ndiani? (My daughter, who is uncle Chase?)

Me (surprised): Sei mabvunza? (Why do you ask?)

Mum Dearest: Nekuti mwana wako anogara akamutaura (Because your son always talks about him)

Me (relieved): Oh, imwe shamwari yangu yandakambogara nayo ku London (He is just a friend I lived with in London)

Mum Dearest: Well, Nyasha doesn't like him

Me: Sei madaro? (Why do you say that?)

Mum Dearest: Because Nyasha says, when he grows up he wants to buy a gun and kill Uncle Chase because he made my Mummy cry.

Silence on my end as my heart shutters into a million pieces.

Fast forward to when my son was 15 years old, here in the US. We were watching old home movies of us in the UK and Chase was in the background of one of the movies:

Nyasha: Mama, murume uyo ndiyani? (Mum, who is that man?)

Me (quickly remembering my conversation with Mum Dearest a few years back): Why do you ask?

Nyasha: I don't know why but ndakamumaka (my spirit doesn't sit well with him)

Me: Ahh hameno (I don't know). Liar! Liar! Pants on fire!

Heart shuttered again into more million pieces to think that I exposed my son to that way of living. Lord help me!

Our children may not verbalize it, but they are impacted by domestic violence regardless of how well we think we are at hiding it. They know more than they let on and eventually, it catches up with them in unexpected ways.

> Sidebar: To my fellow single parents, I know life is tough doing it alone with a significant other but hang in there. It is much tougher to clean up the mess of an abusive relationship. Sometimes children who are exposed to abuse become abusive partners later in life. Let us protect our children by making conscious decisions to prioritize their welfare. End of Sidebar.

Experience Seven

Sometime between the traditional marriage in Zimbabwe April 7th, 2016, civil marriage on May 26th and our scheduled August 19th wedding ceremony, our marriage broke irreversibly.

> Sidebar: Briefly and oversimplified - In my culture, as described in a) of the various ways of marriage above, my fiancé sends his people to represent him to my people to inform them of his intentions to marry me. In the proceedings, my sister stood in my stead and his wife in his since neither my fiancé nor I could travel to Zimbabwe at

> the time. During the proceedings, he is then charged roora (dowry) as a token for bringing families together, appreciating the gift of a wife thereby sealing the deal. The dowry is a combination of cash, livestock and grocery items previously provided by my Mum. Payment of these items signified marriage in my culture. So for all intents and purposes, we were now married. He then asks for the right to do a white wedding, which they may or may not oblige. In my case they did. End of Sidebar.

It is after this traditional ceremony that we announced our plans to the church congregation. Majority were genuinely happy for both of us but mostly for their pastor. A lot of them had prayed for this day to happen for their pastor. But there were one or two who showed their disapproval of our union for their own personal reasons. This small group of people took what was going on between my husband and very personal even before our problems began to manifest in the flesh. However, one of them went to the extreme and tried to evoke some spirits from the dark world through witchcraft. Sometimes, truth is really stranger than fiction. If this wasn't happening to me, I too would have a hard time believing these events.

As I was driving to work one day, I was on the phone with my husband when our call was interrupted by an unknown number. I excused myself from the call to answer the incoming:

Me: Hello

Caller: Is this Teresa Dangwa?

Me: Yes, it is. Who is this?

Caller: My name is Martha Chimombe (real name withheld for privacy), you don't know me but I got your number from Jessie Nehanda. Do you know her? She said you are good friends.

Me: Yes, I know her. How may I help you?

Caller: Like I said you don't know me but I have something I need to tell you. Is this a good time or can I call later?

Me (curiosity getting the better of me): Now is good, we can talk.

Caller: Well, I just returned from Zimbabwe and wanted to tell you something important.

Me: OK

Caller: Do you know Chido Mazoredze?

Me: Yes I do, we go to the same church

Caller: I know you do. Well, here is the thing. While I was in Zimbabwe Chido called me asking me to for a favor to pick up a package for her from her mother and bring it with me.

Me (not sure where this is going): OK

Caller: I had delayed to pick it up till last minute because I was busy so I was on my way a few days before I left Zimbabwe when Chido called. She was telling me her Mother had told her I had not come by as expected but she was expecting me. She wanted to know where I was. I told her I was on my way to her mother's house. Chido then assured me the package was small, just a long envelope with stuff in it. And before I asked her what it is she decided to confide in me. She asked me if I knew you, Teresa Dangwa, and I told her I didn't. She told me that you were trying to get married to her husband, she is the one who is supposed to be getting married to that man. Have you had your wedding yet?

Me (in complete shock and dismay, I managed to mumble): Not yet.

Caller: Chido told me kuti wakabvisirwa mari asi muchato hausi kuzoita (dowry was paid but there will be no wedding) and that package her mother had prepared will help with that.

Me (still in disbelief): Really?

Caller: Chido wanted me to bring mushonga waiva mu envelope from her mother wavakapiwa nen'anga yekumba kwavo (she was being asked to bring some witchcraft in an envelope to be used on me).

Me: Is this a joke?

Caller: No this is not a joke. I gave you my name, my address is So-So in The Bronx. You can ask Jessie she knows me very well. And if you want you can put me on a three-way with Chido and I will say the same thing in her presence or if you want you can pick me up and we can go together to her house to talk about it.

The reason I am telling you this is because when Chido mentioned your name, hana yangu yakarova zvakandivhundutsa (my heart became heavy and unsettled) and I just knew that I could not participate in the matter. I know you are a praying woman because of what happened in my spirit at the mention of your name. It made me very afraid so I made a U-turn and have been ignoring Chido's calls ever since hoping to reach out to you first. So, Teresa I am telling you this because of the way my heart became uneasy with fear at the mention of your name and also to warn you to be careful with these women you pray with. That is why you have never seen me at that church. I am sorry to shock you but I had to tell you. Feel free to call me if you choose to confront Chido and please pray because the forces of darkness are against you on this union.

Me (not knowing what to say after all that): OK, thanks.

Caller: I am so sorry, but Jessie said it was best you know. Bye.

Me: Bye

After the shock I took a few minutes to pray and then I called Jessie and she said she was expecting my call. She apologized for handing out my phone to the Caller without asking my permission, but she knew I would need to hear for myself what the Caller had to say. She told me the Caller wanted her to deliver the news to her, but she thought yakanyanya kukora muto (euphemism for 'way above my pay grade'). I later called my husband to narrate this stranger than fiction encounter and we prayed. I also narrated this to my mentor and prayer partners.

Like I said before, church folk, we are our own worst enemy. *If this stuff was not happening to me, me too I would have a hard time believing.*

Did we Just Get Excommunicated?

AFTER I CALLED off the wedding I seemed to have ruffled many feathers in the local church. There was no doubt that the congregants loved their pastor, Munyaradzi. From what I was told, he had been their only constant and consistent pastor for about 15 years. He had been loyal to them, so naturally, they guarded him jealousy and rightfully so. I was a new kid on the block, having been in the church for less than two years and I have not only swept their pastor off his feet, but now I have sent him into seclusion. From their perspective, I was the one who was in the wrong. None of them came to me to ask why I had called off the wedding, let alone ask if I was okay. Women, especially, sneakered and whispered behind my back. The few friends I had there kinda drifted into the crowd.

One Saturday, I received a call from one of the pastors at the church looking for my husband. He said he had tried to call my husband several times, but it seems my husband was not picking up his phone. I told the pastor my husband was actually on his way home. I could have him call the pastor back when he arrived unless he wanted me to take a message for him. He wanted me to tell my husband that because of the personal issues we were having in our union, a decision had been made to ask us (my husband and I) to step down from our leadership roles. At the time, I was the church secretary and a member of the board. He went on to inform me that the church, which had been having some issues way before I started attending there, was now coming together and our situation will just be a hindrance to the progress.

He also went on to say that we were welcome to come to the church, but for now if we could sit in the back and allow the church to heal from this situation it would be greatly appreciated.

He asked me if I had anything to say and I remember saying, "Well, if the decision has already been made, there really wasn't much to say. I didn't realize that one needed to be perfect in order to serve in the church, but my husband and I will respect their decision and we will get back to them after I had discussed with him". We later wrote the board an email on the matter and needless to say, that was the day my husband and I ceased to be members of that church.

My husband and I felt that rather than getting help from church leadership, we were being punished for being imperfect human beings. I get it that there are certain standards that pastors and church elders are to be held accountable to. I am totally in agreement with 1 Timothy and Titus on what those standards are. However, we felt this situation could have been handled with a little bit more sensitively and with a certain measure of compassion. In my opinion, the best thing to have been done was to call my husband as a fellow pastor to an in-person meeting, then bring us before the board and in partnership formulate a plan to share with the church members at large. You see, as a non-pastor at the time, I honestly didn't see why our personal situation needed a community sit-down and kangaroo court. We were not in Kansas anymore (if we were in Zimbabwe maybe to some level if these individuals were our relatives we would need to have a family meeting to figure out what was going on. The operative word here being 'family'). I didn't and still don't believe that we owed "the church" a play by play of the reasons why we were where we were at the time. I felt like there was a certain level of entitlement the church was asking for which was crossing the line of acceptable boundaries.

Now, do not get me wrong, in retrospect, I get the intent of the pastor who called me. Admittedly, our situation was unique to a lot of people - truth be told, I am still trying to figure out what the heck was going on, like for real for real. So, because it was uncharted territory, most people didn't know not only how to help us but how to react under such circumstances.

> <u>Sidebar: I remained very good friends with that pastor till now. We have forgiven one another and we are co-laborers in the Vineyard. He is my unofficial mentor, if there is such a thing. End of Sidebar.</u>

So this specific situation and other experiences by other pastors became the backdrop of *the Diaspora Pastor*, created to be a practical solution to the question I asked myself many months from that season of trials, *Where do pastors go when they are hurting?*

Arise Oh Zion Arise!

GOD IS RAISING UP A NEW caliber of pastoral leadership who will usher in the second coming of Christ. I believe the Church has been barren for a long time. A lot of stories we hear of compromise at the Pulpit. In *Matthew 6:10* Jesus taught us to pray, "*Thy Kingdom come, Thy will be done on earth as it is in Heaven*". We cannot expect the will of God to be ushered in by the world and using worldly systems. The Kingdom of God will be on earth as it is in Heaven through church leadership and believers who make a deliberate and conscious decision to worship God in Spirit and in truth. We cannot continue to keep playing church and expect different results.

I believe somewhere along the road, we as believers gave up our rights and even responsibility to the government and worldly political systems. As believers we seem to be contradicted in our attitude or views of the government systems. Part of us expect the government to be the end all of worldly issues. When it comes to our expectations of what the government can or cannot do, we have seized or have chosen to be ignorant of what the Word says. When Isaiah prophesied the coming of our Lord Jesus, he said, *"For a child will be born to us, a son will be given to us and the government will rest on His shoulders and His name will be called Wonderful, Counselor, Mighty God, Eternal Father, Prince of Peace". (Isaiah 9:6).*

Many of us know this verse from a Christmas carol and it is possible that it is also the only time we pay much attention to it. However, there are many of us who have not taken the time to consider this profound statement, *"the government will rest on His shoulders"*. Meaning Jesus is the ultimate political ruler who will rule the world as a Wonderful Counselor, Mighty God, Eternal Father and Prince of Peace.

In my experience in healthcare as well as in social services, we have counselors who help patients and clients navigate various systems. They seek to make plain otherwise complicated and confusing processes for their targeted constituency. Counselors by nature are advisors and carry a certain level of trust and wisdom. In some instances, clients and patients present with chaotic situations feeling helpless and counselors help unravel the chaos by identifying solutions, resources and tools. So now bring it to the spiritual realm with the King of kings as our Counselor, our Advisor, our Prince of Peace. Because He dwells in us, we too have the power to advice and counsel in our spheres of influence, including governments. Sadly, we have relinquished our power and allow governments to determine our actions and how we worship God or serve the communities around us. Imagine, we have pastors who when government officials visit their churches, they physically relinquish their authority at the pulpit and allow the politicians to address the church as if they are some type of authority even in the things of God. Then when the politicians quote one verse, even out of context, we the congregants go wild with Amens and Hallelujahs. Lord help us to have the wisdom to discern the spirit of those we allow to speak into our lives from the pulpit. When politicians come to our churches, we must take that opportunity to preach and minister Salvation to them recognizing that a politician who knows God is more likely to have real integrity and consider the Word before participating in enacting policies that are contrary to the Word of God. Jesus is the source of all truth and His counsel has no confusion or uncertainty rather there is order. It then follows that since He dwells in us, being that the same Spirit that raised Him from the dead, is the same Spirit that dwells in us, we ought to be more like Him. Shouldn't we, believers, then be bringing order into our homes, churches, communities and the world at large?

CHAPTER 5

Blessings in Disguise

"Behold, how happy is the man whom God reproves. So do not despise the discipline of the Almighty" Job 5:17

"For momentary light affliction is producing for us an eternal weight of glory far beyond comparison." 2 Corinthians 4:17

"All discipline for the moment seems not to be joyful but sorrowful; yet to those who have been trained by it yields the peaceful fruit of righteousness." Hebrews 12:11

— ∞ —

WHEN YOU ARE GOING THROUGH A ROUGH PATCH IN life, it is hard to see the blessings behind it. Often the blessings we seek from God come in packages we don't anticipate or, quite frankly, don't like. It is rare that God reveals the endgame of every trial. Truth be told, even in instances where He does reveal it, we can't see the forest for the trees.

A lot of times we expect blessings to come our way when we have been praying and fasting for them. We believe that we have received the blessings because we prayed, that is why we tend to judge others when they seem to not be getting blessings that we see with our naked eyes. There is an error in Christian circles that looks at a seemingly poor person or one who seems to see calamity after calamity and we believe they are not praying enough or are not Christian enough. Many times, I have found myself in a place of want for everyday needs to be met and yet be at peace and content. Sadly, we have some in the Body of Christ who equate worldly wealth with a prayerful and righteous life. This couldn't be further from the truth. I like the encouragement we get from Apostle Paul in *Philippians 4:11-13, "Not that I speak in respect of want for I have learned, in whatsoever state I am, therewith to be content. I know both how to be abased, and I know how to abound: everywhere and in all things I am instructed both to be full and to be hungry, both to abound and to suffer need. I can do all things through Christ which strengtheneth me."*

In all instances, blessings come to us because the timing is right- not our timing, but God's timing. Ecclesiastes 3:1 says, "There is a time for everything and a season for every activity under the heavens." Blessings come in different packages. Some come through pain, trials and tribulations and it is not always easy to recognize them as such, hence, I like to call them 'Blessings in Disguise'. Allow me to share with you some of such blessings that the Lord has brought my way in packages that did not resemble blessings.

When God Does What God Does

"Sorry we have to let you go."

"It's not working."

"It's not you, it's me."

"I don't think you fit in with where we are trying to go."

We have all heard these statements said in one form or another. If you haven't, well good for you…keep on living and you will hear them soon enough. I am not wishing them on you. Far from it. As a matter of fact, I pray that you don't get to hear them ever. However, I also know that in *John 16:33* Jesus says to us, *"I have told you these things, so that in me you may have peace. In this world you will have trouble. But take heart! I have overcome the world."* So you see my friend, you do not have to find trouble; trouble will know your address when it's time. Thank God that we don't have to face trouble alone, if we so choose to trust in His Sovereign plan.

No matter how you slice rejection, it is painful. Even when you expect it, it still sucks. Perhaps you know you haven't been pulling your weight on a project and letting the rest of your team do all the work. Then when promotion time comes, you are informed, "Maybe next time"; or worse, you are told, "We no longer need you". Those words of rejection are painful. I have had the privilege of being fired at least three times in my life. I have the luxury of saying, "privilege" now in retrospect but trust me it wasn't fun and games at the time. Every position I have been fired from has ultimately opened up opportunities that I otherwise would not have considered at the time. I can trace my career growth and success to that one day while I was working for a certain NGO in Upstate New York, and I was in the 11th hour of being vested. Who does that? Fire people at such a pivotal moment? It turned out some entities do that so they do not have to pay retirement. I am not saying that this particular NGO did exactly that. I don't know why they fired me 5 seconds before I was vested. I just know that I received a call that the Executive wanted to meet with me and the appointment kept getting postponed throughout the day. Apparently, that was a tell-tale sign but I clearly missed the memo on "Behaviors Exhibited by Those in the Corner Office Just Before They Fire You". I found out later that it was their attempt at being humane. *Or, were they afraid of the perceived "Angry Black Woman"?*

It turned out it wasn't Executive who was going to deliver the news, it was my immediate supervisor. He called my office line, early evening after everyone was gone. I didn't know until I went up to his office that everyone else had gone and I was the only one, save the Executive and my boss left in the building.

"There is no other way to say this so let me get right to it. We are letting you go."

"Letting me go from where?" I inquired, my naïveté showing. I had never been fired before so how was I to know he meant I was being fired?

"Your services are no longer required with immediate effect", he opted for the more direct way.

"Oh, really? Why?" I inquired

To this day, I don't know if he gave me a meaningful response because it all went blur. All I know is, I asked, if I had messed up something and the answer was a short, "No" with zero emotion.

<u>Sidebar: I think when one fires someone, it is not only kind, but the right thing to do, to give them the real reason they were fired, if it is safe to do so, of course. When firing someone, there really is no need for political correctness because withholding information on areas of improvement is doing a disservice to the individual and to the public. So, if you are a boss, do the right</u>

<u>thing, give helpful criticism, and always end on a good note by telling employees what their strengths are as well. End of Sidebar.</u>

It was clear that my boss was not quite as prepared as Executive thought because he was a nervous wreck and he said something like, "HR will be in touch and you will get a packet in the mail. Please pay attention to it and make sure you respond in a timely fashion. It was a pleasure working with you. I will now escort you to your office so you can gather your things and leave the building per company policy". *Wait, what policy? Was that in my employee manual?* Clearly, I had not remembered reading that part. *I mean, with all the excitement of getting a job at an organization with a mission I truly believed in, it slipped my mind. Of course, I didn't read it! I was too busy mesmerized by the annual salary they had offered me, which at the time seemed like a million bucks. Or it was in the fine print? Who reads the fine print? Seriously?*

Any-who that was that. I was out of a job. You see, for a while I had contemplated going to Grad School, but the timing was never right, Until I got fired. Now I had all the time in the world. I immediately went to register for Grad School. I probably would not have done so while I worked at that job.

Fast forward to my next job from where I was fired. I had just been given a stellar review about eight months into this position at a hospital when I got a call to come upstairs and sure enough, 45 minutes later security was escorting me out of the building. *Why do they do that?* I have never understood the reason behind this security escorting business. If they think you will lash out, why don't they call you at home in the evening and say, "By the way, tomorrow, don't bother coming to work – we will send your personal effects to your last known address?" It would save a lot of people the aggravation and unnecessary humiliation.

While I was at this hospital job, I knew I needed to leave and do the fellowship that I had been checking out at my university. I had applied for it, gone through the process, and I had been accepted. Dina Refki, the Executive Director for the fellowship was awaiting my acknowledgement of whether or not I accepted the opportunity. There were a couple of catches to being in this fellowship – a) you couldn't be employed. It came with a stipend, but the stipend barely covered the bills and b) it was only for 6 months, then you are back into job hunting with the hope that the fellowship would open doors for you for bigger and better opportunities. I could see from the fellowship outline why these two stipulations needed to be there, that 6 months was no joke – it was rigorous. Most of the fellows, like me, were still taking other graduate classes, independent from the ones required for the fellowship.

My hospital job did not have a direct growth development line. The best you could hope for at the time is increase pay-wise and that's about it. The pay wasn't bad so I was comfortable. There was a pension if I stayed long enough. It was steady…you can't go wrong with healthcare. *I can really retire here*, I would tell myself.

What UAlbany Center for Women in Government & Civil Society Fellowship was offering, more than made up for the meager stipend. The lessons learned, the friendships nurtured, the doors opened and still opening is priceless. Fear of the unknown can be paralyzing at times to the point where one is afraid to spread one's wings and recognize one's full potential or at least get a glimpse of that potential. We as humans talk about faith, but we don't want to fully exercise it because it takes away the control, we think we have. Faith by nature is not only believing but trusting in something that you have not seen in the natural. There are some of us who, like Thomas, need to see before we believe. Jesus in John 20:29 responds to Thomas' unbelief by saying, *"...Blessed are those who have not seen and yet have believed"*. *Hebrews 11:1* teaches us what faith is, it says, *"Now faith is the substance of things hoped for, the evidence of things not seen"*. The ESV puts it this way, *"Now faith is the assurance of things hoped for, the conviction of things not seen"*.

When you are at a job you somehow think getting to work on time every day, not hanging out with the wrong crowd, not calling in sick frivolously, meeting all your deadlines, presenting excellent work ethics and going the extra mile at every turn somehow absolves you from crap happening to you. How wrong we are. Sometimes bad things (a.k.a. crap) happens to good people like you and me and there is nothing we can do about it. Other times, we may not realize it, but that stuff happens to us to push us into the next level God wants us to be. I know for a fact that had I not been fired, I would have missed a window of incredible growth not just in my career, but spiritually too. Of course, when the firing happened I wasn't amused, although I do remember having peace in my spirit as I drove out of that employee parking lot for the last time. At the first firing, I had palpitations and anxiety, but not this time. Without being fired at that first job, I would not have gone to graduate school which was one of the qualifications to be in the fellowship. Without being fired at the hospital job, I would never have gone for the fellowship. See nothing is wasted, Romans 8:28.

Not every bad thing that happens to us originates from the enemy's camp. Sometimes it has come from the Holy of Holies. Take for instance, Job. Job had every calamity known to man befall him. Loss of wages, business, material things, loss of livestock or worldly wealth, loss of friendships, loss of children's lives and even loss of confidence from the person who was supposed to be closest to him – his wife. Everything Job went through was orchestrated by God. I know it is hard to think of a loving God as one who would set in motion your deepest trouble. Oh, but He did and since He is no respecter of persons, what He did to or for Job, He can do to and for you and me. I encourage you to read Chapter 1 of Job to see how God orchestrated the trouble that came upon Job.

Job 1:6-12 is pretty profound. Here is what it says, *"One day the angels came to present themselves before the LORD, and Satan also came with them. The LORD said to Satan, "Where have you come from?" Satan answered the LORD, "From roaming throughout the earth, going back and forth on it." Then the LORD said to Satan, "Have you considered my servant Job? There is no one on earth like him; he is blameless and upright, a man who fears God and shuns evil." "Does Job fear God for nothing?" Satan replied. "Have you not put a hedge around him and his household and everything he has? You have blessed the work of his hands, so that his flocks and herds are spread throughout the land. But now stretch out your hand and strike everything he has, and he will surely curse you to your face." The LORD said to Satan, "Very well, then, everything he has is in your power, but on the man himself do not lay a finger." Then Satan went out from the presence of the LORD.*

So next time trouble knocks on your door, ask God for a spirit of discernment so that you will be able to resist hitting the panic button, knowing that God is always in control, even when it seems like He is fumbling in the dark and having a hard time in locating your GPS coordinates.

While I was working for the initial NGO that fired me unceremoniously, I had written in my diary that one day I was going to work for the NYS Department of Health, AIDS Institute. I used to write things I wanted to accomplish way before vision boards were a thing. Before vision boards, there was *Habakkuk* 2:2-3, *"² And the LORD answered me, and said, Write the vision, and make it plain upon tables, that he may run that readeth it. For the vision is yet for an appointed time, but at the end it shall speak, and not lie: though it tarry, wait for it; because it will surely come, it will not tarry."* I had written out my vision and now it was about to unfold.

In addition to attending graduate classes and special presentations by various experts in both government and civil society, we were to select three entities we were interested in to do the practical part of our fellowship. The choices could be from any government agency or NGO and needed to be approved by the Executive. Since I only had one entity I was really interested in, I wrote:

1. NYSDOH AIDS Institute
2. NYSDOH AIDS Institute and
3. NYSDOH AIDS Institute

Ms. Dina looked at my selection and told me to revise my list because as much as they would try to put us in our 1st choices, it is sometimes not possible. I informed her I didn't have other choices. We went back and forth as she tried to help me "to be more realistic". I understood where she was coming from, but my mind was made up. We agreed that I would think of alternatives if I couldn't be placed at my choice agency; so she let it be and made arrangements for me to be interviewed at the AIDS Institute. I met with Ms. Sue Kline, my mentor, and we hit it off. Let's just say I ended being there for three years as a fulltime employee after my fellowship ended. On Day 1, at my full-time job, I wrote in my diary that I wanted to be at the AIDS Institute for three years. Sure enough, my next assignment came along right on time. How that came about was nothing short of a miracle. One day, I woke up earning about $50K/year and the next I found myself in a 6-figure position that I didn't apply for and was certainly not qualified. I had an incredible boss who took a risk and with whom I found favor and the rest is history.

OH, BUT GOD!

My career growth would not have happened if it wasn't for that deportation from the UK. Being deported is worse than being told "we are letting you go," in my humble opinion. It turns out being deported and losing almost every material thing I owned was where God needed me to be in order for His name to be glorified in and through my life. Without the deportation, I would never have met the man who said to me in a hotel lobby in Harare, Zimbabwe in July 1997, "Are you the woman I am looking for?" I would not have seen Joel 2:25 come to life and I being the recipient of such restoration. It says, *"And I will restore to you the years that the locust hath eaten, the cankerworm, and the caterpillar, and the palmerworm, my great army which I sent among you."*

Delay is not denial! For me, getting fired in all those jobs turned out to be what I needed for God to push me to the next level of my purpose. Truth be told, if I had not been fired from my last job, I would not have written this book any time soon. Being rejected by man is a set up for God to elevate you! There are no coincidences in life, everything is orchestrated. #trusttheprocess (Thank you Dr. Marquita Smith Blades for the lesson).

Are You The Woman I am Looking For?

ONE BEAUTIFUL SUNDAY afternoon in July 1997, I had just come back from church and was relaxing at my rented cottage, taking in the day and preparing for the upcoming week. Little did I know that my life was about to take an unexpected turn. I had been in Zimbabwe now for 6 months since my unceremonious departure from UK, aka deportation. With that knowledge in mind, the more profound the story I am about to share shall sound. I could not have written this script even if I tried. It is also these kinds of heavenly moments that helps me recognize and appreciate the meaning of such verses as Jeremiah 1:5; Psalm 37:23; Romans 11:29, Jeremiah 29:11 and of course Romans 8:28. The July to September experience helped me begin to see why the Holy Ghost had me stand on Joel 2:25 and Romans 8:28 for the better part of that year. Keep reading and you too will be amazed at what seems to be foolishness in our eyes and is revealed as God's wisdom.

One of my really good friends, Misheck, called my landlord's house to ask me if I could accompany him out of town for an errand and to return same day. Within an hour he had arrived at my house with two African-American missionaries, mother and son. The mother happened to share the same name as me, Theresa. This duo was the errand. They needed to be driven to Murewa Mission which was about an hour and a half away. When they arrived, I was ready in my jeans, a t-shirt and flat shoes that I had changed into after coming back from church earlier. As I walked to the car I heard a still almost inaudible voice say to me to change my clothes. I ignored and continued to advance to the car. I had an inside conversation with the voice arguing that it made no sense to change into anything else after all we are going to the rural areas to drop off the guests and come straight back. As I arrived at the car and was being introduced to the duo, I heard the voice and this time the voice was so loud I thought everyone had heard it. As if to answer my unspoken question, simultaneously I saw a vision of the exact outfit that I was supposed to wear. It was a cream pencil skirt and top suit that either my mum or sister-in-law had made for me many years prior. In the vision, I saw the whole outfit including stockings and shoes. I excused myself and informed them that I needed to change my outfit. To my surprise they were okay with it even after I told them that the outfit I needed to wear was in a suitcase somewhere and needed to be retrieved and ironed. I couldn't even remember the last time I had worn that suit, but it had definitely been while I was in England. After a while, I came back to the car looking like I was off to a business meeting. Everyone in the car complimented me and I remember noting that none of them seemed bothered by the wait or the dressing. Even Misheck, who would have protested because he always complained about women taking too long to get ready, seemed okay with this seemingly bizarre behavior I was exhibiting. Misheck turned out to be a destiny helper before the term was coined.

As we were driving towards the city center, the guests requested to visit two places prior to leaving for their final destination, the Kopje and the Sheraton Hotel. The Kopje is a small hill just outside the city center dotted with some of the most spectacular naturally balancing rocks I have ever seen. It also offers the best panoramic view of the city of Harare. The Sheraton Hotel & Conference Center was one of the landmarks (I believe it still is) that exhibits architectural wonder built by the legendary architectural Serbian couple, Ljiljana and Dragoljub Bakić. It has since been renamed to The Rainbow Towers Hotel and remains the most luxurious hotel in the nation. So naturally, it made sense for our guests to want to visit these landmarks prior to embarking on our missionary assignment. Misheck obliged and I found myself climbing the Kopje in my stiletto heels trying not to complain.

When we arrived at the Sheraton Hotel it was swamped with police and plain-clothed security people. We had no idea what was going on. As we approached the entrance, we were informed that we could not get in for security reasons. Apparently and unbeknownst to us there was a big summit taking place and President Robert Mugabe was a keynote speaker, hence the security. Misheck tried to sweet talk the policemen explaining that we had international guest tourists who were just interested in seeing the inside to take a few pictures and we would be out in no time. It didn't work. We started to walk back to the car a bit disappointed. Then something amazing happened. Misheck decided to turn around and ask a different policeman who asked why we wanted to go in that day instead of just coming back the following day. Misheck proceeded to inform him about our missionaries' agenda in Murehwa. He then summoned us to follow him. He directed us to a side door and told us to wait there. Sure enough, in a few minutes, he reappeared from the inside, and hurried us through that side door and we parted ways.

An angel on assignment! Let me just say when God has an appointment for you nothing can stop it. Of course at the time I didn't realize the appointment was mine and everyone else was an angel on assignment in my movie.

We got to the lobby and I was exhausted from running around in heels so I let them go about their exploring while I rested my feet. Why I didn't find a seat right away, as tired as I was, is a miracle in and of itself. As I stood there watching people, I was wondering what all the excitement was around this place which was so swamped with police and security detail that we almost didn't get in. Lost in my thoughts, I didn't realize a man had snuck up to me and invade my private space. I almost jumped out of my skin.

"Are you the woman I am looking for?" He inquired.

"No, Sir," I responded.

He walked a few feet away from me but kept turning his head towards me.

"Are you sure you are not the woman I am looking for" he inquired again, not believing my initial response.

Now I am curious, but not enough to ask him who he thought I was. I began to walk away from my "spot" getting impatient that my friends were taking too long. *Have they forgotten I just walked up and down the hills of Kopje in my stilettos, seriously?* I thought to myself. As if on cue, the man approached me again, this time a bit more forceful.

"Ma'am, are you sure you are not the woman I am looking for?

"Sir, I am very sure that I am not", I responded with equal force.

At that moment, as he began to walk away, he stopped, looked me in the eye as one who had read my mind and said, in a more controlled and almost begging voice, "Ma'am, it is not what you think". Possibly thinking I may scream at him, he didn't give me a chance to say anything and he continued, "My name is Bill Tumbler, I am an American here with my wife, Dr. C. Deloris Tumbler, and other Americans for a summit". I relaxed as soon as I heard, "my wife". He went on to explain that he had requested the hotel to provide him with a young lady to help him distribute some materials at his table outside the auditorium. So when he saw, "A well-dressed young woman" he assumed I was the lady he was expecting. Mr. Tumbler went on to explain that the summit was coming to an end and he had some materials he wanted to distribute to the summit attendees as they left the last session. Apparently, this was the last day of the summit and they were leaving for the US within hours. I ended up helping him out after checking with my friends. Later he introduced me to his wife who was among the summit guest speakers sharing the podium with then President Robert Mugabe. I guess I impressed them so much they presented me with a job offer within an hour of meeting them. It was pretty surreal. I didn't believe it at first because who does that? OH, BUT GOD!

— ∞ —

More Angels on Assignment

IT WOULD BE ALMOST two months later that I made contact with Mr. Tumbler (or Mr. T as he was affectionately known). I had almost given up on calling them because most of their calls were going unanswered. It turns out Dr. Tumbler, his wife, had some health challenges upon returning to the US so she was at home recuperating. If it wasn't for Misheck who insisted on us calling one more time, I may have missed an opportunity. This time Mr. T. answered the phone and he instructed me to take my passport to the US Embassy. Apparently, he had already called the Embassy in advance because he wanted me to come immediately. He told me that his wife wanted me to arrive during the Annual Conference so I was to go to the US Embassy with my passport ASAP. Sure enough, a day or two later, I went to the Embassy with my passport. The officer was expecting me but he flipped through my passport and informed me that I needed a new one because the one I had was about to expire. He went on to tell me that my passport needed at least 6 months of life prior to getting a visa.

From the Embassy, Misheck and I made a b-line to Kaguvi Building to see about applying for a new passport. We got there and completed the application form. As we paid, we were told that it would not be available for another three months. I explained to the clerk that I didn't have three months to wait, she didn't seem to care. I took my receipt and we left. As we approached the gate, a man came and tapped Misheck on the shoulder and said, "Mati mwana arikufanira kuenda kuAmerica svondo rino?" (You said she needs to be in America this week?)

Misheck: Yes.

Man: Ndipei receipt ndione (Let me have your receipt.)

He took it and looked at it and told us to meet him at this same spot at the same time tomorrow. The following day we were there as instructed and the man came out to meet us. He handed me my passport. We thanked him and Misheck tried to give him some money in appreciation but the man politely declined. He said the fact that I had gotten an opportunity to go out and better myself was gratitude enough for him. With my passport in hand, we drove to the US Embassy and the man gave me my Visa in my passport and envelope right away. He asked me if I knew the address on the envelope, I confirmed that I did. It was a travel agent in the city center. I took my passport and the envelope, thanked the officer and we drove to the travel agent. I was issued my ticket and the following day, September 11th, I was on the plane to the US. ONLY GOD!!!

I was so excited about this opportunity that when I arrived at Baltimore International Airport, just outside Washington, DC, I didn't think much of it when the same man whose wife had offered me the job in Zimbabwe took my passport. I was told that they needed to submit my passport to authorities so that my work permit may be stamped into the passport.

When we arrived, the organization was in full swing preparing for the National Congress of Black Women Annual Conference that had already started. The night before Janet Reno, former US Attorney General, was to speak, Dr. Tumbler asked me to prepare a speech because she was going to have me as one of the guest speakers sharing the podium with Janet Reno. Of course, at the time I had no idea who Janet Reno was. Dr. Tumbler wanted me to speak on a specific topic, "The Effects of Rap Music on the African Child". I was honored, except I did not know what rap music was and whether or not it had reached Africa yet. The Internet was not a "go-to" resource for information at the time. I accepted the challenge and prayed for osmosis to take place from the heavens. The download came in the form of an article in Parade Magazine at home as I sat in my hotel room in the early hours of the morning asking God how I was going to pull off this speech. My hotel room phone rang. It was Misheck, my friend from Zimbabwe. After pleasantries, I informed him of the humongous task before me.

As I say throughout this book, if this stuff was not happening to me, I too, would be more than skeptical.

Misheck, hardly able to contain himself, went on to inform that he had just come from the newsstand where he had seen and purchased the current Parade Magazine that had that very article in it. If I wasn't sitting on my bed, I would have fallen to the ground. I could not believe it! He started reading the article to me. It was the most incredible thing. I asked him to fax it to the hotel after I ran downstairs to ask for the hotel fax number. I don't know why I went downstairs rather than calling the front desk. I don't remember. I ran back upstairs, gave Misheck the fax number, and hung up so I could go to the reception area to wait for the fax. I spent the rest of the night copying the article on a computer in the lobby. I read that article so many times so the speech could at least flow. The last time I gave a public speech of similar magnitude was in high school. It was a school-wide competition which I won. My topic, "The Effects of Alcohol". My father, a veteran in speech delivery, had coached me. So had my uncle, Clifford Tserayi, who was a couple grades above me.

Later that day, I gave my speech just before Janet Reno, who was the current Attorney General of the United States and I remember her words as she approached the podium after the people were done giving me a standing ovation, "Now, that is a tough act to follow". I couldn't believe what had just happened. Thank you, Misheck, Parade Magazine, and of course, God for orchestrating everything!

– ∞ –

As time went on, I began to notice some things that were a bit odd. For instance, I realized that the position that they had offered me was actually taken. They claimed they were planning on firing the young lady. I started off doing odd jobs until they realized that I actually knew my way around computers, something I had informed them when they hired me back in Zimbabwe. Three months went by with no contract, no salary, no mention of any payment of any kind. After staying in a hotel for two weeks – at their expense, I was moved into an apartment. It turned out the man was a landlord of many properties in Washington, DC and Philadelphia. I refer to him as he was affectionately known, Mr. T., out of respect. So I was put into a studio apartment in one of his buildings in Washington, DC. I was informed that he would be taking me back and forth to work until I was ready to use public transportation on my own. Every request for a contract was met with either, "As an employee, you don't really need a contract in America unless you are a consultant" or "We cannot have you sign a contract until you have a social security number". When I inquired about how to obtain a social security number, I was informed that I needed to receive my work permit first and that takes time for my passport to be returned to me. So it became the song and dance that went on for almost 2 years.

This couple was not your everyday people, if you will. They were very prominent in American politics, especially in the African American community. Mr. T., as I said, was a real estate mogul and the wife, Dr. C., was the political figure. When I first met her, I was mesmerized by her representative, aka, who she wanted people to see or think she was. Behind closed doors she was just as mesmerizing, but with a rather dark side. To the African American people around her, she was the best thing that ever happened to women's liberation since Rosa Parks and Sojourner Truth. She was known for representing the rights of women and children, and yet, here I was in her care and I was starving with no adequate access to food. When I complained of hunger, she and her husband would joke about, "It can't be as bad as it is in Africa or where you come from". I wanted so bad to remind them that when they approached me in that hotel in Zimbabwe, they did so because I was well-dressed and after less than an hour of interacting with them, they seemed surprised, but at the same time, intrigued by my "command of English" to which I kindly but sarcastically pointed out, "Zimbabwe was a British Colony"! This clearly went over their heads because they asked if I had learnt to speak English from studying in London since I had "a strong "British accent". Sometimes it is okay to leave people in their chosen state of ignorance and pray for another opportunity to try and educate. On this particular date, for this particular subject, I chose the latter. In that brief encounter in Zimbabwe, they asked about my educational background and career which clearly impressed them, for they hired me on the spot. So where is this implication that I was coming from a place of starvation coming from? As a matter of fact, I did not know what it was to be hungry to the point of starvation until I came to America. I never knew what it meant to go without sanitary pads till I came to America where I was forced to use paper towels to manage my periods. Another fact they seemed to choose to ignore was that the Zimbabwean dollar in 1997 was much stronger than the American dollar.

When I mentioned earlier that living in a country without proper legal immigration status leaves you vulnerable to abuse, I am speaking as one who suffered incredible covert racism by people who not only looked like me but also claimed to fight against the very thing they were exhibiting and subjecting me to. Outsiders would be told how they brought this "poor African" to America as their protégé and how "generous" they were. This always got them cheap praises. When an individual has your passport in a foreign land, you pretty much have nowhere to run, especially when they constantly show you how powerful they are and how well-connected they are. With the colonial background that Zimbabwe had, as well as a black leadership that was beginning to allow their newly found power (post-Independence) to go to their heads, I was very familiar with individuals made to disappear by the very same people sworn to protect them. As educated and as exposed as I was before I came to America, I was also pretty naïve. I trusted this couple. My life was dependent on them so-to-speak. I was not allowed to make friends, not even with my co-workers. Even though they knew I was a Christ Follower, they barred me from going to church. They began to emotionally abuse me as well as isolated me even from my family back home. Back then you needed calling cards to make international calls. In the first few months, they would give me $20 cards which were supposed to last me at least a week. They were very aware that I had left my 7-year-old at home, as well as my retired parents who needed my financial support. Eventually, they just stopped giving me the cards and before long I was completely shut out. I then learnt that I was not the only foreigner they had done this to and now, in retrospect, I recognize

I was involved in a human trafficking situation, before it had a name. I am grateful that I was spared from sexual abuse. Unlike a significant number of individuals involved in human trafficking, there is almost always sexual abuse involved. I must say there were times where I wondered if they brought me over to be Mr. T.'s concubine. I cannot explain it, but it was always a thought in the back of my mind based on conversations and behaviors exhibited. My reality and their abuse of choice was overworking me to the point of physical and mental exhaustion, as well as constantly reminding me how connected they were not only here in the US, but also in Zimbabwe and they could make not only my life, but my family's lives a living hell. If I wasn't working on database management and fundraising campaigns, I was working in Mr. T.'s office or in their homes (they had two homes, in Washington DC and in Philadelphia), I was also working in any of the buildings they owned.

I was trapped. The emotional abuse was incredibly brutal that sometimes I thought it was better to be physically beaten because at least I knew how to deal with physical wounds - my father had dished me more than fair share as a child.

One day, as had become the norm, they had gone out of town and instead of coming by the office to pick me up, they had forgotten about me and I had no way of going home. It was way after midnight when they finally answered my calls and informed me they had gone to bed forgetting to take me home after their day trip to Philadelphia. They asked me to come over to their house which was not too far from our Silver Spring, Maryland office. Dr. C. asked me to bring a report of what I had worked on all day. I made my way to their apartment on 16th Street where we spent about 45 minutes going over the report along with me being berated for calling them in the middle of the night. Mr. T. then gave me $20 to take a taxi to go home. "The security guard downstairs will call a cab for you", he said. I went downstairs and the security guard tried his best to assist me, but there was no cab that was willing to take me to Southeast DC due to perceived violence that happened there. I lived in that apartment for almost 2 years and quite honestly I did not encounter the violence people seemed to speak so much about. But then again, I was not home enough to know my neighborhood. After attempting to get into a few cabs and being kicked out once they realized my destination, I had no choice but to walk. It felt like I was walking for eternity. I wasn't adequately dressed and was so cold I couldn't feel my feet or my fingers. The first wrong thing I did when I got home, was run a very hot bath in an effort to "thaw" myself. Unbeknownst to me I suffered from frostbite. All I knew was I was in excruciating pain like my whole body was on fire. I was in bed for a few days before the building manager, Mrs. Gaine, knocked on my door and let herself in because I couldn't get up from the bed. Mrs. Gaine. ended up nursing me to health. It was during that time that I made a resolution with myself that I needed to get out of this situation. I could have been mugged that night or worse and since I travelled around with no ID, who knows if the Tumblers would have had the guts or the kindness to claim my body and ship it to my parents. I started praying for a way out. Fasting had become an everyday occurrence, albeit unintentionally, but fasting nevertheless.

As God does, He answered my prayers. One day I was cleaning Mr. T.'s office and noticed that one of the desk cabinets was unlocked. This had never happened. This is the one cabinet he always made sure was locked, even when going to the bathroom. So needless to say, curiosity got the best of me. *Why does he always have this cabinet locked? I know we are supposed to respect people's privacy, but hey, I am only human.* We, office staff, always suspected it was filled with alcohol because he enjoyed an occasional sip of his drink-nothing crazy- just once in a while. Sure enough, when I looked in it, there were bottles of alcohol. Nothing to write home about. But there was something else in there that looked familiar- my passport. I cannot tell you how I was able to think so fast, except for God's wisdom. All I know is I reached for it very quickly, put it in my bra and locked the cabinet door. At that very moment, as I turned my back towards the door away from the cabinet and dusting the conference table, Mr. T. walked back in. He walked over to the cabinet, tested the lock and saw it was locked, mumbled something, and walked right out. I finished cleaning, locked the office door as usual and went back to my office. Even though I seemed okay to the naked eyes in the office, my insides were shaking like a tropical leaf by the Montego Bay seashore. I kept my passport in my bra until I got home that night, occasionally tapping it to make sure it was still there..

That night I did not sleep. I called one of my co-workers, Angie, who was a believer and asked if it was okay for me to come live with her family until I figured out a plan. Her parents agreed. I then asked her to pick me up that night. I began to pack my few belongings then sat down with a pen and paper to write a letter to my "hosts". I informed them that I was leaving and would not be returning. I laid down how I had kept my side of the bargain by working tirelessly for them and they had failed to keep theirs. I told them that I was uncomfortable with them continuously threatening to return me to Zimbabwe knowing that the political situation had deteriorated significantly and it wasn't safe for me to return. I reminded them how they continuously used parts of my story that I had shared with them to force me into submission, claiming they were in direct contact with the government officials back home. This wasn't far-fetched since I had witnessed part of their encounter with President Mugabe in Zimbabwe. I thanked them for their time and I left the letter on the table as well as the keys. Angie came and that was it - trying to avoid prying neighbors and alerting Mrs. Gaine, we snuck my belongings through the window and drove away like Thelma and Louise, without the husband/boyfriend, cliff and the famous Thunderbird. That was the last time I had anything to do with them…so I thought.

My new host family and any other American I shared my challenges with could not understand why I just didn't walk into a social security office and obtain a social security number. It seems pretty simple to locals. When you are an immigrant there are protocols you have to follow that most natives are not are not privy to, understandably so. Why would natives have the need to know the immigration rules of their country? I didn't know the immigration rules of Zimbabwe. Except that one time when they were going to deport my British-born son, Nyasha when he was a toddler visiting my parents. Immigration system anywhere is not always straightforward and it is not always clear where to get advice. It was during this time that I realized that my passport had never left the custody of Mr. T. All the time they were giving me all the song and dance about my passport having been sent to immigration were all lies-and deliberate ones too.

Eventually, I started meeting people at church who gave me advice, from an American perspective, which didn't always align with immigrants. Of course, they all meant well. After a while of knocking on various doors, I finally knocked on the right door and obtained a social security number. I also met a lovely lawyer called Theresa with whom I shared my story and she, in turn, introduced me to a labor lawyer. Up until that time, I didn't know that I had rights, even without legal immigration status. I didn't know that labor law required me to be paid for work done regardless of whether I had a work permit or not. So after meeting with the labor lawyer, Mr. Robert, he assured me we had a case. We began months and months of depositions. I was literally afraid for my life because I felt intimidated by Mr. T. and his wife. At this point I was living alone in Maryland. Because my address was documented in the deposition papers, Mr. T. would just randomly appear in my complex, follow me with his car and not say anything. I spoke to my lawyer and I eventually left the Washington, DC area and moved to Albany, NY.

My day in court

Finally, we were given a date to come to court. I was so nervous, but at the same time I needed someone to vindicate me because these people who bought me to the US had been spreading untruths about me. One of the most hurtful untruths they had the nerve to share in court was how they had intercepted my letters while I was employed by them. They tried to use the information in the letters to put my character into question, stating that even my father had complained in the letters that I had not only neglected my parents, but I had, in essence, abandoned my son too. My father had a right to write such because in our culture, our parents look after us so that when they are older and we are adults, we can look after them. While I was working for the Tumblers and not receiving a paycheck, I wasn't in a financial position to do anything for myself, let alone my parents and son. So on that day, as I sat in court being asked if I recognized these letters, it broke my heart that these individuals who had presented me with what seemed like a great opportunity, were being this vindictive towards a person they hardly knew.

It's important to understand that these individuals were not "you and I" kind of people. They were well-connected and revered in communities throughout the country as civil rights movers and shakers. This was always funny to me because, here they were treating me like crap, denying me food and access to proper sanitary products & health care, fellowship with brethren, and any kind of friendships, and yet, their circles were the likes of Dr. Dorothy Height, Coretta Scott King, Mrs. Hilary Clinton (when she was the First Lady), Rev. Jesse Jackson, Dick Gregory, Dr. Shirley Chisholm, etc. Dr. C. had this blown up photo of her with Martin Luther King, Jr. marching for civil rights in Selma, Alabama in 1965. Of course, at the time I didn't fully understand, nor did I fully appreciate it, being that my own civil rights were being violated every day. As I sat in that courtroom, I couldn't help but think of how people like them, who brought foreigners into this country, treated them badly and had zero consideration for how their actions impacted not just the individuals they bring, but their families by extension. If you had told me back then that I was involved in some form of human trafficking, I would have denied it because it didn't look like what you see on TV. It was much more sophisticated than that. In their minds, they really believed exposing me to the high life and famous people should cancel out the discomforts they were subjecting me to; not knowing that where I come from, we are not a culture that gets star-struck or mesmerized by celebrities and political figures. When we run into them on the street or restaurants, we greet them and keep it moving - no groupies, no pressure - we respect their privacy.

It reminds me of an experience I once had. My boss, Dr. C was part of the VIP at the Million Woman March of October 25, 1997 in Philadelphia, Pennsylvania. So by default, I too, was counted among the VIP and was seated on the stage with all the celebrities and guest speakers that included, my shero, Winnie Madikizela Mandela, Dorothy Height, Congresswoman Maxine Waters, Attallah & Ilyasah Shabazz (Malcom X's daughters), Jada Pinkett Smith and Sista Souljah. Among the celebrities was one Blair Underwood. Some of the people who were part of my team were busy taking pictures while I people-watched. So as they were taking a picture with Blair underwood, one of them asked me if I was not interested in taking a picture with Blair Underwood. I said I wasn't because I didn't know who he was. Mr. Underwood heard me and turned around and asked, "You don't know me?" I answered that I didn't. He seemed shocked and annoyed that there dare be someone in the crowd who didn't know who he was. Sensing his disappointment, I asked if he knew me. He was taken aback and responded, "I don't believe I do". I politely stretched my hand to shake his as I said, "I am Princess Teresa Dangwa of Njanja Zimbabwe, who are you?" "I am Blair Underwood, nice meeting you," he responded still looking shocked. I went on to ask him, "Would you like to take a picture with me"? Still seemingly shocked and maybe bruised a bit, he obliged and my colleagues snapped a picture as a groupie photo-bombed us (I still have that picture hanging in my house for posterity). Of course I knew of Blair Underwood, I grew up watching LA Law but answering, "Yes, I know you," would have been false. I knew his character on LA Law, Jonathan Rollins and that's about it. To date, by nature/nurture, I do not go gaga over celebrities. Perhaps the only famous individuals I would go a little gaga over would have been Nelson Mandela, Viola Davis and Tyler Perry, for inspiring us to break the proverbial glass ceiling.

– ∞ –

As deliberations proceeded on that day, my best friend, Iris and her Mum, sat in the audience listening to these people's lies about me. Ironically, I met Iris through the Tumblers.

> <u>Sidebar: Iris was the young lady who was working in the office the day I arrived and I was "assigned" to help her with the media packages she was putting together for a conference that was about to start at Hotel Washington within hours. Iris, seeing me dozing off – had been kind enough to allow me to nap on the couch. End of Sidebar.</u>

As I narrated to the judge how I went for days with no access to food, Iris' Mum knew exactly what I was talking about because she was the one who was feeding me. She didn't know then, but she always told the story of how one day as she was preparing lunch for Iris something in her spirit told her to prepare more than Iris could consume. Iris then jumps in and says at first she protested that it was too much food, but then Mum always won. Iris started to bring food and would offer me some without realizing that what she was giving me, was the only real food I was guaranteed a day most of the times. Sometimes. Mr. T. would distastefully joke that I should be used to a little hunger because of where I came from. Apparently, I was supposed to be grateful for them bringing me to the US, because there are a lot of people who would kill to be in my shoes. *Not if they knew they would be denied access to basic things - no they wouldn't*, I thought. *Not if they knew they would need to use bathroom tissue for sanitary towels, in the land of plenty, absolutely not*, I continued to say to myself. They always got surprised when I explained to them that I grew up with running water, access to more than enough food, and freedom.

Anyway, we expected our case to be heard and ruled on the same day, but as we were in the middle of deliberations, someone came to whisper to the judge that we needed to evacuate. We were not told why, but were informed we would be given another day to come back to court. As we walked out of the courtroom we saw swarms of people trying to make it to their cars and others huddled up. Iris and her Mum left soon after to beat the traffic. I was planning on driving back to Albany the same day; however, I ended up spending a few days at another friend's house because traffic was just bad. My lawyers and I needed to chat a little, so they suggested we go to the nearest bar. There was hardly a place to stand. It was swamped and people were visibly shaken. Some were crying. It was then that we noticed no one was drinking or eating. They were all glued to the TV screens in the room. *What is going on? What happened?* Then, we found out. Two planes had flown into the Twin Towers in NYC. America was under attack. Strangers huddled up, all shaken at the core. A moment whose sole purpose was to destroy and divide people living in the US was, for that moment in that bar in Maryland near the courthouse, was defeated. We stood there as members of the same species feeling the pain of the attack, confused together and seeking understanding together. In that moment, the enemy was defeated. Strangers were hugging each other as if acknowledging that we were alive together. We were hurting together. We were under attack together. It was September 11, 2011.

Indeed, there are some experiences that we go through that make you go, "Ha!" But in the end, they are blessings in disguise!

CHAPTER SIX

The Blessing of Motherhood

"Children are an inheritance from the Lord. They are a reward from Him" Psalm 127:3

"For God is the one who gives seed for the farmer and then bread to eat. In the same way,. He will provide and increase your resources and then produce a great harvest of generosity to you." 2 Corinthians 9:10

– ∞ –

ANOTHER DATE THAT WOULD FOREVER BE ETCHED IN the center of my heart, is the day my son was born. When I got pregnant I didn't know I was pregnant for almost five months. I didn't get the usual morning sickness that is the tell-tale of most pregnancies. I didn't gain weight. As a matter of fact, I distinctly remember getting on a bus in London one time and finding no empty seats because it was full. I stood in the middle aisle pushing my stomach as far out as possible to try and show I was pregnant and needed someone to courteously offer me their seat. It didn't work - that's how small my stomach was throughout my pregnancy. I didn't have cravings until I was told I was pregnant at five months, which leads me to believe that, for me, cravings were more a psychological thing than a physiological thing, but that is neither here nor there, I suppose. "Well, didn't you miss your periods?" you ask. I did, but that wasn't anything new for my cycles. I had a messed-up cycle history in which I could go for months without seeing my period and then, at times, I would bleed heavily like all blood was being drained out of my veins and with serious cramps that paralyzed me. So for me, missing my period was no sign of "you are pregnant". Missing periods for months was my normal.

But that early morning in January of 1991, my Mum knew. Call it intuition, but she knew. We were walking down Muzari Avenue in Chinhoyi towards my big brother Emmanuel's house. He is my cousin but, in my culture,, we don't have cousins, remember? That word doesn't exist in my language. All our cousins are either brother or sister and they are treated just like our siblings.

As we walked down this long street that had no significant bends, it stretches as far as the eye could see. The weather was beautiful, not too sunny, but a welcomed change since it would have been the rainy season at the time. As we briskly walked, we talked about life and other general things. We also shared the excitement of my upcoming journey to London. UK. My Mum wanted us to go to Mukoma Manu, as we affectionately call him, so he could share with me some insights on living abroad. Mukoma Manu had studied and resided in Scotland years prior.

Mum was giving me advice to listen intently to what Mukoma Manu had to say, "Nekuti vakambogara kumhiri kwemakungwa" (Because he lived overseas), she said. So when my Mum, out of left field said, "Teresa, unenhumbu iwe (Teresa, you are pregnant)". It threw me off completely. It was not a question but a very firm statement. Like a doctor confirming to a patient who had come to inquire why they were throwing up every morning.

"Aah, handina nhumbu ini. (I certainly am not pregnant.)", I responded with 100% conviction and in shock that she would say such a thing. I was incredibly naïve. Mum, always the gracious woman, said nothing else and went back to other things. I don't think she let the matter go because I had denied her claim, but I think she was stunned at my vehement denial and naïveté and perhaps considered slightly that she was wrong. Or, perhaps - the most likely explanation - she, in her wisdom figured, "I have said my peace, now let's wait and see". Or, maybe, she thought not to rain on my parade of the eminent journey to London that would open lots of possibilities for my future being the unwanted child who had been rejected by my father a few years back. Or, it's possible that she thought to not push it, lest she drives me away since she had just gotten me back after having been disowned by my father years before. I will never know why she didn't push me for answers or ask me to "prove it". I am sure if she had asked me to prove it, I would have taken my naïve self to the doctor right away because, well, "Of course I am not pregnant".

— ∞ —

Nyasha, My First True Love

I named him Nyasha, a Shona name meaning "found favor with God"

ACCORDING TO MY DOCTOR I was not due for another week. We all know that technology is not 100% accurate; it makes assumptions based on information we, humans, feed it. So on the evening of June 15th, when I was seated on the couch, relaxing and possibly watching pre-recorded episodes of the Australian based *Home & Away*, Ryan, Wendy's toddler son jumped on me like he always did out of excitement whenever he saw me. Except this time, I had not braised myself. He jumped right onto my belly and I lost the ability to take consistent breaths. I felt like, well, someone had punched me in my stomach. Within the same time, I felt like I was going to puke all my insides. Wendy was my landlord and Ryan was her son.

"Ryan! How many times have I told you to be careful?" Wendy screamed at her toddler who was now sheepishly looking at me with his big blue eyes and his overused pacifier in his mouth as if to say, "Please save me".

"Oh, he is fine Wendy. He didn't mean to," I defended him.

"He is too rough. He has to be careful," retorted Wendy.

She turned her attention to me because I was now bent over due to the discomfort in my belly.

"Are you okay, Teresa?"

Not wanting to get Ryan into more trouble than he already was, I managed to painfully assure Wendy that I was just fine and this feeling would pass. I didn't want to tell her that I had felt the impact right through to the lower part of my back. I mean, I was in so much pain that I needed her assistance to get upstairs to my bedroom. I tried to assure her that it was just a little shock; it was nothing that lying down would not cure. I said it, but I didn't believe it. I was in pain.

I got to my room, Wendy helped me settle on my bed and down the stairs she went to prepare Ryan for bed. She was hosting a little party that night and needed to get ready fast. I could hear her tell Ryan, "You have five minutes" and it would be bedtime, the first of several warnings. I lay on my bed in the fetal position for what seemed like a lifetime. Slowly the pain subsided and at some point I fell asleep. I thought I had been sleeping for a while but it turned out it was only a few hours. I remember being annoyed by the fact that I needed to go to the bathroom. I got up and felt a weird wetness in my panties. *Really, I wet myself?* I scolded myself. *But I didn't have "the dream". Or did I?* I stood there trying to remember if I had "the dream" or not.

I bet you are wondering what dream? Well, you know the dream we all have, those of us who are crazy enough to admit it anyway. "The Dream" presents itself in many forms for different people. For me I am at my grandmother's home, in the rural areas of Manyene in a place called Marondamashanu in Chivhu.

<u>Sidebar: This is my maternal grandmother's home. My parents always sent us there during school holidays. I had a love and hate relationship with spending time at my grandmother's home. I enjoyed being there because it meant being spoilt by my grandparents and being encouraged to try some foods we generally didn't eat on a</u>

regular basis, especially the wild fruit and mushrooms. I have never been one to enjoy manual labor. To this day, I absolutely hate it. Being at my grandparents' meant serious manual labor. You see, everyone in the rural areas' livelihood is largely dependent on the land. That is called subsistence farming. This is a type of farming that is done for personal and communal consumption. There is a lot of tilling the land, nurturing the crops and then harvesting the crop – all depending on what time of the year or season we visited. It is during these times that I developed this hate relationship with manual labor. It meant waking up at an unholy hour before dawn and walking the 3-5 miles to where my grandparents' field was located. The walk was fun, though, because I really loved the challenge of crossing the stream we had to cross to get to the field. We had to figure out the best spot to cross. Sometimes when the river was low, we could pretty much cross anywhere and taunt fate a little, under the watchful eye of my grandparents. However, when it is the rainy season, that river can be extremely angry and sometimes unsafe to cross. The safe crossing spots have strategically placed, huge rocks that we jumped on to get to the other side. On occasion, our cousins who resided in the rural areas throughout the year, would let us know of stories where someone decided to fight nature and was swept angrily by the river to a sure death. Once in a while, we would hear stories of some who lived to tell the tale. Some would speak of the God who

<u>caused them to be swept straight into a floating log that they held onto and were "spit" out of the raging river. End of Sidebar.</u>

Okay, back to the dream. In this dream, I am in another dream and find myself in need of going to the bathroom. It's always a wonder to me how this never applies to #2. It is always #1, pee. (I am in no way suggesting that I would like for it to be #2 at times because that would be a gross disaster - just wondering is all). I find myself looking for the best spot behind a bush where I can do my business without any interruptions. In my dream, I look at every possible route that a person can intrude my space. After I am sure no one is coming, or is likely to see me, I then look for a nice clear space where no one else has had their business and where there are no likely creepy crawlies to find their way up my unmentionables. Then I prepare myself to stoop low enough not to splatter but not close enough for my unmentionables to touch the grass. I am now ready to do my business. Wait!!!! Wake up! Wake up! Don't do it, it's a set up! You are dreaming…that's "the dream".

In that moment on June 16th, as I am trying to figure out if the wetness I am feeling is a result of "the dream", I feel a warmth traveling down my legs inside my nightgown. *Wait, am I in "the dream"? No I am not! Holy mackerel, I'm peeing on myself but I am awake...what in the world?!* I shuffled as fast as I could to the bathroom. My legs are completely soaked at this point and as I sat on the toilet I see the trail of where I had walked. *That doesn't look like pee*, I marveled to myself. I try to wipe myself and this substance is feeling a bit different than regular pee. The consistency reminds me of the agile from the river near my grandmother's home. *That's weird*, I tell myself. Then I remembered my mother's letter. I run back to my room. *Where did I put that letter* which had become like a Bible to me? I was referring to it more often lately. *Where is it? I just read it yesterday. Where is it?* Now I am beginning to panic. *Oh there it is, right in the side pocket of my baby preparation bag where I had neatly placed it.* The letter! I read it slowly as if for the first time. It's written in Shona, my native language, with a cursive handwriting that I grew up reading all my life. I feel a warmth just looking at the words neatly penned throughout the pages. The letter was penned with great concern and deliberate usage of certain words, some repeated for emphasis. I know deep down this was a hard letter to write but it had to be written. I felt the love that went into every stroke as the sentences came together to form what had become my manual to motherhood.

"Mwanangu", the letter starts after the date at the top indicating when she had written it. Mwanangu simply means, "My Child". It was full of a lot of advice but the passage that was of utmost importance in this moment was the one that read, "Ungwarire nekucherechedza mvura dzinobuda kusi. (Be on the lookout for unusual liquid from down under). Dzinobuda seweti asi haisi weti. (It feels like pee but it is not). Ukaibata inenge ichirembuka kunge mazerere kana madziwa. (It feels like mucus or algae). Color yacho inenge brownish, imvura yakasangana neropa" (It has a brownish color because it's mixed with blood). *That's it, that was the substance coming out of me! What does that mean again?* I knew the answer, but I needed to be sure. "Ukaona mvura idzi, ziva kuti mwana avakuuya, ibva waenda ku hospital" (This means your water has broken and you need to go to the hospital).

> Sidebar: You have to understand that this was a difficult letter for my Mum to write because generally, in our culture, mothers do not have these kinds of conversations with their children. Anything that has to do with monthly periods, the bees and the birds, reproduction, childbirth, issues in marriages, etc. is almost taboo to discuss with Mum. It is reserved for your aunt, not just any aunt but your father's sister. So my Mum was breaking all kinds of rules to make sure I have a safe birth in a foreign land where there were no Aunts. My Mum may not admit it but she is an underground radical. End of Sidebar.

The baby is here, oh my God, the baby is here! He is here! I need to call the hospital. We don't have a house phone. OMG, this liquid is coming out hard. I need to wake Wendy up. So I stuff some soft toilet paper in my panties and walk across the hallway to knock on Wendy's door. We had a plan that we had practiced many times. When it happens, I get Wendy and she goes next door or to the nearest public booth to call an ambulance while I watch Ryan. *Why didn't Wendy have a home phone?* I don't remember, but in that moment it seemed weird and inconvenient that Wendy didn't have a phone in the house. Wendy doesn't answer the door. *I need to pee, I go to the bathroom but it's not pee – it's the water. My water broke.* My mum, in the letter, had emphasized the need to keep calm so I was practicing calm. Then it hit me, *I needed to pack my hospital bag.* I go to reach for it and notice that it is already packed. I pick it up and throw it on the bed. I open it. I reach for the piece of paper with the list I had received from the prenatal classes.

The list had things like a night dress and gown, panties, comfortable bras - nursing bras if possible (*who has money to buy a nursing bra on a minimum wage job, seriously?*), stuff for the baby (vests, sleep-suits, hats, mittens, socks, booties, napkins, baby blanket), slippers for mummy, etc. Okay, all is accounted for. I had packed this bag 2 months in advance and would check it at least once a week just to ensure I had everything on the list.

I went back to wake Wendy up, but she still wasn't waking up. I lie down because now I am feeling a little pain in my lower back. *Okay, breathe, Teresa. You can handle this. Your period pains are worse than this. That is absolutely right, this pain is nothing compared to the cramps.* So I start to breathe again. The pain is not that bad. I keep needing to go to the bathroom, but nothing comes out except this slippery liquid. Every time I go to the bathroom, I stop at Wendy's door and still she doesn't wake up. I decide the pain is not that bad, that I can wait till 5:30AM when she gets up. I go back to my room to pack my bag for the umpteenth time. It feels like the Christmas list song,

<u>"Santa Claus is Coming to Town"</u>:

You better watch out
You better not cry
Better not pout
I'm telling you why

Santa Claus is coming to town
(Santa's coming to town)

He's making a list
He's checking it twice
He's gonna find out
Who's naughty and nice
Santa Claus is coming to town
(Santa's coming to town)

Except I am checking my list more times than I cared to count. Wendy finally woke up. I calmly told her to go and call the ambulance.

"Oh my God, is the baby coming? Why didn't you wake me? Are you okay?" she threw questions at me in succession.

"I tried to wake you several times", I calmly tell her.

"How can you be so calm, you are having a baby?"

"I don't know but you need to hurry up because I don't know how long before the baby is born after the water breaks".

"How are your contractions? Are you breathing?" she kept calling out questions as she changed out of her pajamas.

"I don't know, I can't tell how far apart. Yes I am breathing. Please go and call the ambulance", I insist without showing any panic but with a sense of urgency in my voice. It didn't help to have two panicked individuals at this moment. My friend/landlord was panicked enough for both of us.

Wendy ran out to the nearest telephone booth and the ambulance was there within minutes. When they came, I had already wobbled downstairs to the living room with my suitcase and Ryan in tow with his pacifier in his mouth. I swear he slept with it all night long. I had lived here for a few months now and I was yet to see it washed. *That's gross. Why am I thinking of this stupid pacifier at this time really? I don't know. All I know is that my son will not be using one.* As I am carefully being strapped in the ambulance, I am asked some basic questions and the driver made a radio call to the hospital to ensure my consultant was available when I got there.

As long as I can remember, I have always heard older women talk about the pain of child-bearing. Therefore, I am mentally ready for this pain. I am expecting it and I wait. I wait for it to feel more than my regular cramp and it still doesn't go any further than my mild to moderate cramps. I am thinking, *it has to get worse because if not it will make all those women liars. Where is this pain? I want to feel it. Or do I? Heck no, I want this process to be smooth, no pain.* See, my pain threshold is pretty high, but because of those women's stories, I am expecting crazy, bite-your-partner's thumb off type of pain…without the partner part in my case. Bite someone's thumb off. Nothing! No pain to write home about. I am so busy having a conversation with my pain that I don't realize we have arrived at the hospital. Sirens and all. It dawns on me that this is the first time I have ever been in an ambulance. As they whisk me into Northwick Park Hospital, my consultant is at the door to meet me. As soon as I see him, it hit me that this is really happening. Then panic took over now I really don't want to feel that pain because I turn to him and say, "I want a C-section." My consultant looked puzzled. "I have heard the stories of pain. I have excruciating pain with my periods so if it is more than that type of pain, I definitely want a C-section. Besides, I really don't want my 'yard' to be any wider than it is right now." He seemed to get my point. As calmly as he could muster, without laughing out loud, he says, "My dear, we don't give C-sections on order, but I will manage your pain effectively and you won't feel a thing. Just as we discussed numerous times during prenatal classes".

"No, no, I don't want the pain, nor the thought of my 'yard' being opened wider than it is," I protested vehemently.

"You will be fine," he said patiently.

I was whisked into my private room and strapped to all kinds of machines. Hospital personnel were going in and out of the room with each of them wanting to monitor this, to take that info, to fix my pillow, to give me water, a towel for my sweating forehead. So much activity. I began to pray, *Lord let this cup pass me by. I really don't want to go through this birth naturally.* When I didn't get an obvious response from God, I turned to my son, "Listen, Nyasha, it's you and me. We can't go down like they are thinking. We need to do this a bit differently". *Did I feel a kick? Wait, it wasn't a kick. I haven't heard him kick in a while.*

I was monitored for a few hours, got an epidural, even though I didn't really need it, but the consultant wanted to give it as a preventative measure because the pain would definitely come, he had declared. Well, it wasn't pain that came, but panic. The nurse came into my room and looked at the monitors. I told her I had not felt my baby kick, she assured me that all was well, and then, all of a sudden, her demeanor changed as she looked at the monitors. She dashed out of the room without a word. A few minutes later, she was back with my consultant and other professionals in tow.

"What is going on?" I inquired. No one answered me.

I gave them a minute and I asked again. It turns out my son agreed with my preferred choice of him making an appearance into the world. The next thing I knew, I was being told I needed an emergency C-Section. Fetal distress, they called it. *More like Mother and son had an understanding. Way to go Nyasha, you and I will get along just fine!,* I thought to myself as I was whisked to the operating theater.

In an effort to put my mind at ease, my consultant asked if I was expecting, a boy or girl. I told him, I wanted a boy and if it was a girl I didn't want it. He laughed it off and assured me I would love the baby no matter the gender. I told him I was very serious. He ignored me and we discussed other things. I can't tell you why I didn't want to know the gender of my child prior to his arrival, but it could be because my conscience battled:

a) I didn't want it to be a girl – *that* much I knew. My life growing up as a girl was tough. No one disowns a male child and sends them to be married off to some stranger. Whatever happened to me was not going to happen to my offspring.

b) The very minute I was told I was pregnant, I somehow knew it was a boy, but I didn't want to perhaps jinx it by knowing.

c) Besides, part of me thought that a girl was more likely to suffer the same fate as the one I had, and I couldn't see myself getting over my daughter being molested, raped and abused.

– ∞ –

My son loved going to church. As a matter of fact, for a very long time in his earlier years, he claimed that he was going to be a pastor and doctor when he grew up. He was so sold on Jesus that he used to get upset when his Pre-K teachers tried to convince him that his heart was a blood pumping organ. He insisted not his heart, for "Jesus is in my heart". The teachers would try to convince him and he would cry to the point of the school calling me to come and get him.

"Mummy, Mummy, they are saying there is blood in my heart, but I know there is Jesus in my heart, right Mummy?"

The teachers were not winning this one. "Yes kiddo, Jesus is in your heart".

Oh well, that settles it then and all is well with the world.

One time, in Kindergarten, his teacher was trying to explain to the kids the purpose of the skeleton in human bodies. In as simplified a way as she could muster, she told me how she tried to ascertain if the kids understood what she meant. So she posed a question, "Does anyone know what would happen to them if they didn't have any bones?" She expected for them to say things like, "You will fall to the ground" or "You will have no power" or "You will disappear". Instead she got blank faces staring at her from all the kids, except of course, Nyasha. He had his hands up excitedly as one who was convinced his answer was what the teacher was looking for. "Okay, Nyasha, what would happen if we didn't have our skeleton?"

The teacher told me how my son stood up and very confidently said, "God will give us new bones!"

Drop the mic! That's my baby! So with a son that I loved and adored, who loved God in his special way, to hear that some church folk were referring to him as Ishmael completely broke my heart. Imagine such cruelty from the very same mouths that worshipped God and claimed to be Christ-like! Church, folk are some of the most judgmental individuals on earth.

My son and I used to go to a local branch of the same church I attended when I was in Zimbabwe. I figured the same belief system but different crowd would give us a much needed fresh start without a total overhaul of our preferred form of worship. Well, I suffered ridicule, being spoken about behind my back, and rumors being made about who my son's father was. I could handle that. What I couldn't handle was learning that discussions would happen in which my son was referred to as "an Ishmael", implying he was not a child of the promise because he was born outside of wedlock.

Sidebar: Ishmael was Abraham's first born before Isaac. In Genesis 15, God had promised Abraham that not only was he going to have a son, but he shall be a father to many nations. As the years went by and Abraham and Sarah grew older, they began to lose hope of God's promised son. Sarah tried to help God so she gave Hagar, her slave maiden, to her husband. Abraham and Hagar conceived. God then appeared to Hagar letting her know to give her son

<u>the name Ishmael which means "God who hears". Later on, in God's time, Sarah conceived at 99 years old and conceived a son whom they named Isaac. End of Sidebar.</u>

— ∞ —

Errol, Gogo's Prince

IF ANYONE HAD TOLD ME I would be Gogo (grandmother) before my son was established in his career, I would have told you that you needed your head examined. Like most parents, I had so many dreams and aspirations for my son. I wanted him to finish college, enjoy life, travel the world and figure out his God-given purpose before he settled down to have a family. Lie most parents, totally disregarding the thought that it is very well possible that Nyasha's purpose is to be the best parent for Errol he can be. We have been conditioned to associate purpose with everything else but parenting. Oh how wrong we are.

In Shona, we have a proverb that's similar to, "Those who live in glass houses should not throw stones". Mugoni wepwere ndeasinayo, literally translated, "it is those without children who have the luxury of speaking in ideologies". When you have a child, you do not go around boasting that your kid won't fall into this trap and the other because life has a way of making you eat humble pie.

Graduation season of 2012 was upon us. New beginnings in the air, with graduates excited to go out into the world to make their mark in their chosen field. I had been invited to be one of the speakers at the Center for Women in Government Graduation and 30th Anniversary Kick-Off. I was excited to travel to Albany because it also meant that I would get to see my sons and have an impromptu early dinner. My two sons, Nyasha and Yaw were in college in Albany. I had moved the previous year to Westchester, NY, about 2.5 hours from Albany.

I was so nervous but excited at the same time. Just as we were about to start the program, my phone rang. It was Nyasha. I excused myself and ran to the restroom to take the call. Nyasha then said, "Mum, I have something to tell you but you are not going to like it". Normally, I would give my little speech of there are only three things that are unforgivable, everything else we can work ourselves through it. 1. You have deliberately killed someone; 2. You were arrested for an alcohol-related infraction or 3. You have made a girl pregnant. Thank God, I didn't say anything of the sort. I almost did, but the Holy Spirit arrested my mouth and instead I said, "Whatever, it is we will work through it". He repeated that I was going to be disappointed and I encouraged him to spill. He said, "I made a girl pregnant". I managed to mumble, "Are you sure and how old is the girl?" It was important to me that the girl was at least above 18 because I couldn't handle the possibility of my son being charged with statutory rape. He assured me she was older and I was incredibly relieved. I told him I had to get back to the event but I will speak to him later and not to worry.

Even though I sounded calm, I was not calm. My heart was screaming. *Where had I gone wrong? Had I not taught this boy better than this? What am I going to do with a baby right now? Who is this girl and who were her people? Was she house-*

trained? Did she have good manners? I had so many questions that I needed answers to. *Had Nyasha run out of condoms?* Okay, I had no time to ponder too much on these and other questions, at least not for now. I went back to the auditorium and did my speech shortly afterwards. People reported that they enjoyed my speech, even gave a standing ovation for me and my fellow guest speakers. I couldn't tell you what I spoke about because it was purely the Holy Spirit which sustained me during that 8-10 minutes.

I went to dinner with Yaw. Yaw, is my "adoptive" son...long story for another day. It was supposed to be Nyasha's belated birthday dinner. He had turned 21 years old exactly 10 days prior to this day. My son was a kid himself, how could he be having a kid? He can barely look after himself. Nyasha had given his brother some excuse for not coming to dinner with us. I suspected he was either afraid to see my reaction or too embarrassed to face me or a little bit of both. After dinner I dropped Yaw off and got to see Nyasha briefly at the house where they stayed.

That night as I drove back home with nothing else to do but think, it felt as though while I was at the event in Albany, the department of road works had come out and diligently worked to extend the road just to aggravate me some more - the 2.5 hour drive seemed longer. I continued to ask the questions, not to anyone in particular, but I needed answers. Nyasha had mentioned something about the girl going to the doctor to confirm the home test she had done. I prayed that it be a false alarm because my goodness, how can these kids be having kids? Then the biggest question, the one I feared the most - *what are people going to say?* I was a devout Christ follower. Before I moved, I was involved in my church as part of the care ministry who were responsible for intercessory prayer. *How am I going to explain this to people?*

Sidebar: What are people going to say? That question, if one is not careful, can make you lose your mind. It is a question designed by the Devil. It serves no purpose but to depress you and lead you nowhere but a dark hole. So let's think about this for a minute. What are people going to say? What people? Why are the people in your business? Why should I worry about what people say? Have they helped me in bringing up my child? What exactly are people's roles in my life and my son's life? Why do we put so much emphasis on what people will say? What about what does God say? Now there is a question worth seeking because no matter how you slice this one, it ends at love because God is love. God knew this day was coming and He had already prepared the exit strategy. Jeremiah 29:11, "For I know the thoughts I have towards you, thoughts of good and not of evil, to give you an expected end or

<u>to give you hope and a future". End of Sidebar.</u>

While I was lost in my thoughts, the phone rang. It was Nyasha. "Mum, are you home yet?" "No, I am almost there, should be about five minutes", I answered trying not to show my emotions.

Silence.

Neither of us spoke for what seemed like forever, although in reality it was a few seconds. After the awkward silence, Nyasha said a line that will forever ring in my head. "I bet you are not the proudest mum right now".

Those words pierced through my heart like a spear. I quickly answered, "I am just really disappointed because that is not what I had envisioned for you." I also reassured him that there was nothing he would ever do that would make me love him any less. By this time I had parked at my house and we devised a plan on dealing with the matter.

For months, I went through a time where I was devastated, depressed and just couldn't stop blaming myself. In times like these, I had three trusted individuals that I could confidently talk to with certainty of my privacy being respected. They were my youngest sister Janet, my best friend, and my big sister Caroline Manyika. Unfortunately, Janet had passed away years back so I reached out to Sisi Caro and Iris. These two ladies, although not related by blood, we were connected by the most precious blood - the blood of Jesus Christ. They both started as friends but they quickly became sisters. I knew that neither of these two ladies would judge me. So I called and sure enough, to their character, they prayed with me, cried with me, allowed me to cry some more and encouraged me. With them, I felt free to tell them exactly how I felt inside. They used scripture to encourage me and bring me out of the rut I was in. They gave me the space to pour out my heart, to speak out loud my innermost fears. At my job, I had three other sisters who I eventually confided in after they had witnessed my demeanor changing. Ninna Sarpong, Latia Johnson and Tsitsi Tafirenyika became my local anesthesia. When I eventually shared the news with them, they all reacted the same way, "We will get through this. We are here for you.

Whatever you need." And true to it, they were there when I needed them - more angels on assignment.

Even with this incredible support system around me, my thoughts when I was alone at home would get the better of me. There is a reason why the Word of God encourages us to take authority over our minds, because, left to its devices, the mind is a battlefield. *2 Corinthians 10:4-5 says, "For the weapons of our warfare are not carnal (flesh) but have divine power to destroy strongholds. We destroy arguments and every lofty opinion raised against the knowledge of God and take every thought captive to obey Christ".* For a while I forgot this Word. I couldn't eat. I literally went through a phase where I would wake up, go through the motions of the day, come back home, go to bed and do it all over again. At work I would "act normal", but inside I was tormented. I could not stop blaming myself. *How could I let this happen?* In all my planning and giving my son freedom to reside on his own while he attended college, I had never considered the possibility of my son becoming a dad at 21. How could I? We are a good Christ following household? OH, BUT GOD!

Sidebar: To all the great parents out there, I want to encourage you and say this. When a crisis hits your family, your initial reaction is not going to be Biblical. All the theoretical scenarios we go through in abstract are so far removed from reality. No one prepares you for the mind games the devil brings to your doorsteps. You cannot help but blame yourself - it's a given. What helped me in this season was what the Holy Spirit whispered in my ear, when I allowed myself to hear Him beyond the devil's loud shouts, **"When you know you have done all you can to lay a solid foundation for your kids, when you have given raising them your best - not from a material point of view but from a values point of view - you will know that the decisions they make as an adult, are not**

on you. They are now responsible for their own actions. When you stand before the Father on judgment day, you will not be judged for the decisions your children made as adults. You will be judged on the type of foundation you laid out for them, whether or not you taught them the law of the Lord so that when they grow up they will not depart from it? *"Train up a child in the way he should go: and when he is old, he will not depart from it." -Proverbs 22:6* **Our kids, will stray, it is inevitable as they try to figure out their sense of being outside of us. All we can do is pray, be there when they need us, and trust that the Jesus foundation you gave them is solid and that they will always find their way back to base. End of Sidebar.**

January 22, 2013 was a huge snowstorm. It was also the night my son received a call that Tahj, Errol's mum, had gone into labor. We woke up, got ready, and drove the 2.5-hour journey through the blizzard. At that time, I had pulled my kids out of UAlbany and they were attending a local community college. I figured they needed more monitoring, given the results of what they had gotten into when left to their own devices. My car, a Volvo station wagon, did not have heating so we bundled up really good and made our way.

We got to the hospital and I met Tahj and her family for the first time. *They seem like nice enough people*, I thought to myself. Between her mum, her grandmother and me, we were hovering over her making sure she was comfortable. Eventually, the baby came. January 23rd Errol Isaiah Dangwa was born and I was instantly healed from self-diagnosed depression, shame, feelings of isolation and all the negative things I had allowed the devil to deposit into my mind. There is nothing like a new birth that just brings with it a new perspective. All the things I worried about seemed to be a non-factor from that point on. I was mesmerized. I was in love. There is a certain level of love that is unexplainable.

It is like God created another layer of love that only grandparents get to experience. It is an intense type of love. Like I said in my dedication above, it is not that I loved my son any less; it was just that the love for my grandson was heightened. Errol Isaiah "Tendekai" Dangwa is no doubt, the love of my life and for that, I am forever grateful.

Sidebar: When Errol was 6, he asked me why he didn't have a Shona name. "Your Dad didn't think to give you one', I replied rather amused.

"Oh", he said before he thoughtfully continued, "Gogo, can you teach me Shona Gogo?

"Sure Errol, I can teach you Shona", I answered.

"How do I say Errol in Shona?" he inquired.

> "Errol means Nobleman and in Shona that means Tendekai", I told him thinking pretty quickly.
>
> "Good, from now on call me Tendekai. My name is Tendekai", he declared proudly and began to write the name everywhere after I taught him how to spell it. End of Sidebar.

It was very important for me that Errol's DNA was tested for paternity immediately after his birth. I am sure it made Nyasha very uncomfortable to have to make such a request to Tahj but it needed to be done. Since this book is about bearing it all to shame the devil and for God to get the glory of the testimony, that is my life. Yes, part of me wished and hoped it wasn't his child, not because I didn't want Errol, but because I wanted and desired for my son to not be a dad at such a young age. Another even more important reason for the DNA test was multi-pronged and very practical:

a) Every child deserves to know their true identity - who his/her people are...his/her tribe.

b) Every person deserves to know and must know their health DNA. I imagined if he was to be sick at some point in his life, in order for the doctors to give a well-informed decision and provide a true diagnosis, his health DNA needed to be as close to accurate as humanly possible. I could see the potential of a wrong diagnosis where certain aspects may be dismissed because his given history "does not support" such a diagnosis. It is very scary how, in general, we tend to dismiss or not pay attention to our health and mental DNA. There is no one who enjoys completing their comprehensive health assessment forms at their doctor's offices, but for better healthcare outcomes, it is a necessary step towards a healthier lifestyle. There are certain diseases that are known to run in the family, such as diabetes, heart disease - including high blood pressure, asthma, cancer, cystic fibrosis, sickle cell anemia and hemophilia, to name a few. Knowing your health history, can help the doctors to work with you in preventative medicine to reduce the chances of either getting the disease or making it worse. Having Errol miss out on better health outcomes due to an intentional faulty diagnosis was a risk I wasn't willing to take.

c) In my Shona culture, even where people "adopt" children from strangers, it is still very important to find out as much information as they can about the child's people. When people do not believe in the Word, or are ancestral worshippers, not knowing where one comes from can be detrimental; especially when that individual dies in your custody. It is believed that the spirit of that individual never rests and can also cause some bad omens in generations to come. Again, this is where belief systems are not the same or tradition is important. In instances where grandparents do not have the same belief system as yours, like in my case, my dad is a traditionalist and I am a Christ Follower. If Errol was to somehow end up with my dad when his DNA is not part of our clan, Errol may be seen as a bad omen if my family continued to see one calamity after another. This may cause some serious tensions among families. It is important that I state that I don't believe in these things, however, there is a whole huge population out there that doesn't share my belief systems.

As it turned out, Errol's DNA proved without a shadow of doubt that he is indeed my descendant. All is well with the world!

I am a better mother, grandmother, sister, friend, pastor and human being because of Errol. His being in the family causes me to want to be a great role model for him, not in my speech only, but more importantly, in the way I conduct myself. I am blessed beyond measure, my cup runneth over!

CHAPTER SEVEN

Betrayal & Forgiveness - a Necessary Partnership

I have deep sorrow and unceasing anguish in my heart - Romans 9:2

For if you forgive other people when they sin against you, your heavenly Father will also forgive you. But if you do not forgive others their sins, your heavenly Father will not forgive your sins.

- Matthew 6:14-15

— ∞ —

WHY DO PEOPLE ALWAYS SAY, "TAKE IT ONE DAY AT A time"? Seriously, is there some kind of alternative for which I somehow did not get the memo? What page of the "life manual" is that on, because I really could have used that alternative during one of the darkest seasons of my life?

One of the hardest things that we as Christ followers are called to do is forgive. We are to emulate Christ in that, even though we were yet sinners, He died for us (*Romans 5:8*). The whole point of Christ coming to the earth in the form of man, was to teach us by example that forgiveness is possible, not because people have shown remorse, but simply because the Word says so. Forgiveness is not a weakness; rather a strength. It took strength for Christ to endure the Cross so that our sins may be forgiven. Therefore, when we are wronged, we too are to exhibit that same strength.

Unfortunately, society has taught us that when we are wronged, we should seek revenge or seek to exert as much pain, if not more, to the person who has wronged us. We forget that our just and faithful Father says vengeance is His. *Romans 12:19* says, *"Do not take revenge, my dear friends, but leave room for God's wrath, for it is written, "It is mine to avenge; I will repay" says the Lord".*

Besides, when we seek vengeance, we are NEVER taking into consideration that person's soul and their eternity. As a matter of fact, we pray for God to destroy them with the "Holy Ghost Fire". That is why God says vengeance is His because not only does God dish out punishment from a place of compassion and healing, He does it justly, never losing sight of the fact that He desires that no one should miss Heaven. *2 Peter 3:9 says, "The Lord is not slow in keeping His promise, as some understand slowness. Instead, He is patient with you, not wanting anyone to perish but everyone to come to repentance."*

Forgiveness is hard, especially when the hurt or betrayal is deep, but it is not impossible. We can do it through the assistance of the Holy Spirit. However, I must say, when you are going through it, it is very hard to remember these precepts and if you do remember, it's tough to follow through when you are hurting.

Falling in Love is a Beautiful Thing

I ALWAYS THOUGHT that when I fell in love I would feel the romanticized butterflies and all that pizzazz we see on the TV screens or in Hollywood movies. Boy, was I wrong! Like every girl out there I had my proverbial list. If truth be told, when I fell in love with Munyaradzi, I had given up on love. Not in a bad way, but in the "I am not trying anymore, let the chips fall where they may" kinda way. I had had a very frank conversation with

God concerning a life partner and had surrendered to His plan, whatever that was. I asked Him to shut down the feelings I had of wanting companionship and the feel of a man's touch. Okay, maybe not totally shut them down, but to put them on hold until He was ready to reveal His choice for me. I stopped trying to manipulate the narrative.

December 30th 2015 was a real paradigm shift for me spiritually. I travelled to Canada with the intention of "helping" God out in my love life - to rekindle a relationship with an old flame. The events that took place upon landing in Toronto were nothing but God communicating with me in a more profound way that this trip wasn't going to end the way I had envisioned it. I can't say I know what my host was planning, but it wasn't as relevant as what God had planned for me. When my first love arrived at the airport, not only was he late, but he had not made any effort on his appearance or his car. I entered the car and couldn't believe he had not made an effort to at least get it cleaned or pick up the mess in the car. The plan to get my groove on over this particular visit was shut down right there. We got home and his house was absolutely spotless with the table set for a romantic dinner. Quite frankly, I was very impressed. This was the man I fell in love with many moons ago. It was all beginning to come back…aaah the memories. I even started to tell myself that maybe he didn't get time to make himself presentable or to clean the car because he was busy cleaning the house and making it nice for me.

Well, even though that evening went down well with great conversation and great food - *my goodness he was still a great cook.* Although the meal made me salivate, I just couldn't shake the feeling I had at the airport. Let's just say, the extended long weekend didn't go down as I had planned in my head. My itch wasn't scratched but I was content.

Back to the proverbial list. I know most of it was only possible if I married Jesus Himself, but there were five top "conditions" I placed on my list that I wasn't quite interested in compromising:

    a) The gentleman had to love God with all his being;
    b) His spiritual maturity had to be above or equal to mine, he couldn't be a baby in Christ;
    c) He had to be Zimbabwean. The thought of explaining culture and, most importantly, jokes, to my significant

other all the time just did not appeal to me (I love to laugh and some jokes tend to get lost in translation);

d) He had to have a mother who was dead (morbid, I know but the thought of having a mother-in-law around scared the daylights out of me. I have heard way too many stories of horrible mothers-in-law) and I could do without the hassle.

e) He couldn't be a pastor or any version of a man of the cloth. I lived in enough pastors' homes in my early years as a Christ follower and witnessed enough challenges they faced to want to be a member of that elite squad. Needless to say, God gave me all but the 5th of my wish list. I wanted to be normal but God had other plans.

When I started going to the Zimbabwean church in Harlem, finding a husband was not even in my peripherals. I wanted to reconnect with "my people" while serving God at the same time. I felt really strongly in my spirit that I needed to be among my countrymen. As destiny would have it, I found myself working closely with the pastors behind the scenes to establish a leadership program. Little did I know that something miraculous was taking place in the heavenlies! I remember one time having a conversation with Pastor Tembo, letting him know that I was off the market for a husband and that I just wanted to come to church and serve God. Pastor Tembo asked me to keep an open mind and the rest is history. This goes to prove the Word of God concerning our lives, *Jeremiah 29:11, "For I know the thoughts I have for you, thoughts of good and not of evil, to give you an expected end."* And *Proverbs 19:21, "Many are the plans in a person's heart, but it is the LORD's purpose that prevails."*

One of the most heart-wrenching, emotionally-charged, and bowel-moving (literally) 3 weeks of this process was the struggle I had in how to tell my son, Nyasha of this love journey I had embarked on. It was tough because for the past 25 years, my life had revolved around my son (save the past 6 years since my grandson, Errol was born). Nyasha had been the man of the house. I had never introduced him to any man. This is not to say I never had boyfriends; lest you mistakenly think I was a saint...I just never had one worthy of the introduction. Munyaradzi and I prayed countless times for God to give me courage and the right setting for this conversation. In the end, it wasn't as bad as I imagined. Apparently, he already knew. Nyasha claims he saw the signs of a happier me, being secretive and always smiling and acting like someone in love when I picked up calls from "Munyaradzi" (my caller ID showed in the car).

Sidebar: Most of the times when you think your kids don't know, they know. They know when you are happy. They also know when you are being abused. All this affects them accordingly, so watch what and who you bring around your kids. End of Sidebar.

My son was so happy for me. It was the most beautiful thing to behold and feel. God is faithful and is concerned about the seemingly insignificant concerns.

The Sign

MUNYARADZI DID NOT ASK me out in a traditional sense. I fell in love with Munyaradzi's spirit!!! A ministry-related conversation somehow transitioned into a getting-to-know-each-other type of conversation. As I spoke to him, I knew in my spirit that something was brewing. But as a good Christian girl that I am, I did not want to be presumptuous. The more we talked, the more I felt a deep sense of connection to him.

On that 1st night, I asked God for a sign because what I was feeling was foreign to me. I have never felt such a sense of security and spiritual connection with any man. I needed to know from God Himself that what I was feeling was the real deal. I did the one thing I knew to do, pray. That night, God showed me a vision similar to a recurring dream I had had for years. In the vision, I saw a sky full of sheep, so many of them I couldn't number them. While in this vision, I felt a sense of responsibility to those sheep but it was not total responsibility. To my right, at an arm's length, was a man standing in front of me but a little on the side. This man was looking at the sheep seemingly oblivious of my presence. I sensed that the full responsibility for these sheep was upon this man and my job was to help this man. This vision was both scary and calming at the same time. For two more nights I kept asking God for a sign and He kept saying "I gave you a sign already". I had the vision two more times.

> Sidebar: Sometimes we ask God for signs and He gives us visions which are not related to the matter for which we asked a sign. But in our minds, we think we are seeing this vision based on what we prayed for, when in reality, God is giving us a vision for His plan for our lives, not necessarily related to the prayer we just sent up to the Heavens. In hindsight, given all the other related dreams, I have concluded with a peace in my heart that God, at the time, was not referring to my relationship with Pastor Munyaradzi, but with the calling that is upon my life. Sometimes, we do see

<u>what we want to see because it makes more sense to us. End of Sidebar.</u>

Not so long after that, Munyaradzi asked me on a date and the following Saturday we went to one of my favorite restaurants (alternative to Denny's), IHOP. Brunch ended up being more than four hours. As we talked, it was as if we had known each other for years. One of many amazing moments is when God quickened our spirits at the same time about *Joel 2:25, "I will restore all that which the cankerworm has eaten".* As late bloomers on this marriage journey, we both felt a sense of having "missed out" but it turns out, right before our eyes, the Lord's Word was becoming alive. From that point on we were traveling on Restoration Highway.

As we got ready to walk out of the restaurant, I was still asking God for a sign under my breath. I excused myself to go to the restroom and left Munyaradzi standing in the lobby. As I walked through the restaurant, I still asked God for a sign. God said, **"What sign? I already gave you one three times"**. I said, "I need a specific sign". He asked me what I wanted. I said, "As long as I have been talking to this man, he is yet to say he loves me". Don't get me wrong, he had said everything else to show how he felt, but never those three words. Given his reserved personality, and add limited experience in relations with the opposite sex at this level, I recognized and understood that there were some things that may not always be verbalized. So I put a demand on God that I needed to hear him say those three words. I handled my business in the bathroom and walked back still mumbling that demand. As I walked back to the lobby, I continued to make that demand. I got to Munyaradzi and he asked me if he could hug me. I obliged, then he whispered in my ear, "I love you". I was done! Talk about incredible emotions...I was overwhelmed.

Our journey felt so natural, as if we had known each other for years. A way of life was born on this day. Everything we asked God, His response became instant. No one but God deserves all the glory for our story! OH BUT GOD!!!!!

The Dress

OH, THE DRESS! Where do I start?

All of a sudden all those ideas I had whenever I envisioned my wedding gown disappeared. I had no idea what I wanted, how the dress would look. Like everything with this process, I gave it all to God to give His guidance. I asked three of my closest friends at the time, my prayer partners, to accompany me. These ladies blew my mind away with the way they availed themselves to me. They carved out whole Saturdays just to dedicate to helping me find my dress. We prayed, we praised, and we went on a mission. Even Emma, who had only been in the country for a short while at the time, learnt to navigate the subway system for my sake.

We went to David's Bridal store and we had so much fun. I tried on the first two dresses and on the third dress, my body started shaking and my spirit was filled. I started to cry uncontrollably and knew right away that this was my dress. I proceeded to try on many other dresses, and as beautiful as they were (Some of them, just okay), none quite gave me the reaction like that third dress. Fast forward to a few weekends and a couple of bridal stores later, we found ourselves back at David's Bridal. Between Pink, my maid of honor and confidante, and my attendant bringing all kinds of gowns, I lost count of the number I tried. Then there were two left, but still nothing close to that third dress. A little discouraged but still having fun, I tried on the last dress. I walked out of the booth feeling rather excited in my spirit. Come to find out that last dress was that same third dress. My friends and I were ecstatic. I was shaking, crying, snorting, goose bumps everywhere. An emotional rollercoaster. Needless to say, after gathering with my friends in a circle, we prayed, danced, and sang-still snorting and all. The attendant helped ring the bell (David's Bridal tradition when a bride finds their dress)! I paid my deposit and we went to celebrate over a meal.

A couple weeks later, I was driving to work as I spoke on the phone with my brother Calvin, giving him an update of what the Lord was doing in my life. Calvin is my late best friend Iris' husband. We talked and prayed and hung up. A couple of hours later, I am sitting at my desk and I get a call from David's Bridal with a bad news and good news situation. Bad news was that they only had one dress in the warehouse and they were not sure if that was mine or another bride's. I told her clearly it was mine and she needed to do whatever she had to do to make sure that was mine. She tried to tell me there were new dresses coming and I could get another one, but I wasn't having it. After back and forth supervisor conversations and 40 minutes of holding, she said she'd secured my dress. The good news was someone named Calvin had paid off my gown. I have no idea how I managed not to faint. My debt of a significant amount was paid off! All I could do is cry and praise God for my brother. What an incredible gift. I still cry thinking about it...sometimes the words "thank you" just seem inadequate. Thanks, Bro (and Iris, my dearly departed Sister, who trained him well)!

If this wasn't happening to me; even I wouldn't believe it!

A Deep Betrayal

I HAVE COME TO REALIZE that in life there are some betrayals that just cut way too deep. Betrayal by a family member – in my case my father – but, it could be any relative, is tough, because you think of family as your first line of defense. So when that first line is infiltrated by a betrayed trust, you lose your bearings. For me, I lost my sense of identity and belonging. Somehow, I had gotten my mind and heart to believe that who I was and what I was to become was one in the same. Then, there is betrayal by church-folk, that is deep too because you think they are in the Word, therefore, they ought to know better. I place betrayal by church-folk in the same category as betrayal by a close friend. They just ought to know better. When you get married, your first line of defense shifts a little and it becomes your spouse. Your ride or die. The jelly in your peanut butter & jelly sandwich. Betrayal by a spouse is one of the worst kind in my book because the expectation is when you get that close with someone your vulnerability scale is quadrupled. You loosen up; you become an open book figuratively and literally. You're at your most vulnerable. You open up about your fears, your aspirations, and your deepest thoughts because now you are the same flesh with this other person. You are them and they are you, so no need to hide anything. You lay it all out, again, figuratively and literally. So when one betrays the other or when one feels like they are betrayed, it is hard to return from there.

<u>Sidebar: Don't get me wrong. I said it is hard, but not impossible. Restoration can happen but it cannot be done on your own. Only the Holy Spirit can heal and restore fully – nothing and no one else. End of Sidebar.</u>

I went through days where I told myself, I've forgiven my spouse until I was alone in the car, stuck in traffic as I navigated down 287 East to I-95 South, onto the ever-congested Throgs Neck. I've never really understood how that bridge, or any other, has such a bottleneck when traffic is moving fine five minutes before the toll booth. Any-who, I would be driving to or from work and I would start screaming how I hated him and would cry my eyes out for feeling this way towards someone I had chosen to love and spend the rest of my life with. You hear a lot about a "very thin line between love and hate". You just don't know what it feels like until you are treading that line. I was walking this line for months. It was so bad that I could not recognize myself. I mean, I've been hurt before by a member of the opposite sex-molestation, rape, and all kinds of abuse-but I never felt this way. The emotions along the thin line were foreign. I honestly didn't know how to deal with how I was feeling. I also didn't know who I could turn to. Who, on this side of heaven, would understand how I was feeling? I didn't know anyone who had been where I was. I'm not saying no one has had experiences similar to mine, far from it. I'm saying I didn't know anyone in my life who had gone through what I was going through. I needed to speak to someone who would at least give me a preview of what was to follow and who would help me understand this type of pain. I didn't know that there was a deeper type of pain that existed until it knocked on my door.

The closest I can equate it to is grief. When you lose a loved one; I mean someone you are really close to, you feel like the walls are closing in. I've only felt this for five deaths in my life - my brother Russell; my youngest sister, Janet; my Mum's youngest sister, Mainini Middie "Aunt Mildred", my Dad's young brother, Babamunini Eriya "Uncle Elias" and my best friend who became a sister, Iris. Even writing about them many years later reminds me that we are truly never "over it". Contrary to some teachings that eventually you get over it, we don't "just get over it". Maybe for someone who didn't mean as much to us, we may "get over it" but we really don't. We learn to live at peace with their absence from this side of Heaven. Thank God as a believer when I'm going through one of those moments, I lean on the Holy Spirit. Without the help of the Holy Spirit, I don't know how I would have survived with my mind and heart relatively still in place.

During that season of betrayal, it wasn't me per se who did the leaning on the Holy Spirit because I honestly don't remember doing so subconsciously. How could I? I was angry at the Trinity! It was more like the Holy Spirit was leaning on me and watching from a safe distance.

I went through moments where I would pick up the phone to call Munyaradzi, because even though he was the source of this incredible pain, I felt like he was also the only one who could understand the pain. You see, for many years prior to 2016, I had lived a life where I consciously chose not to go to bed angry. Literally, before I fell asleep, I forgave anyone who might have wronged me on that day-real or imagined-I would pray for forgiveness from those I would have wronged. I even wrote them text messages or emails and then I would forgive myself. It worked for me for the most part, save the instances where I felt I needed to punish self a little longer because I just couldn't believe what I'd done, again, real or imagined.

One of the things that confused the heck out of me was not only were we both born again, sanctified, speaking in tongues, and part of our church's leadership, but also that he was a Pastor. I just couldn't reconcile what was preached at the pulpit with what I was going through at home. If I had $5 for every time I asked him how he justified what was happening to us based on the Word and got a simple, honest, and yet defiant, "I can't", I would have built the clinics and the college I had been wanting to build in the rural areas of Chivhu for years. In retrospect, I honestly believe that he too was not sure how to deal with what was going on to us and around us.

Sidebar: It is important that I mention that I do not take away from him the calling that is upon his life. Making bad judgement calls in one's journey does not negate a) the calling of God on one's life; b) the work they have deposited into the Body of Christ, c)nor does it stop one from being used by God in the present and in the future. Remember the Apostle Paul writes in Romans 11:29 that, "For the gifts and calling of God are without repentance". God does not change His mind in mid-life to remove that which He has deposited in us, regardless of whether we choose to utilize those gifts and calling or not. Apostle Paul encouraged Timothy in 2 Timothy 1:6 to "stir up the gift within him" meaning it was

<u>already deposited by God at his creation. The same applies to us, God deposited in us the gifts and calling before the beginning of time for He says, He knew us before we were formed in our mother's womb (Jeremiah 1:5). At the end of it all, my husband is a Pastor, a servant of the Most High God and that is not up for debate. I choose to honor that. End of Sidebar.</u>

When my husband and I were courting, one of the things we made a commitment to was, "No matter what was going on in our lives, the Word of God will always be what we would turn to for guidance. We agreed that the Word of God will have the last word over our opinions and/or feelings". My goodness, making commitments and promises is very easy when love is in the air, so to speak. Let life happen and even the Word goes out the proverbial window. My goodness, did it go out the French door. Perhaps, what we should have added out loud to that commitment was the Holy Spirit's guidance in our inevitable differences in interpreting the Word of God.

So here are two God-loving and fearing people - him 53 and I about to hit 50 – with neither of us having ever been married. We had ideas of how marriage should be, naturally influenced by our parents' marriages and other couples we had encountered along the way both collectively and individually and what we believed the Word says about it. We were both entering unchartered territories with very limited personal experience. We went through the required sessions on pre-marital counseling which were helpful to a certain extent. Not because the Pastor leading them was not spiritual enough or not anointed, to the contrary. He is a God-fearing man and a dear friend to both my husband and me. I just don't think that he was equipped to help us work through our issues because, quite frankly, they were foreign to him too. We had a counseling script, that we went through (guided by our Pastor) – at least I did – each week diligently. There was just something that was not clicking in my husband's brain. It could be that the pressure was too much for him, I didn't know then. I chose not to acknowledge its possibility because, "well, my husband is a pastor – he ought to know better". Even during the time when challenges were presenting themselves, I chose – maybe not consciously, but my choice nevertheless – to look at it for what I wanted. I chose to look at this whole drama entirely from a selfish point of view. He, on the other hand, took a more religious approach. He really believed that Jesus would fix it all, without us making any effort.

You see, when you are a single pastor teaching and preaching on marriage God's way, it is very easy because it is all theoretical, at least from your perspective. For instance *Genesis 2:21-24* which describes the initial and foundation of all human marriages, God's way is very utopic and very romantic. God caused Adam to fall asleep under the anesthesia of the Holy Spirit, surgically removing one of his ribs and neatly fitting into Eve's rib cage like it belonged. Watch what Adam says upon coming to, *"This is now bone of my bones and flesh of my flesh, she shall be called woman for she was taken out of man" (Genesis 2:23-24)*. Seriously, how romantic is that! I have heard of engagements that were broken because of uttering someone's name other than the fiancé's as one comes out of anesthesia induced sleep.

Marriages have been placed on 'Rocky Mountain' for gibberish that seemed to put to question the love one has over the spouse hearing it. Worse still, if one utters a name that sounds like the ex's name – you are in the dog house for a while.

I reached out to some pastors, and in some instances, was advised "not to worry too much, just go through the wedding and all will fall into place". They expressed their concerns on how this would look for the church being that we were part of the leadership. I can tell you without a shadow of doubt that it wasn't made out of malice; they 100% had good intentions. Even when I finally chose what I felt was best for me by calling off the wedding 10 days before it happened, I saw friendships dwindling and the church folk shunning me. At the time I was bitter, even more so when I was asked to step away from a leadership role "until you and your husband sorted yourselves out". This request, although well-intended, was a very hard pill to swallow. I was devastated and slowly began to disassociate with not just church but God. I kept saying to myself, *Isn't church where we go when we are in trouble? Are we not to love each other to health rather than judge and condemn?* Apparently our "situation was disrupting the morale of the church". Wow! I didn't realize it at the time, but ministry was being birthed in me because I kept asking within myself, *Where do servants of God and their spouses go when they are hurting? What "hospital" or "rehab" or "program" do they go to?*

As painful an experience this was, I believe that God allowed me to go through it so I can feel, taste, and see the serious gap in care that exists for pastors, their spouses, and even their children. My children needed counseling of their own to get over what transpired. No church leadership reached out, even though I pointed it out numerous times. We were alone. One or two pastors tried to maintain their connections with me. We are still friends to date, but I could sense the agony they were going through inside. After all, my husband was their friend. They knew him before I knew him. They provided as much support as they could without feeling like they were somehow betraying their loyalty to their friend.

Church folk, are sadly so, the most judgmental group of people on earth. It kinda shakes you because it should be the last place such happens. Church is supposed to be a safe haven, a place of last resort. In healthcare (in the US) there is a health insurance law that designates Medicaid (a government funded health insurance) as "payer of last resort". In other words, "If another insurer or program has the responsibility to pay for medical costs incurred by a Medicaid eligible individual; that entity is generally required to pay all or part of the cost of the claim prior to Medicaid making any payment". (www.cms.gov). In my humble opinion, church, like Medicaid, should be provider of last resort when it comes to complete healing.

— ∞ —

One of the greatest real-life stories ever told is one of amazing love for humans that anyone will ever read and encounter. Everything about love is wrapped up in what transpired at Calvary over 2,000 years ago. Isaiah 53:5-8 gives us a very graphic picture of what was to happen to our Savior Jesus Christ.

"But he was wounded for our transgressions; he was bruised for our iniquities: the chastisement of our peace was upon him; and with his stripes we are healed. All we like sheep have gone

astray; we have turned everyone to his own way; and the Lord hath laid on him the iniquity of us all. He was oppressed, and he was afflicted, yet he opened not his mouth: he is brought as a lamb to the slaughter, and as a sheep before her shearers is dumb, so he openeth not his mouth. He was taken from prison and from judgment: and who shall declare his generation? For he was cut off out of the land of the living: for the transgression of my people was he stricken."

Then when you fast forward to that fateful day at the Cross, Apostle Paul in *2 Corinthians 5:21*, says, *"For he hath made him to be sin for us, who knew no sin; that we might be made the righteousness of God in him."*

So wait, Jesus knew no sin – has never sinned a day in His life, no He is incapable of committing sin because He is Holy. That Jesus, chose to go through Isaiah 53:5-9 for what exactly? For me and you, the unclean filthy rags? (Isaiah 64:6 and Romans 3:19-23). Yes, He chose to leave His comfortable, Holy, and undefiled place – the right hand of the Father – to come and go through hell just for us.

It wasn't enough that He left His Throne in the flesh, but He suffered the deepest betrayal known to mankind. The Word of God says in all four Gospels that Judas Iscariot betrayed Jesus for 30 pieces of silver. Judas was not just an ordinary individual. He was one of the 12 disciples. Jesus had chosen him to be one of the 12 knowing full well that one day this individual was going to betray me. Of this same Judas, Jesus said in *Matthew 26:21-25*, *"And as they did eat, he said, Verily I say unto you, that one of you shall betray me. And they were exceeding sorrowful, and began every one of them to say unto him, Lord, is it I? And he answered and said, He that dippeth his hand with me in the dish, the same shall betray me. The Son of man goeth as it is written of him: but woe unto that man by whom the Son of man is betrayed! It had been good for that man if he had not been born. Then Judas, which betrayed him, answered and said, Master, is it I? He said unto him, Thou hast said".* And people say there are no curse words in the Bible. This was some serious cursing. *"It had been good for that man if he had not been born" (verse 24).*

Wow Jesus!

When I was growing up in Zimbabwe, we used to banter with one another a lot and when the bantering went further than the acceptable norm and one wanted to really hurt someone's feelings, one would turn around and say, "Dai vabereki vako vakatanhaura nzungu musi iwoyo zvaitove nani". In other words, "Had your parents made the choice to labor in the fields, they would have gotten a better yield than taking the time to create you". Serious shade and insult.

Jesus, though He didn't like that Judas was going to betray him, allowed him to complete his assignment – as messed up as it was. Jesus even encouraged him to hurry up and get on with it.

John 13:27, "After [Judas had taken] the piece of bread, Satan entered him. Then Jesus said to him, "What you are going to do, do quickly [without delay]."

Jesus knew that Judas' betrayal was a necessary evil. It needed to happen in the manner in which it happened so that when it happened to us, we would not be shocked. Yea right! I still get a bit shell-shocked when someone close to me decides to betray me. I couldn't believe that Munyaradzi, the man who professed to love me would betray me in the manner in which he did.

I am not delusional; therefore, I am fully aware that where two people brought up under different family systems come together there are bound to be disagreements and some fundamental differences. Like most unions, ours was no different. There were differences of opinion in the date, the venue, the color scheme, the costs, and even the color of my dress. I know…the color of my wedding dress became an issue…I was not expecting that one. There was an antiquated belief held by some of the elders in his family that a woman with a child prior to marriage is not to wear a pure white dress. Insults were thrown. Feelings were hurt. Egos were bruised. I made some bad moves too. Some of them pretty significant. What I did not account for was my husband's reaction or lack thereof. I expected him to defend my honor. To defend me. To choose me. Why? Quite simply, because I had chosen him.

You see, when I first informed my family that I was getting married to a pastor, they were not amused. Some tried all they could to talk me out of it. But I chose him every time. I stood my ground and demanded that even if they did not approve of him, they should at least respect my choice. I was 50 years old for crying out loud! I am sure I had earned the right to make my own decisions without needing validation from the masses. It took a bit of work behind the scenes, outside of my husband's earshot at times (although sometimes it was unavoidable), but they all came around. Every single one of them, including some extended family. Because we live worlds apart, geographically, it didn't seem to take much convincing when I made it clear that their blessings were appreciated but certainly not a requirement for seeing my marriage through. They respected that and based on the love they had for me, they chose to get on with the program pretty fast. They chose to not only accept him, but to love him even before they saw him in person. It is possible that my in-laws and I rubbed each other a lot due to proximity. Their whole family resides merely one hour away from my house. And because they lived together, naturally, their decision-making was intertwined and were, in my opinion, stringent protocols to follow. They had a bond that was just not going to be penetrated, not even by the love I had for their brother. I believe at some point they viewed me as an enemy coming into their lives to disrupt the status quo.

His parents died many decades ago, so it is natural for them to feel they needed to protect one another and to have each other's back in many ways. No matter how the world views any family, there is a certain bond that siblings have that just cannot be disturbed in any way. I was a disturbance. These siblings had lived together pretty much all their adulthood and they had become each other's security blanket. I knew deep down in my spirit that I could commit to my husband 100%. I also knew that it may take a while for my in-laws and me to see eye to eye on many things, because among other things, we were not of the same faith.

What I was unable to do was painfully watch my husband struggle with making a choice between his wife and his siblings. What I didn't understand is why he seemed to have not gotten the memo that our individual roles in his life were not interchangeable. That no matter how hard I may want to, I could not replace them because I could not give him what he got out of the sibling bond in the same way he couldn't replace my siblings in my life. By the same token, our siblings and even parents, cannot be replaced due to marriage because what we offer, as spouses, is like oil and water. If we both could just come to the realization and embrace the fact that oil and water are not necessarily enemies-without either of these two important ingredients, there is no good tasty pepe soup.

My husband knew what Genesis 2:24 says. He understood it theoretically. Even though he preached it from the pulpit, he didn't seem to subscribe to it. I refused to be the pastor's wife who screams loudly with Amens and Hallelujahs in church as the husband preached knowing full well that he didn't practice what he preached. Everyone who knows me knows that I am vocal in church. I am not one to silently agree with the pastor as he preaches. *No, Teresa speaks out loud her Amens and Hallelujahs.* So knowing that about myself, how then, could I acknowledge and cheer my husband on when I felt his preaching was hypocritical? I am a lot of things, but pretending to be happy, is not one of them. I do not subscribe to being politically correct at the expense of my authentic self. In that regard, my husband and I were unequally yoked.

Unequally Yoked, Really?

"Be ye not unequally yoked together with unbelievers: for what fellowship hath righteousness with unrighteousness? And what communion hath light with darkness?" - 2 Corinthians 6:14

When we hear this scripture we often look at it from only one dimension which is literal, and that is, we cannot be yoked with people who are heathens or straight up non-believers. While I was going through this nightmare experience, I came to realize that it is possible to be unequally yoked with someone who goes to the same church with you; hears the same word you hear but has not come to the same enlightenment as you. It doesn't mean that you are more superior that them or vice versa. In my case I was not and am not more superior to my husband, in fact, when it comes to the Bible, he, without a doubt, knows it more than I do. Where it takes me a minute or two to figure out where a certain verse is, he, on the other hand, - has it on the tip of his tongue. One of the reasons I fell in love with him, is because I saw him as my personal teacher of the Word. I was looking forward to doing ministry together. So it is not a question of superior vs. inferior; it is just a question of the capacity and grace we each have in implementing the Word at various seasons in our lives. When we are not careful, in our haste to fit in or to follow what others set in motion for us, we may end up in relationships that God did not intend for us because we misread the signs or we hastened. It could be the right person but not the right time. Or the right time, but not the right person. It is important when we pray for spouses to ask God for that person God has for you to be exposed to the same Gospel and revelation as you while you are in the meantime. It is important for you to be spiritually equal in that when you say the Word is the ultimate decider of any argument, they will not choose to either ignore the Word, disobey the Word, or lose all respect for the Word. I know it is not possible to know someone 100% even when you have been married for donkey years. That is why we must rely on the All-Knowing God, the One who knows the heart of man, who cannot be deceived. Above all trust that, when God says, *"For I know the thoughts and plans I have towards you,"* He really does.

The Marriage That Never Was

FOR AS LONG AS I CAN remember, I've always believed in my being enough in Him. Colossians 2:10 tells us that we are complete in Him yet, there is nothing like being in a valley that causes one to question that belief and lose confidence. Have you ever been put in a corner that shakes your very core? If so, then you have an idea of what I am talking about. It makes you question every area of your life, including your legitimacy as a believer.

So here goes the short version of my testimony. August 19th 2016 is yet another date that will forever be etched in my mind. I was finally going to walk down the aisle in my beautiful white gown…like one of my uncles said jokingly but meaning every word, "Finally, tanga taneta nekumirira for this day", in other words, "We had gotten tired of waiting for this day". Unbeknownst to me, my family - much like many families everywhere - had a secret desire to see me married, but none of them ever pushed me or inquired – except, of course, my Tete Janet (my Father's sister). Culturally, that is her responsibility.

She is one person who was bold enough to ask me directly when I happen to call home while she was around. Our greetings and pleasantries always lasted five seconds and you can almost put a timer to it, the next question would be "Ko mucharoorwa rini nhai Mainini? (So when are you going to get married?") Fellow senior and those of you who married later in life can relate to the societal pressures and you know exactly what I am talking about. I also wasn't aware until after my traditional marriage was done that there were a lot of my cousins and nieces who looked up to me, whose hopes were raised simply by witnessing this event. I had friends and acquaintances who also admired the fact that I was getting married after being a single mother and career woman for so long. "There is hope for us too," they would narrate.

Sidebar: As a child of God, knowingly and unknowingly (notice I am not saying OR but AND), we are a living representative of Christ. So it is very important to watch how we present ourselves all the time. As far as

<u>it is in our control, we ought to do our best to represent Christ. End of Sidebar.</u>

Until I met my husband, marriage was one of those things I didn't pay much mind to. Don't get me wrong, the desire was there, but it was not loud enough for me to lose sleep over not being in one. It was a question of *if it happens it happens, if it doesn't that's cool too...in all things I will praise God.* I had made peace with and was content in my singleness. I was also very aware that God wanted me to do more for the Kingdom beyond being a church member involved here and there. I just wasn't quite sure what exactly He needed me to do, or perhaps I was inactively in denial. See, what the Lord was pressing upon my heart was something I felt was not only too big of an order, but was practically impossible given my current singleness. Like Mary, mother of Jesus, questioned the Angel Gabriel upon being told she was about to have a child without knowing a man. I too was questioning how can it be that I was being called to serve in this capacity He was asking me? I kinda get the idea of being a pastor to people in general but couples in pastoral positions was a very different ball game and in my eyes impossible as a single woman and as one who only dated married men before I got delivered. Like the Apostle Paul, in 1 Timothy 1:15, I too am chief in the sinners department and still am if not for His grace. How many know that God is more concerned about our future more than He is our past? That before He throws us into battle He trains us in the valley? *Jeremiah 29:11 says. "For I know the thoughts I have for you, thoughts of good and not of evil, to give you an expected end".* In other versions it says, *"to give you hope and a future".*

When we first encounter David in the Bible, for instance, it was in his youth, a mere shepherd boy. He hadn't even graduated to being called just a shepherd as in a grown man. King Saul was king at the time but Prophet Samuel in 1 Samuel 16 was sent by God to anoint David, the youngest and least experienced of the children of Jesse. David's training was while he was tending his father's sheep, kumafuro (in the pastures). He was being trained not for the moment of his anointing but for the future; many moons later after King Saul had disobeyed God and fell from grace. All the killing of the lion and the bear that we hear of, as well as the killing of the uncircumcised Philistine, Goliath, was all in preparation for "an expected end". Even the hatred that David's brothers had for him was all in preparation for his future role. But between the anointing and the assignment, David was sharpening his skills through trials and tribulations. I don't even think David had a full comprehension of what that moment of anointing at his father's house meant. The sad thing about the Body of Christ today is that we want the glory but not the labor in the valley. Oh let me not go there!

— ∞ —

When I married my husband at the civil court on May 26th 2016, with a pending wedding celebration on August 19th, I never anticipated that I would be divorced before the ink was dry on our marriage certificate; but there I was practically at the altar – venue, dress, bridesmaids, guests, and all the trimmings – 10 days before I found myself in a place I wouldn't wish even for my worst enemy, if I had one, that is. I called off the wedding celebration. I was done! There were plenty of reasons, which I won't go into at this point. Sorry, kune vanga vateya nzeve (to those whose ears were burning for the juicy parts), but the reasons are really not as important as seeing the hand of God in all of it.

> Sidebar: Important to note that I am sharing this testimony with my husband's permission as he has mine to do the same because our testimonies cannot be told outside of each other. Our collective desire, ultimately, is to be completely open about our experience for the betterment of the Body of Christ. So to those of you who may hear our testimonies in whatever forum and have the urge to activate 911 or 411, keep your panties on. It is well. Just take the lessons and know that we are all good. Also because our journey involves others, you may feel cheated of a story behind the story. It is because we have chosen to respect our loved ones' privacy.

<u>Now that we have the politics out of the way, let's move on, lol. End of Sidebar.</u>

Even though I was the one who called off the wedding, I was not spared on the shame, embarrassment, rejection, and subsequent self-diagnosed depression that followed. For months I cried driving my 1 to 1.5 hour commute to and from work. When I got to work I would stop in the bathroom just to clean my face and do the same before I got into my house just no one would see the pain I was feeling inside. I was surrounded by people, but yet felt so alone in this battle. I even thought God had abandoned me. I mean, how could He allow this to happen to me? What sin did I commit that called for such humiliation and sorrow? I grieved for the loss of a marriage that never was. I questioned my belief system. I questioned my husband's belief system. After all, he was a pastor; so why, if he worships the true God, why would this be happening? Why had he hurt me in this manner? I vowed that not only would I never forgive him, but that I never wanted to see him for as long as I lived. So I began limiting going to places that I may meet him, the church was first to go – as I said he was a pastor. Other places we used to go together I avoided, I cut off as many of our mutual friends as I could.

Now if you don't get anything else out of this testimony get this – the devil's number one weapon, in my opinion, is isolation. He loves to make us isolated because it then makes us more susceptible to his devices. I cannot put into words the hole that I sank into with no one, not even Jesus in sight to pull me out. I began to sink into a place where God did not exist. Because having God exist meant to believe in a Being that is deliberately cruel, uncaring, and was after inflicting the worst pain possible on me. I was so angry at God that I couldn't bring myself to pray, listen to any sermons, or even go to any church. I was in unchartered territory, where I believed there was no one out there who could totally understand what I was going through. Close friends and even relatives seemed to have lost my number and I was very angry at them in silence but most of my anger was directed to my husband, his family, God, and myself. Before meeting my husband, I used to brag that hate is too heavy a burden to carry; but for a season, I believe my anger was sprinkled with a bit of hate too. In hindsight, and with the grace of God, I have learnt to be objective and recognize that everyone I knew who didn't reach out to me, did not do so out of spite or some twisted desire of non-caring, but it was because they, just like me, were in unchartered territory – they didn't know how to help me, what to say to me that could take the pain away. They didn't even know how to be around me and in their own way they were hurting for me too. Another plausible reason is that people have lives and it could very well be that they too were dealing with their own issues. Live long enough and you will begin to see and appreciate that every single person falls into one of three buckets at some point in life, a) those going through a storm; b) those getting over a storm and c) those about to get into one. We each have stuff we are dealing with at any given time. And if as human beings, particularly as the Body of Christ, remember these buckets about life, we will be kinder to one another, we will be more compassionate and more forgiving with one another. We wouldn't be so quick to judge or look down on one another especially in the Body of Christ. *John 13:34-35 says, "A new commandment I give you: Love one another. As I have loved you, so you must love one another. By this all men will know that you are My disciples, if you have love for one another."* Apostle Paul in 1 Corinthians 13, talks about love in that no matter how educated we are, how many accolades we get, how popular we are, how saintly we behave or our ability to speak and interpret tongues, without love, all of it is basically useless. Verse 13 then says, *"And now these three remain: faith, hope and love. But the greatest of these is love."* Amen.

As time went on and my anger became unbearable and too heavy of a load to carry, I remembered *Matthew 11:28, "^{28} Come unto me, all ye that labor and are heavy laden, and I will give you rest."* I didn't know how else to be but I knew one thing: I needed was God back in my life. I began to have a strong desire for God to not only take this pain away, but to restore the relationship I had with Him before I met my husband. My prayer was literally, "take me back to that first love, to that place where you and I talked". I began to remind God of the times Jesus literally sat at the edge of my bed and had one-on-one conversations with me.

Then it happened one day on March 8th 2017. Jesus showed up. In the middle of the night I was awoken by a presence in my room with my sister sound asleep next to me. I recognized Jesus and He was asking me to wake up and sing a song. I said *I don't have a song* and He answered, **"Yes you do. Sing it"**. I still didn't get it for a minute or two. He said, **"You have a song you want to sing, go ahead and sing it"**. Sure enough, I began to sing a song I had never heard before but it sounded so natural. I sang two verses and I woke myself up, grabbed my phone and ran to the bathroom. I felt a strong desire to record it lest I forget it by morning. I recorded it as quietly as possible so as not to wake others. I came back to bed and as soon as I closed my eyes to sleep, Jesus said, **"You're not done"**. And as on cue, I began to sing another verse and in my spirit recognized the one I though was the 2nd verse was actually a chorus. Again I ran to the bathroom to record this next verse. The third time the same thing happened and after recording three verses and a chorus, I went back to bed and fell asleep still feeling the peaceful presence in my room. Then I heard Jesus say, **"That's it. Now sing it."** Here are the lyrics to the song:

<u>I long for your presence</u>
I long for your presence
I long for your righteousness
I long for your Spirit
I long for your love
Chorus:
I long to hear your voice Lord
Feel me with your power Lord
Let me serve you Lord
I long to hear your voice Lord

You are my Master
You are my Savior
You are my Prince of Peace
And you are my God

Chorus

You're Deliverer
You're the Perfect Peace
You're the Alpha
And you're Omega
Chorus

When we woke up in the morning my sister inquired what was going on at night that I kept going in and out of bed. I shared with her what had transpired and I taught her the song. We cried, rejoiced, prayed, and sang again because we both sensed a shift in the atmosphere. That morning marked the first of many mornings where I did not cry from sorrow concerning the loss of my marriage. Between March and April, I continued to have these heavenly encounters while I slept and also while I was driving. By the end of that season, I had seven songs the Lord had given me that I had never heard of. I recorded all of them as it happened. Those of you who know me well know that singing is not a natural gift for me but I have called that collection, "Songs of my Healing".

— ∞ —

Forgiveness is Tough But a Must for the Next Level

IT WAS SOON AFTER the last song was deposited in my spirit that I slipped at work and got hurt on May 11, 2017 I became bed ridden. My hip and back went through the most trauma I've ever had in my body. I was in excruciating pain. Again I found myself angry at God saying, "I thought we were getting along just fine, what is this now?"

At first God seemed to have gone back into 'blue ticking Teresa mode'.

Total silence!

My job had become my safety blanket. I buried myself in my work so much that it began to take at least two thirds of my day, including weekends. Because as long as I was buried in work, I didn't have time to cry and feel sorry for myself and wallow in the loss of my marriage. *Now I am no longer able to work while getting treatment so chava chii futi nhai Mwari? (What now God?) I figured, "God, I too can-do silence"*

and began to watch all the sitcoms I could get On Demand TV. I just binge watched to no end all the shows I had missed. After about three weeks or so, it began to get old. With nothing else to do as I lay in my bed, I found myself reaching for my Bible. I began to read random chapters, just for the sake of reading...so I thought. At the time they seemed random, but God was directing me from behind the blue ticked screen. The whole-time asking God, "But why? Haven't I suffered enough? Now you are allowing me to lose the only thing that seemed to make sense in my life right now, my job? What God? Like seriously? Then one day God impressed upon my spirit that He wanted me to give Him my undivided attention. I began to spend time in the Word and in prayer and the experience I started to have was beyond incredible. God began to download into me through dreams, visions, and His Word the direction He wanted me to take in His vineyard. Scripture began to jump out and come alive. It was as though I was reading the Word for the first time. When I had to leave my bedroom to go to the doctor's appointments, I couldn't wait to get back home to commune with God. I went for a period of time where the Spirit of the Lord impressed upon me to shut down all YouTube videos of sermons or music I sometimes watched. In those times, God began to download sermons in my spirit. He would show me conversations I had to have with specific people. Some people I knew, but some I didn't. He would confirm His Word and all that He was doing and saying through various ways, His Word, servants of God, and random people. I would walk into a new church where I hardly knew people and God would point out people to me saying, "She has a word for you" or "He has a word for you", then I would find myself wondering how they would give me that word since I didn't know these people. I will give you an example.

One time I visited a church and as I was standing at the door, a lady who I later found out was an elder in this particular church, passed by me as she was experiencing some kind of illness and seemed to be throwing up. I remember thinking "veduwe" (why am I at this door) "ndakuzosemeswa nemarutsi" (her belching is going to cause me to throw up). As soon as I said that, God said, **"she has a word for you."** I was like, "How she doesn't know me?" Eventually I went back to my seat and even as she returned to her seat, which happened to be in another section but kitty-corner to where I sat, God impressed upon me that she had a word for me. went on and the pastor began to preach. At some point, he began to pray for people going into the congregation and laying hands on specific individuals. I hardly know the pastor but unbeknown to me, as I was bowing my head in prayer, the pastor directed this woman to come to my section and then directs her to stand next to me and "do what you need to do". At first the woman moved from her seat and just kind of stood beside me but a bit behind me. It wasn't until the pastor then instructed her to "pray for the lady next to you" that I realized he was talking about me. She proceeded to kneel in front of me and asked for permission to pray for my feet. She began to feel my feet as though one washing someone's feet. She then got up and asked if I could come with her as God had given her word for me. Needless to say I was undone. She began to speak into my life confirming the ministry the Lord had been sharing with me. It was an incredible experience. When God wants to speak to you He will do it no matter where you are.

Within weeks of getting hurt, I went from watching TV all the time, flipping through shows to getting bored, and finding myself reading the Bible, then began the most incredible time in the Lord. God started to download first answering why all these things were happening to me…getting hurt at work specifically – His response was simple, "I need your undivided attention". Then the Holy Spirit began to teach me on forgiveness. In order for Him to take me where I needed to be, He needed me to forgive my husband, and his family, particularly. Oh boy!!! I don't know if you have been at a place where you have hated someone that your prayers about that individual was asking God to bring them the most painful hurt possible punctuated with a desire for him to be stricken by "the Holy Ghost fire". I wanted him to hurt as much as I was hurting. Of course, I was operating from the assumption that he was not feeling any hurt whatsoever from this situation. That he was going around enjoying life while I carried all the shame, the humiliation, the anger, the guilt and the depression. Interesting how we as humans always operate from a place of self-interest. We convince ourselves that there is no pain that is more than our own. No one has gone through what I have gone through, etc. We want to help God dish out the judgment we deem fit.

I will not sit here and tell you that it was easy to forgive my husband. It was tough! Boy, was it tough! There was no way I could have done it outside the help of the Holy Spirit. In addition to my husband, God began to show me specific individuals He needed me to forgive as well. While God was asking me to forgive, He was simultaneously downloading

His instructions to me regarding the purpose He created me for and He was showing me that all I have gone through, past and present, had been to prepare me for where He was taking me. That it may have happened to me, but it was about the individuals He had assigned to me from the beginning of time. I should have mentioned that one of the main reasons why I was so mad at my husband was because somehow, I had managed to intertwine the ministry God had placed on me with my marital status. Remember, in the natural, I couldn't see how it was possible for me – in my single status - to do the ministry God was showing me in the spirit. So when my husband came along, I thought "hekanhi waro" (hooray), now I can begin working on that other thing that I had known for years I was supposed to do but kept putting off. Now it was like fire shut up in my bones, nothing else mattered. I thought that being married would give me the platform I needed to "launch" into my destiny; not knowing that in Him I am complete and in Him I live and move and have my being. The calling of God is without repentance so whatever He has deposited in us for the benefit of His Kingdom is not dependent on status – marital, social, or otherwise. Our completeness is not external but internal. When I get married it is not to complete me, but to co-labor in the Vineyard. There is no human being that can complete another – no spouse to spouse, no sister to sister, parent to child, grandparent to grandchild, boss to employee, pastor to sheep – none! ONLY JESUS completes us through salvation and understanding the power of forgiveness. Not just us receiving forgiveness of the Cross, but also through forgiving others and ourselves. The Word of God commands us to forgive so that our Father in Heaven can forgive us too *(Matthew 6:14-15)*. The second aspect of forgiveness is to receive forgiveness from those we have hurt deeply or otherwise. The third aspect of forgiveness is one I believe to be the hardest of the three...forgiving ourselves. This is especially tough because you cannot believe how you, smart as you are, could have allowed yourself to be duped, to be that stupid - so to speak. Somehow, I had subconsciously convinced myself that my role in the Body of Christ was based on my matrimonial status. So as August 19th approached, with the venue paid for, the dress bought, the bridal dresses in the hands of the tailor, civil marriage certificate in place, I began to see and be exposed to a side of my husband that I had not anticipated. Neither of us can share our stories without the other, so it was important for me to get his permission. It was equally important to both of us that if we were ever to share our testimony, individually or collectively, it would be brutally honest. We both recognize that although it happened to us and was painful, it was also for others, so they too, may see the grace and faithfulness of God. Anyway, as life does, one thing led to another and I found myself in unchartered territory, depressed, ashamed, lonely and completely off balance. I even questioned God's presence in my life. You know the usual doubtful questions: God, are you there? Can you hear me? Where are you? Say something? Show me a sign? I have lived a relatively good Christian life. Of course, I am not perfect, but I haven't murdered anyone, nor have I knowingly given someone a deadly disease, so what the heck? I haven't abandoned my obligations, my kids, parents, or siblings? What is going on God? God, I know you hear me, so are you deliberately blue ticking me? A million questions going on in my head that no one could answer for me. And, of course, the "Okay God, I am done with you!" surrendering to what seemed like a one-sided conversation. Part of me also knew He was hearing me but was just 'blue ticking me'. If you, like me, use WhatsApp, you know what 'blue ticking' means. It can be a source of frustration when trying to have a serious conversation or you are anticipating a response and all you see are the two blue check marks indicating the person read your message, but they are just choosing not to respond. That's how I was feeling at this point. I struggled with such verses like *Isaiah 65:24, "Before they call I will answer; while they are still speaking, I will hear"* and *1 John 5:14-15, "This is the confidence we have in approaching God: that if we ask anything according to his will, he hears us. And if we know that he hears us—whatever we ask—we know that we have what we asked of him."* "So He is blue ticking me", I would conclude. Then I would go all religious as if to manipulate Him and quote *Numbers 23:19, "God is not a man that he should lie*". "So, there God, you are obligated by your non-lying nature to answer me and stay true to your Word". It didn't work. I was obviously going to remain in blue-ticked mode until He was ready. So after ending it and eventually dissolving the civil marriage I went into deep self-diagnosed depression. Friends who were once close began to drop off the radar, mentors also dropped off the map and I found myself in a place I could not recognize. I am not saying what I was going through had never happened elsewhere; I am saying for me, I had not seen it happen to anyone I know whom I could call and ask how they got over it.

<u>Sidebar: Important to note that God had never left me, I had forgotten how it felt to be in His presence. God says in Deuteronomy 31:6 and Hebrews 13:5, I will never leave you nor forsake you"</u>. <u>He is omnipresent, so the problem was not with God it was with me. End of Sidebar.</u>

One of the dreams God had shown me included Pastor

Marvelous. As I woke that morning God instructed me to share the dream with Pastor Marvelous but I argued that I was not on talking terms with Pastor Marvelous. She as one of the individuals who had seemed to disappear from my life during my crisis. *So, no God. Give me someone else because I am not talking to her.* I struggled with it till God gave me no choice. I wrote Pastor Marvelous a note and narrated my dream and she said, "I knew you were going to contact me because God showed it to me". I have had many encounters with the Lord. Some painful, but healing, and some would be unbelievable if they were not so real. Sometimes you find yourself attaching your identity to your marital status, like I almost did or to your job, or your social status. God sent me today to tell you that you are complete in Him. God deposited in you your role in His Vineyard/Kingdom before you were formed in your mother's womb. *Jeremiah 29:11 say*s, *"For I know the thoughts that I have for you, thoughts of good and not of evil to give you an expectant end"*. Your completeness in Christ is determined by two main things. Forgiveness and Salvation. Our completeness comes not only at the price of the Cross which brings about salvation but at the forgiveness of sins. Salvation, which comes by accepting Christ Jesus as our Lord and Savior according to *Romans 10:9-10 which says, "That if you confess with your mouth the Lord Jesus and believe in your heart that God has raised Him from the dead, you will be saved. [10] For with the heart one believes unto righteousness, and with the mouth confession is made unto salvation."* My healing and journey to understanding the calling and purpose the Lord has for me was birthed out of understanding that forgiveness is a 3-pronged process which requires three action items:

a) Accept forgiveness from God through faith

b) Learn to equally forgive self. I think of all three, this is the hardest to do. Because forgiving yourself is in some crazy way admitting that you are not as smart as you think you are because if you were, you would have seen this coming. That is a big fat lie from the pit of hell. Even the sanctified, spirit-filled pastors are outsmarted by the devil once in a while. I mean the devil is not called cunning and sly for no reason. Even Peter, Jesus' best friend fell prey to the devil; otherwise Jesus in Luke 22:31-34 would not have had this conversation with him, "*And the Lord said, Simon, Simon, behold, Satan hath desired to have you, that he may sift you as wheat: But I have prayed for thee, that thy faith fail not: and when thou art converted, strengthen thy brethren. And he said unto him, Lord, I am ready to go with thee, both into prison, and to death. And he said, I tell thee, Peter, the cock shall not crow this day, before that thou shalt thrice deny that thou knowest me.*" In other words, even you, Peter, my best friend, my most trusted disciple, upon which rock the very foundation of the church shall be built, yes, even you, are not immune to the devil's cunny ways. So cut yourself some slack, give yourself a break and choose to forgive yourself.

c) Forgive others who have wronged you. You cannot walk in full forgiveness and the fullness of Christ unless you learn to completely surrender and forgive others regardless of whether or not they said sorry. Forgiveness does not start at the point of an apology but of choice by the one who has been wronged. Choosing to extend grace to others when they wrong you is the most liberating feeling I have experienced. Forgiveness does not say stay at the place where you are being hurt, nor does it require you to be friends moving forward, it just gives room for your sins to be equally forgiven. See just like oil and water cannot mix, nor does repentance and unforgiveness. Repentance is the condition of being forgiven, and a spirit that does not forgive is in fact incompatible with a repentant spirit. I know for a fact that had I not made a conscious decision to forgive my husband and all concerned, not just in my heart but sending them messages to say just that, I wouldn't be here writing this testimony.

As Jesus taught His disciples and those present how to pray, He also added this statement that we as Christ Followers tend to glaze over. *Matthew 6:14-15 says, "For if you forgive other people when they sin against you, your heavenly Father will also forgive you. But if you do not forgive others their sins, your Father will not forgive your sins."* I don't know about you, but I want to receive forgiveness from the Lord. Many of us carry the weight of unforgiveness and wonder why God is not using us to our fullest potential. I want to encourage you that today be the day you refuse to go to bed in unforgiveness. Choose to walk and live in forgiveness and you will see God working wonders in your life. If you are to leave an inheritance for your children and generations to come, let not unforgiveness be one of them.

— ∞ —

Why not End it All

I SAT IN MY CAR, parked right outside my house. My kids, sister, and best friend were home oblivious of this dark moment that was stirring in me as if to challenge me. In a way it was because I sat there contemplating what would be the best way I would do it that would bring the least pain to my kids. It's not that I wanted to die. Heaven knows I love life and being there for my son, Nyasha and grandson, Errol "Tendekai", especially. I wanted to see them grow and be great men. I didn't want to die. I just wanted the pain to go away. I wanted to check out from Pain Motel where I seemed to have resided for months now. I just wanted the pain to find residence elsewhere but my heart. I picked up the phone and this time I let it ring. I wanted him to pick it up. I wanted him to tell me what I was supposed to do with these feelings? What was I supposed to do now? Why did he do this to me? What exactly had I done to him for me to deserve this hurt that he was putting on me? He picked up. I started crying uncontrollably and gave him my goodbye speech. I sarcastically told him he had won, that I was done with life and maybe he would be able to explain to my kids, my parents, my siblings, my relatives, and friends what he had caused me to do. He begged me to calm down but he couldn't answer my million questions. I was distraught. In this moment, it dawned on me that I hated him. We often hear of "the out of body experience". I had it on that day. It's like I was watching myself breaking down. I felt like I was hovering over my body watching it as it fell into this deep, dark, and bottomless space. I could not recognize any of the emotions I was going through. The thought of checking out from this world seemed more enticing than feeling the pain I was feeling. It felt like I had an unquenchable thirst that only death can resolve. In that moment all I felt was pain, shame, exposure, rejection, embarrassment, and abandonment. I was back in November 1986 when my father rejected and abandoned me. I felt like God had not only allowed this to happen to me but He has turned His back on me. All those scriptures about, *"I will never leave you nor forsake you" "I will be with you till the end of time"* seemed like a fairy tale. Then Psalm 23:5, *"You I prepare a table before me in the presence of my enemies"*, I felt like I was the enemy and God had put me on a silver platter and displayed me for the whole world to feast on. I was beyond devastated. In that moment, I just could not fathom the loving God I read about in the Word. Where was this God that I have prayed to practically my whole life? Does He care that I'm drowning? Why is He silent? Can He hear me? I began to question His existence. Pain will make you do exactly what you said you would never do. Even now I talk to my best friend and we joke about how we love life too much to freely take ourselves out. But deep down, unbeknownst to her, I was a few inches away from bringing my expiry date to a screeching end. When life seems to be good, one has the luxury of speaking in abstracts of how they would react under certain conditions. The truth of the matter is we all have the capacity to cheat on our spouses, to steal, to embezzle, to kill, and even to commit suicide. It is only the grace of God that sustains us. So here I was with a million questions for Munyaradzi and God and neither of them were in the mood to answer. I hung up on him and cried like a baby, screaming my head off for a good 20 minutes, maybe more. My heart felt like it was broken in a million pieces. My insides were burning. I recognize now, in hindsight, that I had shifted the psychotic scale. I had mapped out what I would say in my final letter to my son and grandson. I had mapped out when I would do it and where. It was not going to be on my King size bed because I knew Nyasha or Errol would sleep on it one day...I couldn't imagine defiling such a comfortable bed; it still had many years to it. It was very important to me that if I were to do it, it needed to be away from home because I couldn't forgive myself if my family couldn't live in the house because it's haunted by the memory of my demise. Our house being in close proximity to a cemetery is eerie enough.

I was stuck on how I would do it. I didn't want it to be messy so jumping in front of a train was a split second's consideration and was dismissed in equally the same speed. Then I considered pills and realized I don't have anything stronger than Aleve and besides, what's the right concoction? Then I considered the possibility of whatever method not working and I end up a medical burden to my son. Then I thought of the pain I would go through before I take that last breath. I thought, "I have a very high threshold for pain". In the end, it was three things that saved me:

a) the pain I would bring to my son and the stigma to my grandson

b) a refusal to give Munyaradzi that much power over me and

c) pure grace. God's grace. Grace located me on that day in March 2017 and I am here to tell the story.

Healing the Children's Bread

<u>*Unforgiveness – a Costly Choice*</u>

I THOUGHT GOD HAD LEFT ME because if He was right here, then where is He? I could not feel Him. It's so easy to speak of forgiveness as a concept. I mean, until you've been through some hurt, you just don't know. Forgiveness as an idea or ideology is easy to do until that betrayal cuts through your core. At this time, I want to go through each of the significant betrayals I experienced and how I came to forgive every single one.

<u>My Father:</u>

My father was a tough one to forgive. I am not going to lie. Actually, truth be told, the thought of forgiving him never crossed my mind. Yes, I said it. I was a born again Christian, albeit young disciple, but disciple nevertheless. I didn't want to forgive him; hence it never crossed my mind. Some people would encourage me to forgive. Preachers would preach about it but I just didn't think it applied to my father. Don't get me wrong, I was hearing what the preachers were saying, my intellect was hearing it but my heart was shut down. I believe subconsciously that I couldn't and still cannot comprehend the thought process that went on in my father's head to take such a strong stance. To be so unforgiving for what he thought I had done even with evidence presented to him to the contrary. So because his reaction and corresponding behavior did not make sense, it seemed forgiving him did not make sense either. Without knowing it, his unforgiving spirit became an inherited trait for me. Generational curses in motion. There are some things as parents that, if we do not address, we transfer to our children – unforgiveness, anger, hate, womanizing, prostitution, etc. Often you hear people say, "Well, what do you expect, his/her father was like that, always angry at the world". Or, "He takes after uncle so and so, he too has children in every zip-code". There are families who pass hatred to each generation like a badge of honor. Some kids hate a certain family but don't know why. Their father hated the family member, and so did their grandparents before them. So it is just something they did.

When my son was born, it dawned on me that I loved him like I had never loved any other human being before. I wanted what was best for him in life. I wanted to give my son what I never had, unconditional love that I didn't have from my father growing up. It was very clear to me from day one that I held Nyasha in my hands that I would never put him through what my father had put me through. I never wanted my son to wonder if I loved him or not. I never wanted my son to feel rejected and unwanted no matter what. Suddenly I felt the need to forgive my father. Not for his sake, but for my son's sake. I forgave my father so that I could be the best mother I could be to my son. *How can I be my best when I held so much resentment in my heart?* I reasoned with myself. I felt that just forgiving him silently in the privacy of my heart was not enough. So I wrote the letter:

Dear Mr. Dangwa,

I hate you! I hate what you stand for. I hate that I hate you but you made me hate you…

I spilled out so much venom on several pages. I told him how I truly felt, without mincing my words.

Sincerely,

Teresa

I folded it, put it in an envelope and kept it in my purse with the intention of taking it to the post office. But it never happened. Instead, a few days later, I found myself tearing up the letter and writing another one:

Dear Mr. Dangwa,

I grew up feeling like you never loved me and for that I will always hate you ...more venom

Sincerely,

Teresa

Several versions of the letter was written, each time taking a few days before "mailing", rereading, and tearing them up. Then one day, I sat down at the park bench as my baby slept peacefully in his pram. I took out a pen and paper and wrote another version:

Dear Baba (Father),

I pray and hope that this letter finds you and Mum well. I am writing because there is something I need to get off my chest. When I was growing up, you used to beat me nemvuu (a whip made out of some animal hind). I never understood what parent would go to the store and buy such a weapon to use on another human being, his children, for that matter. I am sure in your mind you thought you were disciplining me, but for me, it felt like you hated me. I don't remember the last time I felt loved by you or if I were loved at all. In fact, I grew up believing you didn't love me. I felt that most of the time your punishment never matched the crime and half the time you beat me for things I didn't do. Because of your beatings, I always felt like I was never good enough and that I would never be good enough. When we had to leave Bulawayo post-Independence, you and Mum made sure all my siblings were enrolled in school except me. I was left to look after my siblings while you and Mum remained in Bulawayo. When you eventually enrolled me in school, you had to change my birth certificate to make me younger than I really was so you could send me several grades back. My younger sister finished school before I did. I don't why you didn't let my brother be the one to look after all of us. After all, he was the oldest; your first born. Was it because I was a girl? Why didn't you fight for me to go back to school at the same time as my brothers and sisters? Had you decided back then that I didn't matter? I was made to believe that it was my fault that I couldn't be enrolled in school right away because "I was dumb". If I was that dumb, how come I was always placed in the top class? My grades were always lower compared to my siblings, have you ever considered that by you putting me on hiatus, it actually impacted my view of school, subconsciously anywhere?

As if that wasn't enough, you disowned me and sent me to live with strangers who abused me, and when I reached out to you to at least emancipate me so I could get out of this toxic situation, you denied me the freedom.

I may never know why you hated me so much but I want you to know that I have made up my mind to forgive you. I am forgiving you, not for your sake but for my sake because I am tired of being bitter inside. I forgive you for my son's sake because I know if I continue to carry this resentment, I can never be the best mother I should be for my son. My son deserves better. Now that I am a parent, the love I feel for my son, I cannot see how I would treat him as poorly as you treated me.

God bless you.

Sincerely,

Amai Nyasha (Nyasha's Mum)

This is the letter I sent out, without resentment, without anger, just facts. My mother told me over the phone following the mailing of this letter that when my father received that letter, he wouldn't show it to her but he cried. She told me that he kept the letter in his chest pocket at all times, taking it out from time to time, reading and crying. He never responded to me. I didn't expect a response because I knew responding would be regretting that he was wrong, and my father would never do that. I guess, knowing that the letter disturbed him that much was all the response I needed

My Almost Husband

This one, like my father, was tough, but the Word is the Word. I had to forgive him, not because the pain had gone away, far from it. I forgave because my life's destiny depended on it. It was a process that took months, even when sometimes I thought I had forgiven him, I would be triggered by a smell of his cologne, a name sounding like his, or an experience we shared or hoped to share together and I would be right back on ground zero. Eventually, just like with all the other forgiving I needed to do, it took the help of the Holy Spirit, my surrendering to His will and I was able to let go. One thing the Holy Spirit impressed upon me was that I not only needed to forgive my husband for the pain he had caused, me but I was to write off the debt he owed me for the wedding. We had agreed to split the bill with him paying me for what I had already paid for the wedding that never transpired and ended up being a 50th Birthday, unintentionally the most expensive party ever. I couldn't get what was already paid at the venue so a party had to be had...family and friends had come from far and near, so why waste? I laugh about it now, but it was not a laughing matter at the same time. It was painful to have to write off that debt especially since I was now on limited income due to the slip and fall. I really needed that money but being obedient to the Holy Spirit was a more pressing need for me. Sometimes we do what doesn't make sense in order for God to bring us to the next level. I truly believe my calling into ministry was linked to my forgiving the church folk as well as my almost husband.

Church and Church Folk

Like I said earlier, church folk are the most judgmental people on earth. Collectively they choose to bury their heads in the sand the most and pretend their pastor is not cheating on their spouse; the pastor is not misusing church funds and authority; the pastor has no problem with alcohol, other substances, or prostitution; the pastor is not having an affair with the youth pastor or the worship leader. You could place the evidence on the billboard and they would find a way of blaming the person who drew attention to the issue. I chose to forgive church folk for very simple reasons.

Church folk sometimes take for granted the grace of God. By that I mean, there are those of us who God gives us the grace to deal with our issues privately. You know, the choir director who gets impregnated by the senior pastor and they go to abort the pregnancy and come back to church and pick up right where they left off on Sunday with the rest of the church oblivious of their situation. The devil gives them false confidence. Because they have not been caught, they not only go back and continue the affair but they have the nerve to pull the holier-than-thou attitude on some of us who chose not to abort and therefore our sin and humiliation is public. I am grateful that God chose to make public some of the pain, humiliation and sins I have had because by putting them in the open, the devil could not use them to blackmail me and destroy me from the inside. It is the secret sins, secret affairs, secret relationships that I have had that have destroyed my spirit more than the public ones.

As hard as it was to hear people snicker, point, and disassociate, it taught me humility and appreciation of His grace for my life.

I chose to forgive church folk for the simple reason that they, like me, are mere mortals, are fallible. Listen, if Jesus was sent to the cross by high priests and teachers of the Word in those days and still died on the Cross for them, who am I to expect everyone in the church to hold my hand and genuinely sing kumbaya?

Here, I want to point out one specific individual who had done me wrong and I had to forgive. For those of you who know her, please note that she is aware and has given me permission to mention her by name, all so that God's name may be glorified.

Before I knew about Women of Dominion (WoD), God had given me a vision for hosting conferences for women. I had discussed it with one of my pastors, who later became my husband and he encouraged me to reach out to one, Pastor Marvelous, the visionary for WoD. I called her and introduced myself, we hit it off, and I attended my first WoD Annual Conference that year. She ended up being my mentor and so naturally when I was getting married, I reached out to her and we began to fast and pray together specifically for my marriage. When I called her to inform her that I had called off the wedding she was naturally disappointed. Prior to that, I had been providing her play-by-play of the challenges I was having and we would pray. She would give counsel and we would pray again. So, for her to do a disappearing act after I made my announcement to get out of the marriage was beyond disappointing. I was devastated and felt abandoned by the very person I had come to depend on for support. I must say, now in retrospect, it is possible that she didn't know how to help me, but I expected at least for her to just show concern for my broken heart.

Fast forward to 11 months later. As God was working in me to get me out of the dark hole, I was finding myself in, I had a dream. (Dream is narrated in the book). Pastor Marvelous was in that dream and when I woke up the first thought in my mind was, *Zvariri dambudziko rehope kurota kwawakaramba*. Basically, saying what kind of crazy dream is this where you dream of those who rejected you? My next thought was, *God what does that mean*? God responded, but not in a way that I expected or wanted to deal with. He impressed upon my spirit to tell Pastor

Marvelous and let her know about the dream. I protested that I was not talking to that woman. It wasn't happening. Not after the way she avoided me like the plague all these months. It wasn't going to happen! For three days, I struggled with it and figured God had made a mistake because how could he ask me to do that? The Holy Spirit kept impressing upon me to call her so on the fourth day, I sent her a text with the full narrative of the dream hoping she would just ignore it, but at least I had "done my part". Well, she didn't ignore it. Even though she was in the middle of her conference in Tennessee, she sent a quick response that she would call me afterwards because God had spoken to her about me too, and she knew what the dream meant.

Sure enough, after the conference she called me and we discussed the dream. She began to confirm some things God was putting into my spirit concerning the calling on my life. She offered to mentor me for ministry and I reluctantly agreed so we began to have weekly calls. We barely talked about the elephant in the room, we just pretended like it wasn't there.

At some point during the course of that year, I was asked to help coordinate the Zimbabwean community CFI Conference which was going to be hosted in NJ/NY area. As Labor Day of 2017 approached, which was the time for the conference, I reached out to Pastor Marvelous to see if she was planning to attend and she informed me at the time that she had not yet been released by the Holy Spirit to attend and she was praying about it.

Wednesday, the day before the conference, Pastor Marvelous called me and informed me that she had been released and was coming and had an assignment at the conference. It turns out the assignment was about me. I began to ask God for complete healing of my relationship with her in order for me to fully receive "this assignment" and needed a healthy way of addressing the elephant in the room. I didn't know how it would happen but I desired it like a camel desires water on a parched dessert. One thing I knew in my spirit was that this assignment, whatever it was, was significant in what God was doing in my life and it was important to me that I held no resentment or unresolved issues with my mentor or anyone for that matter. I needed to forgive. God had been dealing with me on forgiveness over the past year.

Unforgiveness was not an option a) as a Christ follower and b) given where God was taking me in this season.

So at about 3am on the last day of the conference, Pastor Marvelous asked me to come to her room and asked two other pastoral leaders to be present as witnesses for the assignment. As she was about to reveal what the assignment was about, she asked if there was anything any of us wanted to say. Since they were senior pastors and I knew them, I let the other two ladies go first. They gave their opinions and perceptions of my character, negative and sprinkled with some positives. I just listened intently. After they were done, Pastor Marvelous asked if I had something to say. Me sensing the seriousness of the assignment, I took the opportunity to let all three ladies know how I really felt from my heart. I am learning that owning your feelings and your hurts, as well as taking responsibility for one's role in relationship issues, is a must in the process of healing and forgiveness. I shared with them how angry and disappointed I was with some of the characterization they had expressed but most importantly how they had each abandoned me in my time of need upon calling my wedding off. It turned out there were a lot of assumptions of the level of help they each thought I was getting from other people like local pastoral leadership and/or elsewhere. I assured them that it was not so. As I poured my heart out, we all cried, justified our individual points of view, cried some more, began to see our flaws and how we could have dealt with each other more kindly and better as expected by the Word of God. We cried some more, prayed for healing, cried some more and exchanged apologies, taking responsibility for our part in the breakdown of relationships we assumed we had with one another. We prayed until there was a breakthrough for each of us in our own respective ways. Then, and only then, was I ready and in a position to partake of the assignment Pastor Marvelous had been given by the Holy Spirit for me. I believe that there was a total shift in our lives, a lot of individual reflection for a while after that. But ultimately, and most importantly, what happened in Room 500 that night at DoubleTree by Hilton in Fort Lee, NJ will go down in history and on the Heavenly scrolls as a pivotal moment in pastors exercising what they preached. Forgiveness God's way!

The Tumblers

I chose to forgive the Tumblers because, even though they decided to mistreat me upon arriving to the US, they still were used by God to bring me to this country. The Tumblers were a blessing in disguise. I chose to forgive them because deep down I think they wanted to do the right thing, they had just kinda lost their way a little bit. I am sure if you tell them that what they did was a form of human trafficking they will probably take you to court like they did Tupac Shakur for defamation of character. After all, their lives is synonymous with civil rights in their respective community. I chose to forgive them because unforgiveness was too heavy a burden to carry while at the same time trying to navigate the ropes of a foreign land…I just didn't have enough space in my luggage to carry unforgiveness for this couple.

Self

Forgiving self is the toughest of all because you cannot believe that you were that stupid or gullible. I was able to forgive my husband after the Holy Spirit helped me see that the breakdown of my marriage was not solely on my husband. Unless you are in a place to take full responsibility on the part you played in the breakdown of any relationship, you will walk around with self-righteousness. I know this too well because for a long time, I couldn't see any wrong doing on my part on the breakdown of my marriage, for instance. It really never occurred to me that I too had contributed. As we prepared for the wedding, I found myself sidelining my husband in all the decisions of the wedding. Not only would I talk over him, I would make a decision, act on it and then inform him that I did it. I never really cared to ask for his opinion and if he tried to give it, I hardly acknowledged him. I took my husband's meekness as a weakness, and I, being of a strong personality completely overpowered him. I had not only to beg his forgiveness but to forgive myself for my part in breaking up our marriage. Part of forgiving myself was making phone calls, writing emails and text messages to friends and family, including, and especially, to my in-laws acknowledging my part in the mess and asking for their forgiveness. We are in a good cordial place now and for that I am grateful. I also had to make a very public apology to church folk that was memorialized and will forever reside on cyber world through the beauty of Facebook Live. Like I said, only the help of the Holy Spirit made it possible, I cannot take full credit for it except the courage to choose to walk in forgiveness.

<u>Sidebar: One very important lesson I learnt on forgiveness is that unless you fully understand and acknowledge the forgiveness of sins brought to us by Jesus at the Cross at Calvary; until you know it and walk in that joy of Salvation, it is practically impossible to truly forgive yourself and others. I am convinced that understanding the power of forgiveness at Calvary helps you to forgive yourself which then can be transferred to others. You cannot give what you don't have and that is a fact!!! End of Sidebar.</u>

CHAPTER EIGHT

A Ministry in the Making

"For God's gifts and His call are irrevocable." Romans 11:29

"Father, if thou be willing, remove this cup away from me - nevertheless, not my will but yours be done." Luke 22:42

— ∞ —

YOU'RE ENOUGH! THAT PIERCED THROUGH MY HEART and a light bulb came on. I have heard this phrase before, but somehow today, I heard it differently. Perhaps because these days I am spending more time in the Word rather than aimlessly checking out statuses on Facebook or flipping through On Demand channels to see what I can entertain myself with. In this new state of awareness and realization, I began to view myself in a different light. You're Enough! So if I am enough, then there are some truths I need to tell myself until self gets them. First and foremost, I need to know and understand that "hurt people, hurt others." There are people out there who have not effectively dealt with their own pain and therefore cannot help but hurt others. People cannot give what they don't have. Secondly, there are going to be people around me who will be naysayers just like I will be a naysayer in someone else's journey. Next, I need to learn really fast to shut out the noise and the external voices around me if I am to hear the internal voice clearly. I need to be my own validator, knowing that God and I are a majority. I need to familiarize myself with me, to be a part of my own support system and embrace me; to recognize and acknowledge that no matter what others may think, I am not a sum of my failures. However, my failures can be the catalyst for and to my purpose. My true value is not measured by the jewels in my jewelry box, the type of car or cars in my driveway, the neighborhood I reside in, the type of supermarket I go to, or the schools I choose to send my kids to. My value is certainly not in the length of my hair (real or not), or even the lack thereof, the degrees I hold, or the amount of money I make. All those things are how the world measures value. My value is measured in the intimacy of the relationship I have with Christ, the way I treat those that are less fortunate than me, and the integrity with which I serve those the Lord has put in my charge. Last, but certainly not least, I need to know and be convinced that I matter, that what I bring to the table matters, that I am a significant member of the Body of Christ, and that I am here on earth not to compete with other members…but to compliment them as much as they compliment me.

One more thing, I need to embrace the fact that I am not everybody's flavor and that is A – Okay!

In this chapter, I want to attempt to share my story for those who always wonder what their purpose is and also some who wonder how one knows that they are being called into ministry. A lot of times, we find ourselves with these questions that no one seems to discuss clearly. Like you, I used to wonder if every minister needs to be in Bible school in order for them to be called. Does one get called first, then go to college? Or is it college first, then calling? Is Bible college even a requirement?

<u>Sidebar: When my friend Bruce encouraged me to get a degree in human services, one of his arguments was that without an American education, people in the US may not take me seriously given the things I wanted to do, i.e. work with humans. End of Sidebar.</u>

Full-time vs. part-time, does that apply in ministry, or are we trying to bring what society does into the church, rather than us, as the Body of Christ being the influencer? Have we relinquished our role as the

Church and given it to governments or the world in general? In other words, who sets whose pace? I will share my journey and hopefully you will take from it what God intends for you to take and be inspired to search for yourself in your unique journey. It is important to note that one size does not fit all, therefore, the way God calls you does not need to resemble mine, or vice versa. However, the one thing that should remain consistent is the Word of God.

One statement that the Holy Spirit drilled in my spirit was, **"I have assigned people to you"**, which means not everyone will benefit, or more appropriately, will be open to receive from the calling God has on my life because they are not assigned to me. Understanding that, then helps one to a) focus; b) not see the need to bring someone down so you look good c) will not feel the need to poach from someone's pond, so to speak. I will expand more about this in my other book, *The Diaspora Pastor* coming out soon!

Finding Purpose

<u>Sidebar: Don't mistake your current role for your purpose. You move in and out of various roles but your purpose never changes. Be careful not to fall so much in love with your current role that you lose sight of your purpose - anonymous. End of Sidebar.</u>

One of the questions I get asked a lot is, "how do I find my purpose"? How do I know what it is that God created me for or what I am supposed to do in life or with my life? So I decided to answer that request by sharing a part of my testimony and the journey I took in identifying my personal gifts. This is not to be interpreted as me saying I have arrived - Heaven knows I am still growing, a true work in progress. Neither should this be viewed as the only way there is to identify one's gifts or to unearth your purpose. We all have our individual journeys, some may be similar, but they are certainly unique. However, we can learn from others and hopefully be awakened in our spirits and be motivated to pay attention to the things we perhaps may have thought were insignificant in our lives. I strongly believe we already have in us what it takes to fulfill our destiny because the Word says, He knew us before He formed us in our mother's womb (Jeremiah 1:5), meaning, He had already created us and instilled in us our destinies and the skills, knowledge, and power we needed to see them come to pass. He further says that the thoughts He has for us are of good and not of evil to give us an expected end. (Jeremiah 29:11). He will not withhold any good thing from those who walk upright (Psalm 84:11).

Many years ago, 2003 – 2004, I was at a place where I became dissatisfied by the mundane things of life. I had been in the US for a while and one day I just woke up feeling like there needs to be more to life than waking up each morning, going to work, an occasional trip to the grocery store, meeting with a friend for tea or meal, going to mid-week service and church on Sunday, then doing the same thing all over again the following week. I needed more to my life. So I went back to the source and started asking God questions like: *What is my purpose? Why did you create me? What am I doing in this God forsaken country, away from my son and my family? Is there anything else out there besides "this routine stuff"? Surely there needs to be more to life than "this".* Needless to say, God did not answer me those questions in succession and all at once. It took at least a year of going through the process. Now let me warn you. Asking these types questions requires a certain level of preparation and surrender to the process, something I learnt on the go and was not completely pleasant. Having said that, I wouldn't change it for anything, because it is part of who I am today.

Right around the time I was asking these poignant questions, I was also having conversations with my best friend, Iris (she has since gone to be with the Lord). For my birthday, August 8 2003, Iris bought me a book that she thought would help me answer some of these questions. It was "The Purpose Driven Life" by Rick Warren. It is a 40-day devotional that gives you a topic a day, a point to ponder upon, a verse to memorize, and a question to consider with space within the book to write your responses. If you haven't read this book, I urge you to do so. It really did change my life.

So back to the initial question, *what is my purpose?* Rather than God telling me a straight answer, He took me down memory lane from when I was a little girl. I started remembering experiences of being molested and being abused and I would be taken back to that moment when it actually happened. Many nights I would cry myself to sleep just reliving those memories, which by the way, I had blocked from my mind, possibly as a self-preservation mechanism. For months, the Lord would bring to memory every hurt I ever felt, every abuse I encountered and every time I felt unloved. He even made me see instances where I used sex not for pleasure, but as a way of masking my hurts. This went on for about 8-9 months. Then one day, the memories became about the times where I felt loved, secure, appreciated, wanted, and needed. He showed me how I used to have all these little girls in the neighborhoods at my parents' house so I could do their hair and make them look and feel pretty. How I enjoyed making friends with those others looked down upon. How I would share my lunch with others who didn't have when we traveled on school trips. How I stood up for those being mistreated or were seen as not coming from the "right side of the tracks". The Lord showed me my happy moments. I remember throughout this whole process how I used to leave work with a sense of urgency because I wanted to know what else God would show me that night. The Lord also started showing me things at work that I actually enjoyed doing versus the ones I did not have the grace for. Even sitting at my desk, He would quicken my spirit on things that I needed to pay attention to. One thing I can confidently share with you is that when you build a relationship with Christ, YOU WILL RELEARN TO HEAR HIS

VOICE. I say relearn because, remember, we were created in His image. That means that His voice is already in us when we are formed. Somewhere along the way, and due to sin, His voice became more and more faint. BUT our hearing can be restored!!!!

During this time with Christ:

1. My relationship with God became so strong that many nights I felt Jesus sitting at the edge of my bed as we had conversations.
2. I learnt to sleep with a notepad and pen next to me. I still do, although sometimes I use my notes app on my phone.
    a. Whenever I dreamt of anything or saw a vision, I would wake up and write it down.
    b. Sometimes I was given instructions which I was not even aware that I had written until the morning.
3. I realized that not only was God walking me down memory lane for my purpose, but also for my healing. Brethren, every hurt and abuse I went through, after that season, I was able to recall without feeling pain.

4. One night God started giving me visions of hurting children and had me write things down, verses and all. First He gave me Revelations 21:19 then James 1:27.
    a. Some of the things I wrote ended up being part of the vision and mission of the foundation that I started in 2008. (www.dangwa.org)
    b. He had me draw the logo for the foundation (mind you, I am not an artist by any stretch of the imagination). He showed me that it needed to be a fountain of hope for women and children (in particular the girl-child) who have been impacted by HIV/AIDS. With the image of the logo, Jesus gave me the color codes to the shade (at the time I had no idea what that meant).
5. The day after I drew the logo, I called Iris who had been my confidante with whom I shared the transformation that was going on in my life. She prayed with me and fasted with me and encouraged me throughout the way. (We all need an Iris in our lives – a true friend, who is not jealous of what the Lord is doing for you, who really buys into your vision, who tells

you the truth ALWAYS). Watch what happened when I called Iris that day:

a. She informed me that she was at an even the night before where she "bumped" into an old school mate. During their brief conversation, Iris learnt that the Muslim lady was graphic designer.

b. Iris suggested that I speak to her and maybe she could do the logo for me.

c. By that evening, I had called the lady. I described to her what I needed, informed her of the colors of each item incorporated in the logo without the color codes the Lord had shown me (what did I know, I didn't think it was important). I didn't even send her the sketch I had drawn.

d. In less than a week, she sent me a draft of what she thought I meant by my description over the phone. Her thought was that this was an initial draft to see if she had captured the concept, then we could take it from there. As soon as I opened that email, I called Iris crying because not only did she capture the concept to the T, she had also used color in the objects on the logo that were precisely the colors the Lord had shown me.

e. Needless to say, the 1st draft became the final and only draft, NO REVISIONS WHATSOEVER! A few days later, I received the "color codes" in the mail and they were exactly what the Lord had shown me in the vision!

6. The Lord also showed me visions of me preaching and praying for people. They became recurring dreams for a while and stopped. I didn't think much of these particular visions until 2017 when they started to recur (that's a testimony for another day, the Lord permitting).

One of the questions I asked God was why I always gravitated to those in pain, the underdog, the seemingly forgotten? Even looking at my career, almost every job I did was about taking care of the less fortunate in one way or another. So, one day as I was at a presentation for World AIDS Day, December 1, 2007, I was walking around a handmade quilt that had been spread in the center of the room. The quilt was made of patches of quilts of people who had lost their loved ones to HIV/AIDS. For example, my sister died of an

HIV-related illness many years ago, so in her memory I would have put together some mementos and created a panel of 12"x12". My panel would then be joined to others until a quilt of about 12ft x 12ft was created. So it was this 12ft x 12ft I was looking at and reading the stories of these individuals who had lost their battle to HIV/AIDS. As I walked around, I remembered my emotions changing with each story I read. First from a sense of judgment, as to why didn't they prevent this (an element of righteousness – so unattractive but I felt it nevertheless); then, I was even ashamed for being seen reading these stories as most of them were about individuals who had lived a homosexual life. Then, it was guilt for feeling the way I did and went from feeling sorry for them to myself and back to them. At some point I began to cry and realized I was overcome with compassion. It was at that realization, almost simultaneously, that I heard Jesus' voice deep down and loud enough I thought the person next to me heard me, He answered my question…**This is why?** God was pointing out that it was my compassion that made me gravitate to those in need. I remember, I cried uncontrollably so much on that day I needed to grab a nearby chair. I remember God placing my spirit in a state where I felt the pain and agony of every person whose story I was reading.

The things I was passionate about became my purpose. In this process I found out that I was gifted in certain areas such as grant writing, project proposals, writing in general, teaching, policies and procedures, counseling, coaching, helping others transform their lives (although most of the time I felt like it's my life that gets transformed more in the end). I also found that I am gifted at talking (yes I can talk about pretty much any subject – I was given the gift of gab according to my Irish friends), problem-solving, and computers (taught myself most of the applications). I am a straight shooter,. I am very direct in my approach, boldness (even when I am wrong, I am bold in that wrongness, lol). I take criticism and I give it too. I am not afraid to ask or of public speaking. I am learning to own up quickly to what I don't know, but I am open to learning it if needed. I also found out things I don't have grace for - pain (I cannot do direct care for patients or people), diplomacy- my tolerance can only go but so far. I don't know how (nor do I care) to be politically correct. I don't have grey areas (everything is pretty black and white in my world). I don't always color within the lines either.

A great place to start in identifying your gifts is the Word of God. Here are some scriptural passages to get you started - 1 Corinthians

12, Romans 12 and 1 Peter 4. Proverbs 18:16 says, *"A man's gift maketh room for him, and bringeth him before great men."* So the success you are looking for, the kind that will bring contentment, is linked to that gift. Your job is to ask the Holy Spirit to help you identify it and you will begin to see doors opening for you.

From the beginning of time God has given His servants instructions through dreams and visions. One such instance is the story of Samuel that we read in 1 Samuel 3. Samuel was visiting Eli when one day as he lay down sleeping God called his name, "Samuel". Samuel woke up thinking it was Eli calling him. Eli sent him back to bed. He woke up two more times hearing his name called. On the 3rd time, Eli recognized what was going on and gave Samuel instruction on what to do the next time he hears his name called. "Samuel! Samuel!" The voice called him again. This time he responded by saying, "Speak Lord, your servant is listening". It turned out God was giving Samuel a message that would impact Eli and his family directly in a very public way.

I am sure by now you have figured out from reading my book that God has chosen to speak to me in dreams and visions. Some that I share with others, some He instructs me not to share or He simply removes from my memory until an opportune time. There are some very distinct dreams I believe marked clearly for me the calling upon my life and was, in turn, confirmed by others. God ALWAYS confirms His Word and instructions to us - through others and through His Word. If what you are doing is not supported by the Word or seems contradictory, it is time to consult the Holy Spirit for clarity because God NEVER contradicts Himself. If there seems to be a contradiction, it is never with the Word but our understanding of the Word.

The Forgotten Dream – July 2007

During the time I was seeking God for my purpose, I began to get very vivid dreams and visions. Some of the dreams are recurring to this day. There is one dream in particular I want to share with you because I believe that is when God was showing me this ministry that I am in now, but I didn't know, nor did I ever consider myself in ministry because I didn't want to be poor or a beggar all my life. Yes, the examples of pastors I was exposed to in my early Christ following walk were not the greatest. The full-time ministers were always begging for money. You would be guaranteed that as soon as you see them, after exchanging pleasantries, the next thing would be asking for money – some would downright demand it. It was pretty sad to me. At the time, I didn't understand Proverbs 18:16 but it always bothered me. I am a strong believer that ministries must pay a salary and at the very least health care too, especially for the full-time ministers. I always associated being a pastor with poverty and begging. So, because of that, I missed all the signs, or perhaps, my subconscious was just in denial.

2017, after I fell at work and got hurt to the point where I was pretty much bedridden, and after the season of ignoring God, I began to rebuild my relationship with God. So in my bed, I spent time in the Word and in communion with the Holy Spirit. It is during one of these times that God brought back to remembrance a dream I had in 2007. In the dream, I was at a church where I was preaching. While I was at the pulpit, somehow I began to take stock of the room. I saw that it was filled with people. There were people seated in every chair, some were seated on the floor in front of the podium and others on the stage where I was preaching from. I noticed that there were three rows of seats with an isle in between each row as well as isles at both ends of the rows by the wall which made a U-shape with the back of the sanctuary. I noticed that the isles by the wall, as well as the back wall, were packed with standing people. Then, my attention was drawn to the two middle isles which were completely empty. I thought *that is weird*. All the while, I am taking note of the room as I am preaching. It felt like I was somehow divided into three, even though I was one. I was aware of one part of me checking out the room, one part preaching and the third part having a conversation with the Holy Spirit.

The Holy Spirit was asking me to wrap up preaching and prepare to pray for people by laying my hands on them. I was asking the Holy Spirit how with the place so packed. There is no room at the front of the podium for me to call an altar call. Where are people going to stand? Where are the people currently sitting on the floor going to go while I pray for those who needed prayer? The Holy Spirit said, "You are going to go to them". Then, immediately, I understood why the two isles in the middle were empty. I began to walk to one of the isles. Then the Holy Spirit asked me to stretch my arms so each hand was touching the individual at the end of each row and as I went from row to row, people were getting healed and delivered. It seemed I was doing this for a while and the back seemed to expand as I approached it. At some point, the Holy Spirit then starts pointing out people within the congregation that I could not access at the end of the row and instructing me to go and lay my hands on those particular individuals. I asked again how I would get to them seeing the room was packed and every seat occupied. The Holy Spirit instructed me to jump on chairs since people were standing waiting to be prayed for. I began to climb on chairs and it seems the Holy Spirit was showing me people faster than I could get to them. One time, in my haste to go to the person the Holy Spirit had shown me, I remember stumbling on a chair. I was aware that I hit the front of my thigh on a chair and it hurt but I kept moving to keep up with the Holy Spirit. I was able to recognize a few of those people but the majority were strangers to me. I finally finished and the Holy Spirit led me back to the pulpit where I prayed one last time and was instructed to dismiss the people. Everyone filed out and I left too. The next morning when I woke up, I felt pain in my thigh but didn't pay much attention to it. I took my shower feeling the pain and went to work. When I came back home that evening my thigh was badly bruised. For the life of me I couldn't figure out where I hurt myself. I hadn't been to the gym, which was the only other feasible place I could have hurt myself. The bruise was pretty big. Then suddenly as I showered the next morning, I remembered that the only place I got bumped was during the dream. The bruise lasted for three days and it disappeared.

Over the years I have had similar experiences of getting hurt in the dream while doing some form of ministry and I wake up with pain in that same area that lasts three days and then goes away. Recently it was my foot. I was praying by the river bank and some kids came by with an adult. The adult got out of the car and started dumping kids into the river and drove away. I ran into the water and as I jumped in for one of the two kids, I felt myself landing on a rock underwater. The following day, I woke up with a bruise under the same foot and it lasted three days like the other bruises before.

Ezekiel 12 - July 2017

I had a dream within a dream. In the dream, I was at a conference and sleeping in a room next to the auditorium when I felt God waking me up to go and preach from Ezekiel 12. Instinctively, I knew that I was initially supposed to preach on a Friday, the first day of the conference, but some women began to speak against it and I was taken off the schedule. The woman leading the group that was against my speaking was the same woman I talk about in Chapter 4 above, the one who had ordered some witchcraft in the envelope. Still in the dream, I had been put on the Saturday schedule, but again, she campaigned that I be removed. I was afraid to get up anyway but deep down I knew I needed to do it, so I was still determined to go and share the Word God had given me. Pastor Marvelous was the one who was in charge of the conference. She came to where I was lying down on my bed to tell me that I am supposed to preach, please get ready. She went about her way as I got up to get ready. Now it's a Sunday and I am walking around looking for toothpaste. I knew that the New Yorkers had brought their own toothpaste so I was looking for the toothpaste they had brought. I came to some New Yorkers that I recognized and I asked if they knew where our toothpaste was and they said they didn't know. I turned a corner and it was on the counter behind the witchcraft lady. I asked her for the toothpaste and she told me she didn't have it, someone else had taken it and yet I could see that she had her hands behind her back trying to hide the toothpaste; even though I somehow knew that she had it and had been giving it to the other New Yorkers but didn't want to give it to me. I made a conscious decision not to argue with her and walked away.

As I came from around another corner looking to see if anyone could give me toothpaste, I literally bumped into Pastor Marvelous and she said, "Ndiri kukutsvaga. Hanti urikuziva kuti unofanira kuparidza from Ezekiel 12 saka gadzirira nekuti zita rako rakutodaidzwa." (I have been looking for you. You know you are supposed to be preaching from Ezekiel 12. Please be ready because your name is about to be called on stage). I responded that I was aware but I needed to brush my teeth first and I didn't have any toothpaste. She then opened her pocketbook and took toothpaste out of it, showed me where to go and brush my teeth, and went back into the auditorium. Right there, with a renewed sense of resolve in my spirit, I went to brush my teeth. The fear was still there but I was going to do it nevertheless. I woke up as I got on the stage, walking towards the pulpit saying, "Let us open our Bibles to Ezekiel 12".

<u>Sidebar: When God calls you into ministry, you will face resistance, some of it internal – that is within yourself and from close family members or those whose opinion you value and some external – other people, believers and non-believers alike. Perhaps one of the most hurtful resistances was from other pastors. My naive self expected them to embrace me and show me the ropes, so to speak. I expected them to celebrate a co-laborer in the Vineyard, especially since the Word tells us in Matthew</u>

9:37, "Then He said to His disciples, 'The harvest is plentiful but the laborers are few'". I began to wonder where pastors place the next verse, Matthew 9:38, "therefore pray earnestly to the Lord of the harvest to send out laborers into the harvest." Notice that when Jesus spoke these words He was not addressing the harvest/the crowds (verse 36), He was directing this instruction to the disciples, the pastors-in-training. It then begs the questions to the seasoned pastors out there:

a) Do you subscribe to the Word in its entirety?

b) If so, are you praying for the laborers?

c) When laborers are presented, do you only embrace the ones you like or are within your respective churches or the ones only you have ordained?

d) Whose harvest are you serving?

There is a lot of spiritual warfare that manifests in the physical. I went through this same resistance in its intensity around the time God was revealing His plan for my life. I had resistance from pastors and their spouses - something I never anticipated given we were going to be co-laborers in the Vineyard. It was cutthroat. I received forwarded messages via email and WhatsApp of some very respected generals in the Vineyard speaking untruths and insults not worthy of a general's mouth. I would see them in person or speak to them on the phone as I pretended like I didn't know that they were assassinating my character behind my back. The interesting thing is that God didn't seem to make them stop. If He did, they obviously didn't listen because they kept coming. Instead, God began to deal with my heart to forgive them and not try to get vindication for myself. Not only did He ask me to work as unto Him and not unto man but He also made it very clear that I was not to speak ill of these servants of God to anyone. I didn't listen and God dealt harshly with me immediately. I was on the phone with someone speaking ill of one of the pastors who had written a nasty message about me to various people when I began to feel physically weird. The more I spoke the more I felt my mouth literally shifting to the side of my face. For days afterwards, anytime I mentioned a name of one of the pastors or their spouses in bad light, I felt my mouth shift. It got shifted so bad that one person I was talking to on the phone told me I sounded funny. I could tell my speech was beginning to sound weird. I asked my sister, Pink, to take a look at my mouth, she couldn't see it but she heard my weird sounding speech. My mouth was shifted for about three days after that and then it went away. So did my talking about the servants of God behind their back. After that, and for many months to come, some of those pastors and their spouses owned up to their part in assassinating my character. So, my friends, don't be alarmed when God doesn't respond to you in a way that you recognize. When we pray, He hears and He responds. Even you will be vindicated. It may not be today or tomorrow or even years from now, but God will vindicate you if you trust in His Sovereign plan and ways. End of Sidebar.

The Assignment
Thursday, August 31, 2017

Pastor Marvelous calls: Shalom Teresa, I want you to know that I have been released to come to the CFI Conference so I am arriving tomorrow.

Me: Shalom munhu waMwari (woman of God). That is good news, thank you. I appreciate your support. Please let me know your itinerary so I can make arrangements for your ride from the airport to the venue.

PM: Okay, but I may have a ride. I will tell you if anything changes. But I am calling to ask you if you have anointing oil in your house? I need it for an assignment at the conference.

Me: I do have a little bottle of olive oil that I took from my kitchen and prayed over that I use to rub my back and hip when I am in pain. (She knew I had an injury from work that I was nursing).

PM: It will do. Bring it to the conference. Don't forget. See you tomorrow. Please don't forget.

Me: I won't forget munhu waMwari. See you tomorrow. Bye.

Friday, September 1, 2017

Pastor Marvelous: Shalom Woman of God. I am leaving Indiana. Please don't forget to bring the oil, it is very important. I have an assignment.

Me: Shalom munhu waMwari, I promise I won't forget. Ndakatobata kabhodhoro kacho (I have the bottle in my hand right now as we speak).

PM: Good, because that is the main reason I am traveling - for this assignment.

Me: I understand, I will not forget.

The whole time I was discussing this oil, it didn't dawn on me to or her to mention the size of the bottle. I was assuming that she had been given an assignment by the conference Executive Board to pray and anoint people. Nothing unusual.

After I hung up the phone, with the little bottle of oil still in my hand, something got stirred up in my spirit and all of a sudden I had an awareness that this oil was about me. I couldn't place what it was exactly but I just knew. At the very same moment Pastor Marvelous possibly realized she had not told me whose it was or what it was for. My phone rang. It was Pastor Marvelous and all she said was,

"Teresa, the assignment is for you".

I then made a demand on God, "If this is your will, Lord I want real oil from Israel". I began to call around to Christian Bookstores to see if any carried the anointing oil from Israel, to no avail. Throughout the day, I kept saying the same thing, *God, if this is your will, I want the oil from Israel.*

I went to the hotel where Pastor Lekuku was setting up the PA system in preparation for the CFI conference. We got chatting and I remembered that he had posted on Facebook a few days earlier that he had just returned from Israel. He began to give testimony of some of his experiences in Israel and I shared how I want to go there one day. As I walked out after our chat, I stopped midway and sort of shouted at him with a conviction in my spirit I cannot explain, "Did you bring ME MY OIL from Israel?" Without missing a beat, he responded, "As a matter of fact I did". SAY WHAT?!!! He told me he had bought oil in Israel and had brought the bottle with him so I should bring a bottle of my own so he could pour some in it. Just like that God had answered my request. three days later after the conference was over and as we were saying our goodbyes, Pastor Lekuku narrated to me how in the natural he had no reason to have brought that specific oil with him to the conference. He went on to share how he had bought that oil as his last purchase in Israel right at Lazarus's grave. How ironic that:

a) the night before meeting Pastor Lekuku (Wednesday), I had dreamt of God telling me that He was restoring some dead things in me just as He had restored Lazarus from the dead.

b) Thursday, before asking Pastor Lekuku about the anointing oil from Israel, he had given me his experience upon visiting Lazarus's grave in Israel.

c) Sunday, as we said our goodbyes, he told me that he bought that oil right outside Lazarus' grave with the last spending money he had.

As he held his bottle of oil in his hands (he had dug it out of his bag for demonstration purposes), he showed me how out of the bottle, the only oil he had poured out was mine even though some people who had overheard us speak about the oil throughout the conference had expressed interest in having the oi, they never went back to him to actually get the oil. So basically, God had Pastor Lekuku on assignment to bring that oil specifically for me without any of us knowing what the assignment was. Pastor Lekuku narrated how as he was packing his bags, he went back and forth on bringing that oil with him, taking it out of his bag and returning it several times. God, once again, steering things in motion for practical strangers to meet and fulfill His will in each other's lives.

Sidebar: Prior to this encounter, I had only known Pastor Lekuku from a distance as my husband's friend. I had only met him and interacted for less than three minutes at an event prior to the CFI Conference. I recognized his name as someone who was on my wedding invitation list. Now, when I look back, I see this and many other experiences that were set in motion through that connection with my husband. Our wedding may not have happened, but the connections that came out of the encounter continues to yield great harvests. Once again, God showing that nothing is wasted. End of Sidebar.

Pastor Marvelous' assignment was to pray over me, encourage me, and anoint me for the calling and work God had placed upon my life. She did that during the early hours of Sunday. As Pastor Lekuku and I were standing outside by his car, Pastor Marvelous walked out of the hotel also getting ready to go and catch her flight. The three of us huddled and marveled at the works of God's hands as we each shared once again how He had used each of us for His purpose and will for my life. The assignment was completed and now the manifestation continues.

<u>Sidebar: When God calls anyone into ministry, He confirms it through others, if they are receptive to the Holy Spirit. There are some who believe if they didn't ordain you, then you have no calling. The ordination that people do in various churches, is an outward celebration of what God has already done in the hearts of people He calls into ministry,. In other words, we should not be caught up in religious activities to the point of forgetting that ultimately it is God who gives and orders our</u>

<u>steps, not people. Therefore ordination is ultimately from God. End of Sidebar.</u>

A Season of Dreams and Visions

ECCLESIASTES 3:1-8, talks about a season for everything. During this time that I had now reconciled with God, I went through a season where God was showing me His plan for me. He gave it to me in very specific dreams and visions. A lot of times in our lives, we dismiss dreams and yet, God for years, from the beginning of time, God has communicated to people through visions and dreams. Why would He stop now? He says He is not a respecter of person, so why would he not continue to speak to people in dreams in visions? There are some dreams that God is not expecting to share with everybody. There are some dreams that He expects you to share with certain people. There are some circumstances to express the dreams at a certain time, in a particular season.

That does not mean that I have to parade around and act like I am so special to God that He is giving me this vision. We have a tendency of thinking that when one does not experience God in the manner we are used to or similar to ours, then it means that they are not praying enough or are not Christian enough. God is using everyone He wants to use at whatever given time as long as it is for the purpose of the Kingdom. Even though people think God can't use them, He can and He will.

The Vision Board is also one of those things you can use to put intention into the universe, the things that God has shown you. This book that I am writing is on my vision board. My trip to Israel is on there too. I will talk more about the Vision Board in the next chapter. God has put things into motion. By writing the vision, it is important that when God shows you something, you remember it. If you forget it, it is important to pray to God to bring it back to memory. God is faithful, He will do it. There is something called, "Operating in your Grace". It is operating in the capacity that God says to operate. A lot of people miss their opportunity because they are not operating in their capacity that they are supposed to. Then, there is a time of understanding the timeframe that God is giving us called, "The Season of Grace". There are a lot of times that we think God does not love us. However, God could have been showing us, but we may have missed the season of grace; thus, knowing to operate within the parameters that God has for us. We tend to want to operate outside of the parameters that God has for us and expecting God to change to suit us when it should be the us changing to suit God's order of things. Are you operating in your grace and do you understand YOUR season of grace?

The example that I like to give is that of Prophet Elijah. In 2 King 17. When Elijah was running away from Jezebel, the Word of God talks about how God led him into the desert. There was a time of drought when it didn't rain for three and a half years. Eventually, he ended up at the brook. When he got to the brook, the brook had water when the whole land had a drought. God led him there to drink from the water. When he was at the brook, he led the ravens to give him fresh meat. Ravens usually eat carcasses. For them to bring him fresh meat is a miracle. God was providing. Then, the brook dried up. When the brook dried up, God then spoke to Elijah and said "Get up. Go on to Zarephath. There is a widow woman that I had spoken to and she will take care of you." So Elijah got up. Sometimes, we like to remain at the brook, because it is familiar. We want to stay at the brook, but sometimes God is doing it for a season. Sometimes, we miss God's plan for the brook, we also miss it for other people. Elijah realized that if he stayed at the brook, he would be worshipping the brook, instead of worshipping the God of the brook. On that same day, I want to believe that God spoke to the Ravens and said "your job is done." God led Elijah to Zarephath. When I read this chapter, I cannot think of this experience and not think about how God prepared the woman in advance of Elijah's arrival.

When he gets there, he encounters a woman who is trying to pick up a few sticks and make some food. The plan was for her to wait to die. It was a time of famine in the land. She only had enough for the last meal. She was preparing for her son so that they could eat and prepare to die. Elijah showed up and said "make me a muscle of bread". They go back and forth and the woman is trying to help Elijah see that what he is asking for is crazy.

However, she makes the bread for Elijah. After he has eaten and he is full,. he asked her to go get oil. She became an oil mogul. She began an entrepreneur. She is not only providing for her own child, but also for her community. If he had decided to stay at the brook, all of the people who benefited from this miracle would have missed their blessings.

It is important to know the season of grace. When it is time to sever relationships including business relationships, it is important to do so without delay. Remember, God and Satan cannot occupy the same space at the same time. Light and darkness cannot occupy the same space at the same time, nor can righteousness and sin. So it is with relationships; we cannot continue in toxic and unbiblical relationships expecting to grow in our faith. There is no doubt that some relationships will be hard to sever, especially when you have invested the time, energy, and other resources like emotional ones. But we are not called to do the easy stuff; otherwise everyone would be a Bible-taught and God-fearing believer. Following Christ is tough, but it is the hard experiences that bring us the most significant breakthroughs in our lives. God is looking for individuals who put their weaknesses in His hands to impact others in their Christian walk. The 828 Woman is for the woman (or man) who feels like God is calling them to do great work in the Vineyard, but they feel intimidated by their sinful past, so they can't see how it is that God can use them. It is for people whose pain, humiliation, and shame has been made a public spectacle and are feeling dejected as if their lives have no meaning.

I hope that as you reflect on this book, you too will take a look at your own life and embrace the experiences you have gone through and be open to God using you for His glory. I need you to recognize that God is not a respecter of persons (Acts 10:34), what He did and does for me, He can do for you and more. Although everyone's journey may look similar, we all have different purposes. It is all for the greater good, but ultimately, it is to give God the glory. However, in order to truly find your God-given purpose, you have to have a relationship with God. We need to find our God-given purpose. It is important to figure out what the God-given purpose is, as opposed to the people-given purpose and the self-given purpose. People can define purpose for you. Sometimes, they may be helping you identify what your skillset is and what your calling is. However, after people have provided that to you and before you try any career, any assignment, any business, any way of being, you need to seek God. Seek God and make sure that you are following the instructions that God gives you above all else or, popular, and even, familiar paths.

Further, there is another concern that I want to encourage people to get out of. A lot of times, I fell under that spell too. When God is telling you or giving us instruction, we like to try and match it to what we know. If it sounds strange or unfamiliar, we question whether it is from God. We allow people to even help us question whether it is from God. We want validation from people who God has not even sent or revealed His plans for us. We expect people to validate us from a place of their limitations, prejudices, and even their ignorance. It is not always that your pastor will validate your God-given paths. Contrary to popular belief, pastors don't always know everything...there are some things God will choose to reveal to you alone and confirm through other people who may not necessarily be pastors. We expect people like our pastors and others to validate us all the time and when we don't get that validation, we feel stuck. Would life be easier if God just revealed things to your pastor so you don't have to work so hard in convincing people of the call of God on your life? Absolutely! But it may be that God has not revealed it yet because he is still dealing with you as an individual.

For example, one of the things that God said to me in 2018 was that He wanted me to do two conferences back to back. When God was showing me this vision I said "nobody has ever done it" and I thought "it could not be done". I had never seen that happen before. I allowed the devil to speak to me and have others speak negatively about it. However, out of obedience, we did it. One of the main things that God is looking from us is obedience. We tend to reference or gravitate to what we know or what we are familiar with, opposed to what God wants. God is not obligated to show you what He is showing your pastor and vice-versa. There is a reason why God does not reveal certain things to certain people at certain times. At times it is because we just don't have the grace to handle it at the time.

There are also naysayers to contend with in life. There will always be people that oppose what you say or do. That is an inevitable part of life. It just means those people are not part of your assignment and that is okay. I will say that I did something similar. There will be people who will consider your background, your education, which side of the tracks you are from, who are your parents, what color is your skin, etc. Those will be the people who will try to say you cannot pull this off because you do not fit their norm.

There are too many people who are seeking validation from others. There are people who are in the wrong jobs because a mentor told them they should be in that position. I was once into people-pleasing. There are many people in the church who are people-pleasers. I should know. I was one of them. Thank God for deliverance. You cannot be a people-pleaser and follow what God is saying to you or walk the journey He has set apart for you at the same time. *Matthew 6:24* puts it this way, *"No one can serve two masters. Either you will hate one and love the other or you will be devoted to one and despise the other. You cannot serve God and money"*. There is no doubt that following God is a tough and lonely, but obedience is better than sacrifice. Here are some steps you can follow in finding purpose:

1. Seek to have a relationship with God. How do you have a relationship with God? By being in His Word. *John 1:1 says, "In the beginning was the Word and the Word was with God and the Word was God."* God is not obligated to bless us outside His Word. He does not contradict His Word. If it feels like a contradiction, it is not with the Word of God but our understanding of His Word. Hence, we need the Holy Spirit to make the Word clear in our spirit. When you are constantly and consistently in the Word of God, you will understand how to have a relationship with God.

2. To begin to have a relationship with God, all you have to do is believe in your heart and confess with your mouth that Jesus Christ is Lord and receive by Faith the salvation that is given through Jesus' death at Calvary. He will show you your purpose and reveal to you what you went through or are going through.

3. Be Open. Don't think that because you have the same characteristics as your aunt, you will be like your aunt. Go in with an open mind and say, "Father, here I am."

4. 4. Remember that Pastors are human beings and are therefore fallible. Don't put your trust in men; put your trust in God. Pastors have a responsibility to show people and help them through their journeys, but we are not the Christ. Do not put us on a pedestal that God has not put us. Because God does not like to share His glory. Like Joel Osteen likes to say, "You and God are a majority".

5. You're unique therefore God will have a unique purpose for you and use you in a unique way. Embrace it and inspire others.

The 828 Woman

THE 828 WOMAN is inspired by *Romans 8:28, "For we know that all things work together for good to them that love God, to them who are called according to his purpose."*

We are all born with and for a specific purpose. Most of us miss His purpose because we lose sight and cannot see the forest for the trees. God wants to use our experiences, especially the bad kind, or the ones that we are most embarrassed about. It is important that as women, we come to a place where we do not allow the devil to make us live in secrecy, to make us be embarrassed to the point of being paralyzed by some of the things that happen to us. Things happen, life happens, and even in the Word of God, Jesus even tells us "troubles and tribulations will come." There is no escaping tribulations. God why am I going through this? Why did I go through this or not?

For me, in order to come to a realization, I asked God questions. I asked Him: "Why did you create me? Why are we on this Earth? What is the point of me being here on Earth?" I began to ask God questions. God, Jesus, and the Holy Spirit are gentleman. They are not going to force themselves on you. It is you that has to invite them into your circle. It is you who has to say out loud: "Jesus, I need you to show me my purpose".

The 828 Woman is a woman who has gone through some stuff and is wondering if there is a purpose to the pain, trials, and tribulations. It is a woman who has a desire to see God in all that she has gone through. The 828 Woman recognizes that God made her special, not better than the next woman, but special in her own unique way. It is a woman who recognizes that her life is not a sum of her failures or the calamities that have come her way. This woman may not recognize it, but with encouragement from the Word of God, other women and her loved ones, she is or was being prepared for Kingdom purpose.

Jesus did not sugarcoat life for us. In fact in John 16:33, He lets us know that in this world, we will have trials and tribulations but with that, He encourages that we are to take heart for He has already overcome on our behalf. There is NO escaping challenges. However, the 828 Woman is the woman to whom God is saying that no matter what you are going through, it may have happened to you, but it has happened for you. God is about to use that very experience that the devil meant for bad for His glory. God is about to change the people around you. God is about to change you. God is about to change the perspective that you have regarding the pain that you have been through. There is a shift that needs to happen in your head and your heart to recognize that everything that you have gone through has purpose. God is not going to reveal everything to you in one sitting. It is not possible. There are some things that God must reveal over time. There are some things that God has up His sleeve and must reveal to in doses proportional to our capacity at any given time. If God was to reveal everything to us, then we would not need him. Besides, there are some things that will just blow our minds away into abyss if He were to fully reveal them. Just consider this: If God had revealed to Noah the whole plan, I doubt that Noah would have been onboard with it. If God told Noah, "I want you to build an Ark because there is a huge flood coming and in the Ark, you can only bring your family and a few animals and things I will show you. However, everyone else will be destroyed in the flood. I will start over with just your family and your best friend Sam, or your good neighbor Chloe cannot come, they too will be destroyed". Do you think that Noah would have built that Ark? It would not have happened. That is too much of a burden to carry. Noah would have been scared to have all his friends die just like that. If it were you, you would have been scared too...I know I would have had the heebeegeebees. It's important that we know when God created us, He created us for a reason and that reason will come into fruition if we trust and seek Him. People say gravesites are the wealthiest places on earth. Why? Because there are so many people who died with their ideas, without realizing their purpose. People who were going to be something, but never did.

You think, can God really use you? If God can use Teresa, trust me, He can use you. Don't beat yourself up. Don't allow yourself or the devil to convince you that you are way too broken for God to use you. God is looking for people like you. He is used to people like you and me. The ones that people shy away from, the person that people do not want to be their friend. Those are the ones that God gravitates to. Those are the ones that God wants to use. Why? Because God says that He uses the foolish things to confound the wise (1 Corinthians 1:27). While people dismiss you and pretend like you don't exist or you are not good enough, God knows exactly where you are. He knows your address. He knows you just the way you are and created you just the way you are. He knows all the things you will go through and is confident that you can handle it. He never gives us more than we can handle. Of course, when you are going through it, it is tough. I want to encourage you to say:

As the 828 Woman, you are the individual that God wants to use today and in this season to impact generations to come. God is raising a different caliber of individuals, especially women, to usher in the second coming of Christ. I am not saying that we need to disregard the men who are the Head of our Households. I am just saying that we are living in the end times and Jesus is coming soon. He is looking to raise a different caliber of women who are going to stand up and stand out. Women who are going to say: "I don't care what I've been through. I am not what I went through. I am who God says I am." Those are the people who God is looking for to move forward His Kingdom agenda. You, the 828 Woman, are the person that God is calling to usher in the second coming of Christ.

Stand up high! Lift your head! Shoulders back! Chest out!

Know that YOU are the beloved of God.

You are the 828 Woman. I salute you.

God bless you.

CHAPTER NINE

The Power of the Vision Board

"And the Lord answered me and said, "Write the vision and make it pain upon tablets that he may run that readeth it. For the vision is yet for an appointed time but at the end it shall speak and not lie; though it tarry, wait for it because it will surely come, it will not tarry. Behold, his soul which is lifted up is upright in him but the just shall live by His faith." Habakkuk 2:2-3

- ∞ -

IN 2018, I HOSTED THE FIRST 828 WOMAN: NOTHING IS Wasted Retreat/Conference at Liebenzell Retreat Ministries in New Jersey, USA. At the retreat, we had a session in which we learnt about and created our individual vision boards. I added a little bit of twist to it, my own Holy Spirit-inspired board. I encouraged the ladies to divide their boards into two sections - Vision Board on one end and a GratiBoard on the other. The Vision Board side, common to many, depicts our future aspirations and the Grati' Board is inspired by *Joshua 4* where God instructed His servant, Joshua, to tell the children of Israel to pick 12 stones representing the 12 tribes of Judah as a memorial for future generations of them passing through the Red Sea on dry ground. So, on our Grati' Boards, I encouraged the ladies to put visual and symbolic pictures that show the goodness of God and where the Lord has brought them from. A lot of times we are so focused on what we want God to do for us, we neglect to take the time to be grateful for what He has already done. So 'Grati' in GratiBoard stands for Gratitude.

As you can see on my Board, I had plenty of stuff. The few things I want to discuss briefly in this chapter are marked by red dots in the 2nd picture below:

My November 17, 2018 Vision/GratiBoard

Broken for the Master's Use: The 828 Woman 282

Red dots depict accomplished goals as of the printing of this book and things I am grateful for. Fitness goals of strong body and strong mind continues to be a work in progress.

2019 1st Visit to Israel (what I would write in my diary - if I kept one)

AS I WRITE THIS CHAPTER I am in Tel Aviv, Israel being hosted by two amazing servants of God and their families, Prophet Daniel Bonny and Pastor Solomon Tetteh. The manner in which this divine connection happened is nothing short of a miracle. Like I keep saying, if this wasn't happening to me, I would not believe it. Three strangers meeting via WhatsApp introduction by a mutual co-laborer in the Vineyard, was truly orchestrated by God. I have felt like a long-lost friend coming home. Being invited to minister at their individual churches was an honor and humbling. Here is how this miracle transpired:

July 26th - Purchased ticket to fly to Tel Aviv on Sept 2nd with no idea where I would stay and whether or not to purchase a tour package; trusting completely in God to open doors. I wake up each day expecting unprecedented favor.

August 20th - Divinely led to a YouTube video of an individual I had never heard of, but was drawn to their powerful testimony. Went through video after video, captured by Erica's testimony for which she wrote 2 books, *Erica Part One Seven Years in Hell* and *Erica Part Two Eighteen Years with Lucifer*. I had to buy the books immediately. I think every believer should have these books in their library.

August 21st - I reached out to Erica and connected via WhatsApp. We begin to make plans for a collaboration.

August 26th 8:14 am - Purchased accommodations at Airbnb in Tel Aviv. Still trying to figure out whether or not to purchase tour package - decided it would be my Plan B if nothing else surfaced.

August 26th 4:56pm - Erica's husband, Tim, connects me with Apostle Dr. Marylin Jones of Brooklyn.

August 26th 6:42 pm - I make a phone call to Apostle Dr. Jones and we hit it off. I love it when people start conversations with prayer. We spoke for less than 30 minutes and we just connected. As we shared our experiences she happened to mention that she had just come back from Israel about three weeks prior, so naturally, I informed her that I was leaving for Israel on Sept 2nd. She asked me if I was going alone or with a group. I told her the former. She inquired if I knew anyone in Israel and I told her I didn't. She inquired about my accommodation and tour plans. I informed her of the Airbnb purchase and my Plan B. She asked me to hang up the phone as she had a quick phone call to make. Within minutes she had connected me with Prophet Daniel and Pastor Solomon.

August 26th 11:54 pm- I cancelled my reservation for the Airbnb because I had connected with both Prophet Daniel and Pastor Solomon who were ready to host me in Israel.

August 31st 4:55am - I received an unfortunate message from my airline that there were changes to my flight that would impact my travel.

September 2nd 2:36am – I received more bad news from the airline with further delays that my flight for same day at 9:55pm was not happening. We spent the night going back and forth as I scrambled to find an alternative flight with friends and family all helping.

September 2nd 8: 14am – I purchased another ticket with another airline. At noon, I left my house for the airport.

September 3rd 2 pm - I arrive at the airport and there is something in the air, an excitement, anticipation of all I will experience while I am here. I'm supposed to be tired but I am way too excited.

Pastor Solomon picked me up from the airport as we meet for the first time and yet it feels like we are family. I was eager to see something - anything really - so he kindly drove me to Old Jaffa in Tel Aviv, the site where it is believed Jonah was vomited by the Whale (Jonah 1 & 2), then to St. Peter's Church. Brought back some memories of my days as a Catholic many moon ago.

Wednesday, September 4th - Pastor Solomon drove me to Mt. Carmel where it is believed Prophet Elijah challenged Baal's false prophets to prove the authenticity of their god while he proved his. Needless to say, the false prophets were outshined (1 Kings 18).

As we drove back from Mt. Carmel, Pastor Solomon informed me I was to minister at his church that evening. On our way home to prepare for service, he bought me a phone line for easy communication while in Israel. I marvel at such hospitality. He is like a brother I haven't seen in a while and we are just picking up where we left off.

Ministered on the *Manner or Pattern in which we Ought to Pray* (Matthew 6:9-13).

Thursday, September 5th - Prophet Daniel dropped me off to take the local Kombi called Sherut (minivan of up to 10 people) on a self-guided tour to Jerusalem. Both Pastor Solomon and Prophet Daniel checked on me from time to time suggesting places to go.

This was an enlightening and quite surprising experience. Riding the Sherut brought back memories of traveling in Zimbabwe, except in Israel the seating capacity is not as creative as in Zimbabwe.

Sometimes the Sheruts in Zimbabwe has extra seats that the manufacturers don't know anything about, if you catch my drift.

The Bible literally came to life right before my eyes as I walked through one of the two sites believed to be where the empty tomb is located, the Garden Tomb. It was a very sobering experience to see where it's believed to be Golgotha or Calvary. Just standing there and hearing the guide show and tell how very publicly humiliating it was for our Lord to go through with it when He could have summoned ten thousand angels to destroy the world and set Him free (Matthew 26:53). Jesus chose to go through it all for you and me.

God answered one of my secret prayers unexpectedly. I always used to say I would love to experience a group prayer session and singing like I see on social media. Since I was not part of a group that experience was on my mind as I saw different groups having services. But as I was seating where it is believed Pontius Pilot washed his hands absolving himself of the ruling to crucify Jesus (Matthew 27:24) a group came to join me. We hung out for a while and they invited me to join them. So, I did and then we went our separate ways as I got drawn to the Tomb for longer. As I was getting ready to leave, I bumped into the pastor's wife who insisted I should join them for communion service. I was completely undone! Captured it all on camera. Thank you Jesus!

Following the fourteen stations it's believed the Jesus followed was heartbreaking. On the first day, I went to Jerusalem. I was not necessarily or systematically following the route. I just happened by them. Then, I went back to Jerusalem for the third time, this time to really concentrate on following the route. I couldn't imagine the pain and most importantly the magnitude of His love for us. Gethsemane was the toughest one for me. I was heartbroken by the agony He must have gone through when He prayed that prayer told in all 4 synoptic Gospels, Matthew 26:39; Mark 14:36, Luke 22:42, as well *John 6:38, "And He went a little beyond them (the disciples) and fell on His face and prayed saying, My Father, if it is possible, let this cup pass from me, yet not my will but your will be done"*.

I visited so many places including the Western Wall (Wailing Wall) and the Holy Church of the Sepulcher located in the Christian Quarters in the Old City of Jerusalem. It was one of the interesting places in that it houses, under the same roof, different faiths. The main denominations represented as part of an agreement drawn and signed in the 4th Century, include the Roman Catholic, Armenian

Apostolic, Greek Orthodox and the Ethiopian Orthodox. The Ethiopian Orthodox, whose monks and nuns live on the promises, are believed to be direct descendants of Queen of Sheba.

The experience of the Western Wall was saddening to me. Even though I sensed a very strong spirit of religiosity throughout my visit in Israel, at this place it was even stronger. There are rules to adhere to - women and men pray separately; women must dress modestly (not sure why the same rule doesn't apply to men); men must cover their heads when approaching the wall and on Shabbat, no electronics are allowed. Grateful it's not Shabbat today.

On one end of the Western Wall is the Christian and Jewish section and on the other side was the Muslim side marked by one of the most incredible pieces of architecture I saw, their Mosque. People are to come dressed modestly. Women are to cover their shoulders and knees. There was a lady behind me who was wearing sheer outfit, she was offered a shawl to cover herself or be denied entry. She opted for the shawl.

The spirit of religiosity is just as heavy, except on this side, it is more organized and restrictive, the other side was chaotic. The presence of both plain-clothed security and uniformed armed forces give a false sense of peace and security.

I must say on the Jewish/Christian side, I observed events that made me sad and a bit upset. There were several religious events taking place like initiations of sorts. I witnessed a few families celebrating the adolescent milestone of Bar Mitzvah (entering adulthood/adolescent rite of passage). The man, according to tradition, were on one side, a wide area with big space with tables and chairs along a dividing picket fence type of wall. While the men were going through the rituals, the women were peering over the fence, some on tippy toes - no tables and chairs along the wall. To me, it seemed like women were no different from me, a stranger, observants and not participants of their loved one's significant milestone. I had to remind myself that I was on a self-discovery tour, not on a religious protest tour. *Own your feelings and keep it moving, Teresa.*

One of the highlights of this day, was the visit to the Garden of Gethsemane where Jesus succumbed to the weight and pressure of what was about to transpire, i.e. Him going to the Cross. For me, the whole idea of Jesus in human form is proven in this very moment where He is overwhelmed by His inevitable death and He prays one of the most human prayers, *"Father, if you are willing, remove this cup from me; nevertheless, not my will but yours, be done". Luke 22:42.*

Friday, September 6th - Prophet drove me to Bethlehem where he hired a tour guide to show us the sites. We were able to skip the lines and go straight to the manger. The depictions we have in our imagination are so removed from what is portrayed on the ground. Nevertheless, it was surreal being at the place where our Savior was born. From there, we went to a little two-man operation joint called Shawarma, a few feet from the Church of the Nativity. Prophet Daniel had been talking about this place since morning, that they serve the best Israeli food. I had the opportunity to taste my first Israeli food since arriving in the country. My hosts are Ghanaian so naturally I was fed their tasty cuisine till now. Prophet Daniel was not kidding. The Shawarma Pita I tasted was an incredible mouth-watering experience.

This little nook seats 10 people at a time and it's a small strip of real estate with a tiny passage dividing the eating area and the food prep area. I couldn't help but reflect on how most of the time we wait for a big office space, big monies to come our way and possibly an overinflated business loan, when all God is waiting for us is to use the little that we have and He will multiply it. I am reminded of the faith like a mustard seed told by Jesus in Matthew 17:20-24.

Bethlehem, like Jerusalem, has a huge presence of police and army. The only difference is that in Bethlehem you identify them by their uniform only, but in Jerusalem, they are in full gear with scary looking AK-47s hanging on their sides.

Another observation was the harmony in which all people interact and trade in markets and almost everywhere one goes. Most people are friendly and welcoming. However, it could be frustrating as not everyone speaks or understands English, and a significant number of places, including some tourist attractions are only in Arabic and Hebrew.

This has been an incredible self-discovery journey and I encourage it for every Christ Follower...the transformation is inevitable. The Bible literally becomes alive right before your eyes so it is important, before you leave home, to read your Bible, especially where references of the places you want to see are mentioned, so that it will be more relevant to you.

Monday, September 9th - Decided to take a day tour with a local tour company to Nazareth, Capernaum, and the Sea of Galilee. The architecture in this part of the country is significantly different. It almost felt like a different country, older ruins and structures. Although the houses and buildings resembled Jerusalem and Bethlehem in that they are all concrete and are unpainted on the outside, they looked dingier and a bit dull.

The churches here are more ancient and give you a feeling of "less is more". Visiting St. Joseph Church in Nazareth was revelatory for me. As I walked through it, I couldn't help but note how simplistic it is. Not from a lack of great architecture, because there is plenty of it, but it left me reflecting on how it defines Joseph's humility. For Joseph to have taken an already pregnant wife, Mary, and assume the responsibility of an earthly father to Jesus, is pretty profound. His humble spirit was very evident walking through the church.

The most significant highlight for today was my unorthodox baptism. I had made an advance inquiry on having a Pastor on-site to perform the baptism for me at Yardenit Baptismal Site. This is the site where it is believed Jesus was baptized by John the Baptist. (Matthew 3:13-17). So while my fellow tourists from my tour van were feeding the catfish, I was renting my baptismal gown and bath towel. I cannot begin to put into words the excitement and feeling in my spirit even as we approached the premises. So when I was told there was no pastor around, I was naturally very upset. I went to the river to see if any groups were having baptism and I was going to ask to join them, but no one was being baptized by immersion. I went inside to speak to staff and the manager, Sheba, noting how upset I was, she took my plight and went looking for one of their pastors who was supposed to be onsite to no avail. She then suggested I do it myself. I must say, at first it seemed strange...*who baptizes themselves?* Well, apparently you will today, Pastor Tee. And that is exactly what happened. She led me to a private nook with three of my new friends from the tour van. One of them, Lisa, was my camerawoman; Elena helped carry my backpack while her husband, unbeknownst to me captured all of it on video. I will post it on my website upon my return, www.teresadangwa.com and www.brokenforthemastoersuse.com.

More Angels on Assignment

AS I WALKED INTO THAT WATER, I was so focused on the desire to be dunked in the River Jordan I didn't even feel the cold that others had talked about. I stood in that River, prayed, committed myself to the Lord and sure enough, I baptized myself in the name of the Father, of the Son and of the Holy Spirit. My cup was overflowing, I was so overwhelmed with emotion. I thought I was going to pass out in that river.

Walking out with my friends taking in the moment, I reflected on how God seems to continuously take me through paths that seem unorthodox. Today, I made a commitment to fully embrace that God chooses to deal with me differently, that my path and journey do not have to resemble anything I know or am familiar with or even the status quo. He knew this day was going to happen this way, He orders my steps. After all, He has been giving me this Word from the beginning of my journey:

Isaiah 43:19 says, "Behold, I am doing a new thing; now it springs forth, do you not perceive it? I will make a way in the wilderness and rivers in the desert".

My day ended with the first of three planned appearances on City of David Radio in Tel Aviv to talk about this very book. TV and Radio interviews and hosting are visions God gave to me in the last two years. I just didn't know it would begin to manifest while I was visiting Israel. God is indeed faithful.

The journey continues with more expected Christian Radio interviews to discuss my book, more opportunities for ministering the Word, a tour to Bethany to visit Lazarus' grave, the Dead Sea, River Jordan, Jericho and back to Jerusalem.

Tuesday, September 10th - Rested in the morning and in the afternoon Pastor Solomon took me on a tour to Bethany. My goodness Lord! If I were to list the top three places in which I felt a transformational shift, Lazarus' tomb was one of them. Pastor Lekuku, you were right. It is not like we imagine it when we read our Bible. This place is profound. Standing in that tomb, I was overwhelmed by the miracle of Lazarus' resurrection (John 11) and had to tap into the anointing of all dead things in me being resurrected, the things the devil stole from me being restored. (video on my website, www.brokenforthemastersuse.com). Met Father Michael, a Ghanaian priest who is one of the priests charged with watching over the church built at the ground believed to be Martha and Mary's home.

One of the interesting things I noted during my visit to Israel was how every place of significance in the Word, especially at places where Jesus ministered, a church was built. The churches were built by various entities from St. Helena of Constantinople, the mother of Emperor Constantine the Great to the Catholics, the Orthodox Greek, the Armenian Church, Ethiopian Orthodox (believed to be descendants of Queen Beth Sheba), etc. In some places, like the Church of the Holy Sepulcher in Jerusalem and the Church of the Nativity in Bethlehem, you find more than one faith housed under the same roof.

Wednesday, September 11th - Took a day tour to Bethlehem, Dead Sea, Jericho, and the Jordan River. Since I had already had a private tour of the Church of the Nativity last week, I opted to instead revisit the little restaurant in the strip mall for one last helping of the tasty Shawarma Pita. I returned to the entrance of the church, sat there and people watched while I waited for my tour colleagues.

After Bethlehem, we descended to the lowest region on earth towards Jericho. We drove through some of the most amazing mountains and sites I have ever seen. In this nomadic region, you see homes spread sporadically (at least from the tour bus view) in the dessert. Then, you can't help but be amazed at God's creation when you come across thriving plantations of figs, bananas, and even olive trees. Upon arriving in Jericho, we stopped by the Sycamore tree where it is believed Zacchaeus, the Chief Tax Collector, climbed to see Jesus. Jesus recognized his curiosity and resolve, invites himself to Zacchaeus's home for supper. (Luke 19:1-10). Then we stopped for lunch at a local restaurant and made our way to Mount of Temptation (Matthew 4:8) and the ruins of the walls of Jericho. We rode on the 4,300 ft (1,300 meters) long cable car to get to the mountain and the Greek Orthodox Monastery. At this mountain, where it is believed Jesus was tempted by the devil after 40 days of fasting, I prayed and tapped into the anointing of resisting the devil when he comes near me. I was encouraged that if Jesus could resist after 40 days of fasting, surely, I can do one day of fasting and resist the devil too.

Thursday, September 12th - I came to Israel with an open mind and flexible schedule to allow the Holy Spirit to guide and I am returning home full and eager to do the work that the Lord has assigned to me, serving the people He has assigned especially for me. Much love, life and grace to us all!

In closing…

WRITING THIS BOOK has been a labor of love. I have lost count of the number of times I lost my manuscript. Even with days to the printer, I cried like a baby after the whole book got lost. Thank God for prayer and encouragement from loved ones. Without God and the Holy Spirit, this project would not been done. I had a lot of reasons to give up, seemingly good ones too, but I persevered and I trust that you will be encouraged to persevere in whatever assignment has you today. Be encouraged in knowing that anebhora ndiye anomakwa (in soccer/football, the focus is on the one with the ball). If the devil is not bringing warfare to your doorstep or if you are not doing anything to rattle the devil's cage…it's time to take inventory and see whose team you are rooted in. Check and examine what fruit you are producing? Matthew 7:16-20 says, "**Ye shall know them by their fruits. Do men gather grapes of thorns, or figs of thistles? Even so every good tree bringeth forth good fruit; but a corrupt tree bringeth forth evil fruit. A good tree cannot bring forth evil fruit, neither can a corrupt tree bring forth good fruit. Every tree that bringeth not forth good fruit is hewn down and cast into the fire. Wherefore by their fruits ye shall know them.**

Teresa Dangwa Bio

Teresa Dangwa (or Pastor Tee, as she is affectionately known) is a woman on a mission determined to use her life experiences to change lives. She has gone through her share of trials and tribulations; some of them private, but a significant number of them public. She was denied access to education at a very young age, disowned by her father as a teenager causing her to drop out of high school which impacted her high school graduation, and given for marriage to a practical stranger for all intents and purposes. She managed to escape that situation with her womanhood intact and ran to the church for solace, only to be molested and raped by men in church leadership positions. Pastor Tee was introduced to masturbation and sex after giving her life to Christ by church leadership. She had given her life to Christ in 1984 while in high school. She had a child out of wedlock and was ostracized by fellow church-folk and leadership. Being estranged from her family left her vulnerable, but her vulnerability was often hidden in that "vibrant smile" everyone notices, was often mistaken for strength by some and for confidence by others, but for her, underneath that smile was deep pain and pure survival mode. She hopped from one church leader's house to another having been banned by her father from going to any of her relatives' homes. This house-hopping exposed her to ugly and ungodly secrets within Christian marriages. This experience led to Pastor Tee making a radical decision never to get married.

In 1997, after having been unceremoniously deported from the United Kingdom the prior year due to a series of events orchestrated by Almighty God, Pastor Tee was offered a job in the US while in Zimbabwe. Arriving at BWI that September 12th brought with it raised hopes for a new lease on life and a better future, only to find out later that the American Dream she had been promised was a nightmare. She was caught up in a neatly hidden modern day slavery type of arrangement by the very people who purported to fight for civil rights for the Black community. It is in this situation where she was introduced to two realities: 1. Hunger in the land of plenty and 2. God was all she had and that she had to strengthen her belief system or she would not survive. It is the realization of these things that made her resolve to "running away from captivity". Life was hard as an illegal immigrant and learning to navigate the system by herself after learning of the lies her bosses had told her concerning their "communications" with immigration authorities to "regulate her status". Eventually, with the grace of God, she stabilized her immigration status. Her son joined her after being separated from each other for eight years.

The resentment for the marital institution seemed to go away over the years and although content in her singleness, she would fantasize about it and entertain the idea with three very specific "conditions". "Let's just say when I met the man I was to marry, it was two out of three in my favor…'not bad', recalls Pastor Tee. Her marriage lasted "2.5 hours" due to internal, external, and spiritual forces. She was pretty much left at the altar and was not only devastated, but lost friendships and relationships. The shame, ridicule, and embarrassment she encountered was unbearable. Then, as if that was not enough, she had an accident at work and hurt her back and hip. Now, without her crutch (her work), she became bed-ridden and was really mad at God for allowing such things to happen to her, a relatively good Christ-follower. It was during this period of unbearable physical, heart and spiritual pain that her ministry was birthed. Rehoboth International Ministries' mission is simple, "Renew, Restore, Revive and Release Christ Disciples". God has a sense of humor indeed because He showed Pastor Tee that although her formal education is important, it was not what He wanted to use to be a change agent for the Kingdom.

Her mandate is to serve through Bible-based teaching that is practical to transform the lives of others. God's mandate to Pastor Tee is also to use her life experiences, particularly the ones that caused her the most pain to help others, especially women, to embrace their journey because regardless of what we go through in life, nothing is wasted. Romans 8:28 has been a source of strength and revelation for Pastor Tee. "And we know that all things work together for good to them that love God, to them who are the called according to his purpose."

Prophetess Teresa is the host of a weekly show aired on Facebook, LinkedIn and WhatsApp, *The Dialogue with Pastor Tee.* The show, rooted on the Word of God, addresses everyday life issues such as Salvation, marital relationships, singleness, in-law relationships, relationships in general, love, cultural norms, mental illness, immigration, parenting. Pastor Tee believes the church is as strong as its weakest link. So, if there are unhealthy marriages, there will therefore, be unhealthy families, which turn into unhealthy churches, which produce unhealthy communities. Healthy communities are not a government's responsibility. It is the Body of Christ taking its position to ensure the will of God is done here on earth as it is in Heaven. Pastor Tee also believes that our true identity and relationship with

God is found in the Word of God, not in material things or in societal statuses therefore it is prudent for every Christ Follower to study the Bible and know God for oneself.

— ∞ —

www.ingramcontent.com/pod-product-compliance
Lightning Source LLC
Chambersburg PA
CBHW071105160426
43193CB00029B/1813